'This is a *most* exceptional and unforgettable book – locating, tracing and coherently presenting the debris of a family's efforts to survive the ultimate devastation. Steven Robins steps into that place of densest silence, where death took place, to say the unsayable. One reads it with one's heart in one's mouth, learning the deepest meanings of the word "anguish".'

– Antjie Krog

'An extraordinary memoir ... This deeply moving and brilliantly written account of trauma, history and silence is a layered excavation. What Robins brings to this deeply personal and shattering family story is a scholarly subtext that transcends time and history and finds resonance in contemporary politics and history across continents.'

– Marianne Thamm, *Daily Maverick*

'A personal yet authoritative memoir – an immensely worthwhile read. As an academic Robins has meticulously researched the content, yet it does not read as a lecture. Rather it is a loving family tribute where individual personalities shine through.'

– Gillian McAinsh, *The Herald*

'*Letters of Stone* is the story of the weight of memory, of the burden of guilt and regret; of the obliteration of hope, of identity, of human beings.'

– Michele Magwood, *Sunday Times*

'An absolute triumph of storytelling ... Robins manages this vast body of information with enormous elegance, creating three distinct but intertwined storylines: the story of his need to connect to his family; the story of the family left behind in Germany; and the story of the catastrophe of prejudice and subjugation. Each of these narratives follows its own arc and Robins controls the tension admirably. It builds and builds so that one becomes enthralled to the extent that it is hard to close the book for any period of time.'

– Karin Schimke, *Cape Times*

'Astounding ... fascinating, and infinitely moving ... *Letters of Stone* is a monument to a story which refused to be forgotten. Even if most of the people concerned are dead, their voices have been heard across time and continents to remind us how precariously fragile our ideas of freedom and human rights can be, how every life is a story to be cherished.'

– Karina Magdalena Szczurek, LitNet

'*Letters of Stone* is a moving and thoughtful book and a terrifying reminder of how quickly families can forget their past'

– Vivien Horler, *Weekend Argus*

'*Letters of Stone* is 'n veelvlakkige meesterwerk wat die leser deurgaans boei en lank bybly. 'n Liefdestaak wat Robins meer as drie dekades lank besig gehou het.

Dis 'n roerende elegie wat sy geliefdes uit die dood laat verrys en hul tragiese geskiedenis aan die vergetelheid ontruk.'

– Harry Kalmer, *Beeld*

Letters of Stone

From Nazi Germany to South Africa

Steven Robins

PENGUIN BOOKS

Published by Penguin Books
an imprint of Penguin Random House South Africa (Pty) Ltd
Reg. No. 1953/000441/07
The Estuaries No. 4, Oxbow Crescent, Century Avenue, Century City, 7441
PO Box 1144, Cape Town, 8000, South Africa

www.penguinbooks.co.za

First published 2016
Reprinted in 2016

3 5 7 9 10 8 6 4 2

PUBLISHER: Marlene Fryer
MANAGING EDITOR: Robert Plummer
EDITOR: Alison Lowry
PROOFREADER: Genevieve Adams
COVER DESIGNER: Gretchen van der Byl
TEXT DESIGNER: Ryan Africa
TYPESETTER: Monique van den Berg
INDEXER: Robert Plummer

Set in 11 pt on 14.5 pt Minion

Printed by *paarlmedia*, a division of Novus Holdings

MIX
Paper from responsible sources
FSC® C022948

This book is printed on FSC® certified and controlled sources. FSC (Forest Stewardship Council®) is an independent, international, non-governmental organization. Its aim is to support environmentally sustainable, socially and economically responsible global forest management.

ISBN 978 1 77609 024 2 (print)
ISBN 978 1 77609 025 9 (ePub)
ISBN 978 1 77609 026 6 (PDF)

This book is for my sons, Joshua and Daniel

Contents

‘This Memorial Book gives those murdered their names and dignity back. It is a memorial and at the same time a reminder that every single life has a name and its own truly unique tragic story.’

– Preface of the *Berliner Gedenkbuch* written by the former federal president of Germany, Horst Köhler

‘But the fact is that writing is the only way in which I am able to cope with the memories which overwhelm me so frequently and so unexpectedly. If they remained locked away, they would become heavier and heavier as time went on, so that in the end I would succumb under their mounting weight.’

– W.G. Sebald, *The Rings of Saturn*

The Robinski family tree*

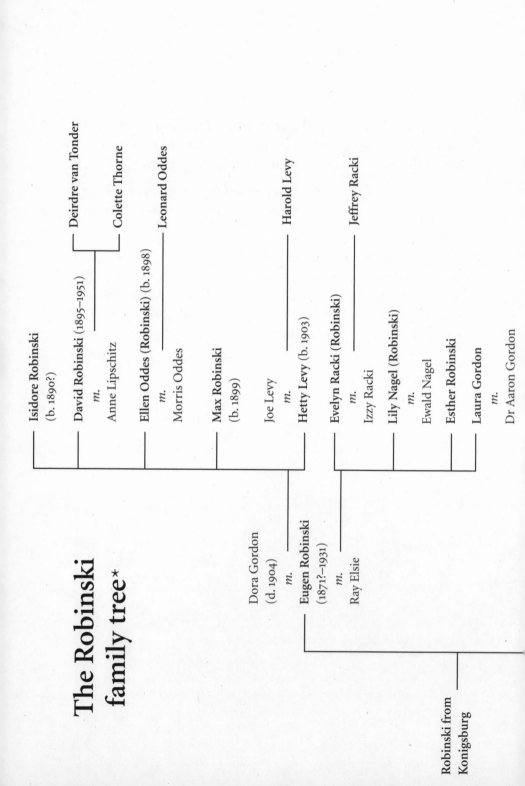

- **Robinski from Konigsburg**
  - **Eugen Robinski** (1871?–1931)
    - *m.* Dora Gordon (d. 1904)
      - **Isidore Robinski** (b. 1890?)
      - **David Robinski** (1895–1951) *m.* Anne Lipschitz
        - **Deirdre van Tonder**
        - **Colette Thorne**
      - **Ellen Oddes (Robinski)** (b. 1898) *m.* Morris Oddes
        - **Leonard Oddes**
      - **Max Robinski** (b. 1899)
      - Joe Levy *m.* **Hetty Levy** (b. 1903)
        - **Harold Levy**
    - *m.* Ray Elsie
      - **Evelyn Racki (Robinski)** *m.* Izzy Racki
        - **Jeffrey Racki**
      - **Lily Nagel (Robinski)** *m.* Ewald Nagel
      - **Esther Robinski**
      - **Laura Gordon** *m.* Dr Aaron Gordon

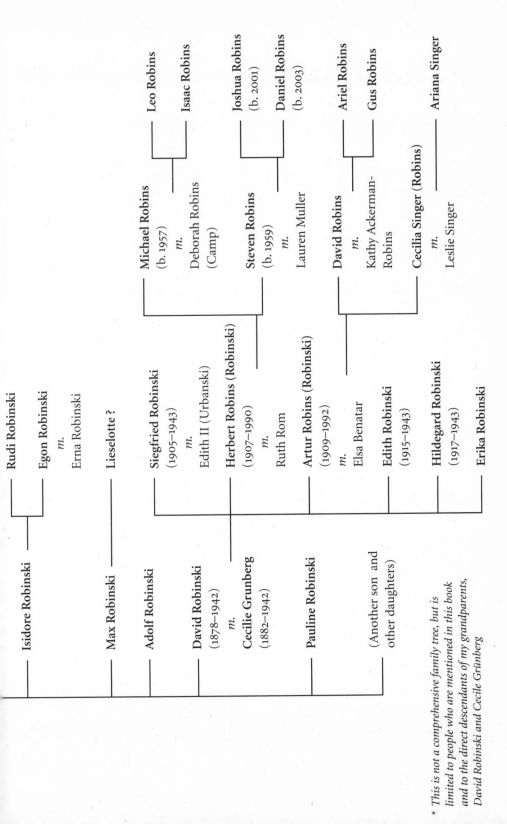

- **Isidore Robinski**
  - **Rudi Robinski**
  - **Egon Robinski** *m.* Erna Robinski
- **Max Robinski**
  - **Lieselotte ?**
- **Adolf Robinski**
- **David Robinski** (1878–1942) *m.* **Cecilie Grunberg** (1882–1942)
  - **Siegfried Robinski** (1905–1943) *m.* Edith II (Urbanski)
  - **Herbert Robins (Robinski)** (1907–1990) *m.* Ruth Rom
    - **Michael Robins** (b. 1957) *m.* Deborah Robins (Camp)
      - **Leo Robins**
      - **Isaac Robins**
    - **Steven Robins** (b. 1959) *m.* Lauren Muller
      - **Joshua Robins** (b. 2001)
      - **Daniel Robins** (b. 2003)
  - **Artur Robins (Robinski)** (1909–1992) *m.* Elsa Benatar
    - **David Robins** *m.* Kathy Ackerman-Robins
      - **Ariel Robins**
      - **Gus Robins**
    - **Cecilia Singer (Robins)** *m.* Leslie Singer
      - **Ariana Singer**
  - **Edith Robinski** (1915–1943)
  - **Hildegard Robinski** (1917–1943)
  - **Erika Robinski**
- **Pauline Robinski**
- (Another son and other daughters)

* *This is not a comprehensive family tree, but is limited to people who are mentioned in this book and to the direct descendants of my grandparents, David Robinski and Cecile Grünberg*

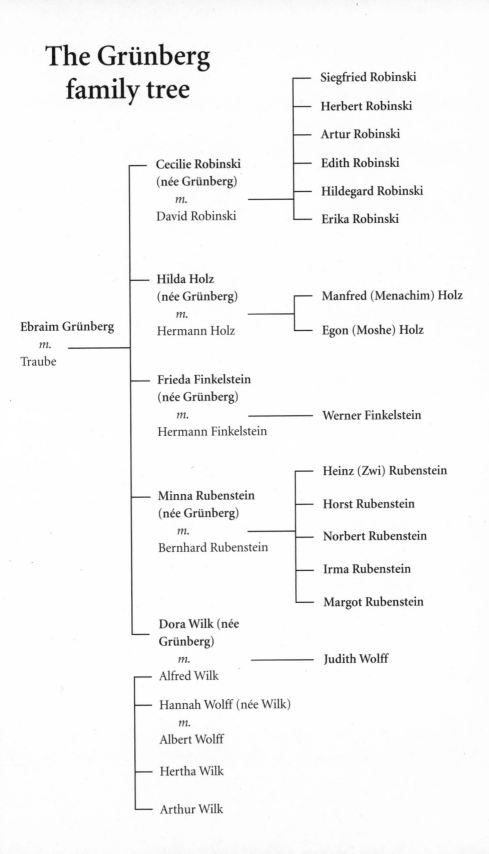

The Grünberg family tree

- Ebraim Grünberg *m.* Traube
  - Cecilie Robinski (née Grünberg) *m.* David Robinski
    - Siegfried Robinski
    - Herbert Robinski
    - Artur Robinski
    - Edith Robinski
    - Hildegard Robinski
    - Erika Robinski
  - Hilda Holz (née Grünberg) *m.* Hermann Holz
    - Manfred (Menachim) Holz
    - Egon (Moshe) Holz
  - Frieda Finkelstein (née Grünberg) *m.* Hermann Finkelstein
    - Werner Finkelstein
  - Minna Rubenstein (née Grünberg) *m.* Bernhard Rubenstein
    - Heinz (Zwi) Rubenstein
    - Horst Rubenstein
    - Norbert Rubenstein
    - Irma Rubenstein
    - Margot Rubenstein
  - Dora Wilk (née Grünberg) *m.* Alfred Wilk
    - Judith Wolff
    - Hannah Wolff (née Wilk) *m.* Albert Wolff
    - Hertha Wilk
    - Arthur Wilk

ONE

The Photograph

Growing up in Port Elizabeth in the 1960s and 70s, I was always aware of a black-and-white postcard-size photograph of three women that stood on a black wooden table in our dining room. I had no idea who these women were other than a vague sense that they were my father's family and that they had lived and died in Germany during the Second World War. By the time I was in my teens I had a sense that they were killed in the Holocaust, but I did not even know their names or exactly how they were related to me. Yet this portrait was to follow me around for many years, its subjects always watching me, hovering in the shadows, waiting for me to notice them, and to respond. The haunting expression on the face of the woman on the left had a particular hold over me.

The women in the photograph are dressed in old-fashioned, formal clothing, the older woman wearing a white ruff, the younger ones white lace bows on their collars. Their expressions seem sombre and despairing. The eyes of the young woman on the right appear to be squint. The older woman stares straight ahead and looks tired and forlorn. The woman on the left, the one who always attracted my attention, appears equally melancholy and defeated.

In our home, it felt as if the photograph was never meant to be noticed, as if someone had mistakenly left it exposed on the table in our dining room. Nobody spoke about its subjects, but neither did I ask about them. My brother Michael does not even remember ever seeing the portrait as a child. The picture always stood out to me, though. Every day, those three sad women would stare at us as we ate dinner.

Only when I was an adult did I discover that the women were my grandmother and my aunts. In 1989, as a young anthropology student who was interested in life narratives, I interviewed my father about his life. I learnt then that his mother was named Cecilie, and his two sisters Edith and Hildegard. Edith: the woman on the left of the photograph finally had a name. My father told me that he and his siblings were born in Poland. He had an older brother, Siegfried, and a younger brother, Artur, all born in the 1900s. His sisters Edith and Hildegard were born during the First World War. Erika, the youngest, died in infancy of starvation as a result of the deprivations of the war years.

The family relocated to Berlin during the 1920s, and my father later took a job as a buyer at a big departmental store in Erfurt. After the Nazis came to power, he escaped to South Africa in 1936 and settled in Port Elizabeth, where he started working as a door-to-door salesman selling socks and stockings. His brother Artur managed to get out two years later and ended up in Ndola in Northern Rhodesia (now Zambia).

The interview, while enlightening, had one gaping hole. While I asked my father questions about almost every aspect of his life in Poland and Germany, none of my questions addressed what happened to Edith and the rest of his family. I knew his brother Artur – or Arthur, as we called him – who had visited with his family many times when I was a child. But there seemed to be an unstated agreement that the rest of his family were not to be spoken about.

Nadine Fresco alludes to this tendency of Holocaust survivors to withhold information about their traumatic experiences from their children – what she refers to as a black hole of silence. The stories of death are never told, and are instead acted out symptomatically between parents and children. This 'forbidden memory of death' finds expression in attacks of pain that are often veiled behind 'a screen of words [and] an unchanging story, a tale repeated over and over again, made up of selections from the war'.[1] The silence in my father's house was even more profound, as he never said anything to me about the war at all until I interviewed him in his eighties, and even then he said nothing about the family who had remained behind. For me, the single photograph of Edith, her mother and sister came to stand in as the repository for this forbidden memory of loss, death and destruction, for the black hole of silence that suffocated any mention of them.

My father in his later years, with his signature beret

When my father died at the age of eighty-three, the year after I interviewed him, it seemed as if the opportunity to discover anything about his family had died with him. But the interview had prised open a window into the Robinski family's past, and I became increasingly determined to uncover the truth about their fates.

It was then that I began searching for archival traces and information about a world that no longer existed. At the time, Edith's photograph was the only access I had to this world. It was, as Roland Barthes put it, an umbilical cord of light, providing a glimmer of hope that would salvage and resuscitate a shattered existence. I looked to this photograph to do the impossible: to mend broken family bonds and bridge my separation from Aunt Edith and my late father. I was asking so much of it.

TWO

White Noise in the Suburbs

With my father and my older brother Michael in our garden

I was born in 1959 in a middle-class suburb in the seaport city of Port Elizabeth. My brother Michael and I were raised in a thoroughly anglicised secular Jewish home, and our childhood was a safe and happy one. We played soccer in our big backyard where we had built wooden goal posts, and although we lived next to a golf course and country club that would not accept Jews as members, nobody seemed to mind, as Jews could always join the bigger and better Wedgewood Park Country Club. Notwithstanding such petty anti-Semitism, my family lived comfortably in our lily-white suburb, my brother and I having no knowledge of our Polish and German ancestry or about what happened to our father's relatives during the Third Reich.

Our surname, Robins, was English, although it had originally been Robinski, also spelt Robinsky.[1] My uncle Artur, who lived in Zambia, told me during one of his visits that a Robinski was skiing in the Swiss Alps one day and lost his skis, and that we had called ourselves Robins ever since. In fact, the name change occurred in the late 1930s, when Artur's cousin David Robinski, a magistrate in the Karoo, decided to anglicise his surname, perhaps in response to the rising anti-Semitism of that period, or, according to my father, to boost his chances of promotion in an English-dominated state bureaucracy. The rest of the family thought this was a good idea and followed suit.

I grew up oblivious to the fact that South African Jews had not always been so secure in their white skins. The working-class Jews from Eastern Europe who arrived here in the late nineteenth and early twentieth centuries were regarded as dirty, unassimilable and not white enough by the ruling establishment, while wealthier Jews were deemed responsible for the economic hardships of the local white population, especially during the 1920s and 1930s. This resentment of Jewish immigrants caused prominent Afrikaner nationalists, including future prime ministers H.F. Verwoerd and B.J. Vorster, to voice their support for the Nazis' anti-Semitic policies. In response to this rising prejudice, South African Jews made even greater efforts to anglicise and fit into white society.

Germany's defeat in 1945 changed everything. The exposure of the death camps, and international condemnation of what had happened to European Jews, convinced Afrikaner nationalists to bury their Nazi affiliations and invite Jews into the white laager. When D.F. Malan's National Party came to power in 1948, its leaders ditched the Jewish Question and turned their attention to the Native Question. Soon after taking office, Malan met with a delegation from the Jewish Board of Deputies and assured them that Jews would be accommodated under National Party rule. Then, in May 1949, South Africa officially recognised Israel, and in 1953 Malan became the first head of government to visit the newly established Jewish state, returning to South Africa full of praise for Israel.[2] South African Jews began feeling like fully fledged members of the white fold and seemed to forget about the war years when Nazi support was rampant in the country. Relieved to be out of the firing line, they embraced their new standing and became silent bystanders as the National Party entrenched its apartheid ideology.

Rabbi Andre Ungar, a young Hungarian Holocaust survivor who led the Reform congregation in Port Elizabeth from 1955 to 1956, berated South African Jews for their lack of identification with the injustices imposed by apartheid. But his uncompromising attacks on the apartheid government were seen by the Jewish community as jeopardising their new security, and when, in 1956, the outspoken twenty-seven-year-old rabbi was sent his deportation orders, the Jewish Board of Deputies did nothing to defend him. The only other Jews who truly resisted the apartheid state were the communists, such as Joe Slovo, Ruth First, Pauline Podbrey, Arthur Goldreich, Denis Goldberg, Harold Wolpe, Ben Turok and Ronnie Kasrils. Of the 156 activists arrested for treason against the apartheid state in 1956, twenty-three were white, and fourteen of these were Jewish. And, in 1963, when seventeen African National Congress (ANC) and South African Communist Party leaders were arrested at Liliesleaf Farm in Rivonia, Johannesburg, all five of the whites were Jewish.[3] As in the Treason Trial, the defence team at the Rivonia Trial was largely made up of Jewish advocates. The Jewish establishment did not protest against the treatment of the arrested activists. Their Faustian pact with the apartheid government had secured the privileges that came with their white status, and it had cultivated a conservative Jewish culture of silence, acquiescence, compromise, and at times outright complicity. By then, most Jews, including my family, had retreated into their white suburban fortresses and kept their heads well below the parapets. The fifties and sixties also saw a growth in optimism and economic prospects for South African Jews, and by 1970, the Jewish population numbered almost 120 000.[4]

Despite the high walls, barking dogs, burglar alarms and round-the-clock policing in white suburbs, I grew up with the sense of insecurity that plagued most white South Africans besieged in the fortified suburbs of a police state whose first duty was to protect white privilege. I can recall the frequent dreams of burglars breaking into our home and double-checking the locks on the doors every night before going to sleep. This was not pure paranoia – our house was in fact routinely robbed when we went away on holidays. We were always aware that we lived in a precarious paradise at the tip of Africa.

The white suburbs were islands of wealth, privilege and ignorance in a sea of black poverty and suffering. My schooling provided me with little knowledge about what was going on beyond the insulated environment of Mill Park, and school textbooks simply retold the official Afrikaner nationalist history of white conquest and domination. I learnt about the 1820 British Settlers, the Voortrekkers' heroic journey into the interior and their covenant with God after their victory over the Zulu king at Blood

With my brother Michael (left) and my parents outside my father's clothing shop in Port Elizabeth

River, and how the Afrikaners came to see themselves as the Chosen People. I had always thought we Jews were the Chosen Ones, but there were clearly other contenders for the crown.

At Theodor Herzl Primary School I also learnt to take pride in Israel and being Jewish. I might have been born in South Africa but I was Jewish above everything else. I venerated Herzl's Zionist movement that had fought so heroically for the creation of the Jewish state. Herzl had concluded that Jews' strivings for assimilation in Europe were entirely misplaced and naïve, and in 1896 he insisted that the only solution to the Jewish Question was the establishment of an independent Jewish state in Palestine. It was this view that animated my Jewish education in Port Elizabeth.

I learnt to have unquestioning loyalty to Israel, which seemed obligatory given Jews' long history of persecution. I was eight years old in 1967 when the Six-Day War was fought and wanted to volunteer my own services in the fight for Israel. Almost 2 000 South African Jews volunteered for non-combatant service in Israel during the war, the largest contribution of any diaspora Jewish community.[5] The South African government allowed Jews to send funds to Israel for humanitarian purposes, and these actions further strengthened ties between the two countries. I remember celebrating Israel's swift, heroic victory, entirely ignorant about the displacement of hundreds of thousands of indigenous Palestinians who had been sacrificed to create Israel two decades earlier.

Following my bar mitzvah at Glendinningvale Synagogue on 24 February 1973, I left Theodor Herzl for Grey High, a 'Christian Nationalist' government school. Exiled from the Jewish sanctuary Theodor Herzl had offered me, I was suddenly thrust into an unfamiliar Christian world where I had to find my feet fast. Soon after arriving at Grey, I dropped any overt signs of my Jewishness, and, determined to fit in, I learnt to submerge my Jewish identity. I had hardly settled into my new school when we were assigned Shakespeare's *Merchant of Venice* for English. The unflattering portrait of Shylock the Jew sent me into spasms of shame and agonising self-consciousness, and gave me even more reason to bury my Jewishness.

Growing up as a teenager in a conservative middle-class suburb triggered a spark of youthful rebellion, but it was my older brother Michael who was the real rebel in the family. He introduced me to jazz, folk and reggae music at an impressionable age, and it was in this that my rebellion found expression. My cultural icons of choice were Angela Davis, Miles Davis, Bob Dylan, Jimi Hendrix, Janis Joplin and Bob Marley, as well as black South African musicians such as Hugh Masekela and Dollar Brand (later known as Abdullah Ibrahim). With my friend Vernon, I would occasionally venture beyond the pale world of the suburbs, visiting our friend Simphiwe, an aspiring black photographer, at his home in New Brighton township. I even attended the celebrations following Simphiwe's return from the bush as part of the Xhosa circumcision ritual. But that was about as far as I went in actually removing myself from the racial straitjacket of my upbringing.

Despite my attraction to black music and culture, I was still ignorant about the realities of apartheid and the struggle against it. Whites were trained to believe that the security forces had everything under control, even as ANC cadres bombed electricity pylons, post offices and police stations. I was born only a few months before the Sharpeville massacre of 21 March 1960, when sixty-nine black demonstrators were killed by police. Then came the banning of the ANC and the Pan Africanist Congress (PAC), the arrest of Nelson Mandela and other ANC leaders, and the exile and imprisonment of hundreds of activists. I was seven years old when, in 1966, Prime Minister Verwoerd was assassinated by Dimitri Tsafendas, a middle-aged parliamentary messenger. Tsafendas claimed he plunged a knife into Verwoerd because of secret messages from a tapeworm in his stomach, and he spent the rest of his life in a psychiatric institution. I remember our black gardener celebrating after Verwoerd's death. Since I liked the gardener and regarded him as my friend, I surmised that Verwoerd must have been a really bad apple.

By my early teens, I had developed an inchoate awareness of apartheid's injustices. I felt an empathy with the oppressed masses in South Africa that probably derived from what I had learnt about the persecution of Jews throughout history. This led me to always champion the underdog, and I remember my father's bafflement whenever I would automatically back black boxers when they fought white opponents. I also supported the black students who took to the streets armed with stones at the start of the June 1976 uprising. I would listen eagerly as our Xhosa domestic worker regaled me with tales of these street battles between the black youth and the heavily armed white police.

In 1978, after completing high school, I began a BA degree at the University of Cape Town. Revolution was raging in the streets at this time, and torture was pervasive in the prisons. My studies were eye-opening, and I soon learnt that apartheid was merely the latest chapter in the centuries-long narrative of conquest and racial domination of black South Africans. Seduced by Marxism and radical politics, I became a member of a long-haired and shabbily dressed crew of pale revolutionaries, who embraced a minimalist, counter-cultural lifestyle in our attempt at showing solidarity with the African proletariat. We read *The Communist Manifesto*, bought our food from veggie co-ops, lived in dirty, rundown digs in Observatory, drank cheap red wine and smoked far too much dope. This way of life was probably not good for our mental

My minor contribution to non-racial football in Gugulethu, Cape Town, c. 1980

health, but most of us somehow stayed on track and obtained careers and middle-class lifestyles. Despite all our rebellion, we were always *shtum* about the fact that our bourgeois parents were bankrolling our bohemian lifestyles.

During my student years, my Jewishness and family history were far off my radar. Many of my varsity friends did not even know I was Jewish. Marx had revealed to us that ethnicity and religion were simply ideological forms of false consciousness, and that it was working-class consciousness that really mattered. So we, the pampered children of the bourgeoisie, committed ourselves to worker solidarity rather than ethnic or religious identifications.

In 1985, after completing my honours studies on the social and economic consequences of forced removals in rural South Africa, I spent a year touring Europe, where I stayed at backpackers' lodges and did piecemeal jobs. In London, I worked as a manual labourer on building sites, but after a few months of loading rubble into dumpsters, my body rebelled and I had to quit this back-breaking job. I decided to migrate to warmer and cheaper southern Europe, finding work at a backpackers' lodge in Athens which, soon after my arrival, was converted into a brothel. Out of work again, I joined a Dutch fellow-drifter on a hedonistic spree of Greek island hopping. Our days were spent sunbathing, swimming, drinking cheap wine in the evenings and falling asleep on the beaches. I eventually tired of this indolent style of living and joined the throngs of drifters making their way across the Mediterranean to Haifa in Israel. We were like Jack Kerouac's Beat Generation, a caravan of wanderers on the road and ready to go with the flow. I arrived in Israel and made my way to Kibbutz Degania Bet on the Sea of Galilee (Kinneret), a literal paradise on earth that became my very own Garden of Eden.

One day, on leave from the kibbutz, I visited the Yad Vashem Holocaust History Museum in Jerusalem. The exhibitions unsettled me, but I could feel no clear personal connection to what I was seeing. I was also indifferent to Israel's Jewish character. As just another cash-strapped backpacker searching for a place to lay my head before moving on, I was definitely not consummating any Zionist longings or religiously inspired commitments. On a visit to Tel Aviv, I bumped into Shiri, a beautiful, dark, green-eyed Israeli I had met briefly in London a few months earlier, and I soon became besotted with her. She lived with her parents in Tel Aviv but would visit me on weekends at the kibbutz, or I would catch a bus to her most cosmopolitan of Israeli cities.

During the week, I worked in the kibbutz kitchen with elderly women who had strong German and Eastern European accents. Some had numbers tattooed on their forearms, but I never asked them about this. I made no association between these women and the three women in the photograph at home in Port Elizabeth. Israel, my visit to Yad Vashem and the elderly survivors at the kibbutz elicited no sense of connection to my family's past, or the Zionist lessons of my youth.

But my idyllic existence at Degania Bet was soon infiltrated by the creeping realisation that my time of drifting was drawing to a close and I would have to make some serious decisions about my future. I would either have to marry Shiri and settle down in Israel, or wander into the big wide world to discover who I was and what I wanted to do with my life. A jazz musician acquaintance in Tel Aviv recommended New York as the perfect place to shake me out of my kibbutz-induced daze, and since I had just enough money to buy a one-way ticket to New York, I sadly said goodbye to Shiri and my paradise on the Sea of Galilee.

In New York, I stayed in a backpackers' lodge in downtown Manhattan. The people there had come from all over the planet, lugging their art and photographic portfolios, musical instruments or film scripts, and all of them were young and looking for fame and glory. Here I found myself in the cultural centre of the universe and I needed to find my own direction or else I would sink into the swamp without a trace.

One freezing winter's day, the city sparkling with crisp, clean snow and lit up by bright blue skies, I visited New York's Natural History Museum. While wandering through the exhibits, I overheard a tall, grey-haired man in a tweed jacket immersed in what sounded like a highbrow, scholarly discussion. I was desperate and walked up to him, introducing myself as a student of anthropology looking for any kind of research job. My *chutzpah* paid off. The man was a professor of East Asian Studies at Columbia University, and before long we were engaged in deep discussion about social-engineering disasters ranging from apartheid's bantustans to Mao's Cultural Revolution before ending with Stalin's collectivisation catastrophe. When we parted company, he suggested I make enquiries at Columbia University's Department of Anthropology about doctoral study fellowships.

A few days later, on another bitterly cold New York day, I stumbled through the thick snow to Columbia's Upper West Side campus, carrying a copy of my honours thesis. I accosted two professors in the corridor of the Anthropology Department who seemed intrigued by this wild-eyed white South African. After reading my thesis, they told me they were impressed with my Marxist-inspired ethnographic analysis of how developments in capitalist agriculture in apartheid South Africa in the 1970s led to mechanisation that resulted in the displacement of hundreds of thousands of black farmworkers and their families in the overcrowded and underdeveloped rural homeland of QwaQwa. The professors advised me to apply for a doctoral fellowship in their department, and my application was successful. I was ecstatic; this was my lifeline. I had found a pathway to a proper career. From back-breaking manual labour in London to chopping vegetables on the banks of the Galilee, I was now about to embark on doctoral studies at an illustrious American university.

I returned to Cape Town in mid-1986 for a few months before beginning my studies. In June, I joined a television news group as a driver and photographer covering political violence in Crossroads, a large shack settlement opposite D.F. Malan Airport. Apartheid security police had been recruiting Xhosa elders, who were known as the 'Fathers' or *witdoeke* (Afrikaans for the white scarves they wore on their heads). The police had enlisted these elders to purge Crossroads of militant ANC youth activists (also known as the 'comrades' or *amaqabane*), who they perceived as a threat to their neo-traditionalist authority. In June these tensions exploded in a twenty-seven-day war during which over sixty Crossroads residents were killed and an estimated 60 000 were left homeless.[6]

I witnessed this violence myself as I walked through the flames and smoke engulfing Crossroads. On 10 June, we managed to capture on film white police arming the *witdoeke*, incriminating footage which was broadcast that evening on British television. The following morning, the comrades escorted us to the smouldering remains of a 'necklacing' victim who had been set alight during the previous night's fighting. I remember looking at the burnt tyre around the neck of the charred corpse and being unable to release the shutter on my camera, so I pretended to take the photograph. Later that day, George De'Ath, a BBC freelance cameraman, was shot dead by *witdoeke*, who, together with their security-force handlers, targeted journalists believed to be allies of the ANC comrades. Those few days in Crossroads were enough to convince me I was not cut out to be a war journalist and should stick to the safer world of academia. I would be better equipped trying to understand the causes of violence as an anthropologist rather than documenting them as a photojournalist.

In September 1986, I began my new life at Columbia University. Studying and living in the Upper West Side of Manhattan exposed me to the heady, culturally diverse world of anthropology, art, film, theatre and music. I met students from many countries and soon realised just how parochial my South African upbringing had been. Seminars by radical African students and scholars at Columbia's African Studies Center were a revelation for this Jewish *boytjie* from small-town Port Elizabeth; so, too, were the student parties. After the suffocating provincialism of apartheid South Africa, the taste of the Big Apple was intoxicating.

It soon dawned on me as an aspiring anthropologist that it was time to show some interest in my own history and German Jewish heritage. And so in July 1989, during a vacation in South Africa, I interviewed my father on tape. I wanted to know about his life in Poland, his early childhood, and what he remembered from his youth and adult years in Germany. He and my mother had moved from Port Elizabeth to Cape Town earlier that year, and I was staying with them at their Sea Point flat. In their living room, with the sound of seagulls and waves crashing down on the beach across the road, I asked my father to start at the beginning. I sometimes replay the tape just to hear his gravelly German-accented voice again. In the background, my mother's voice can be heard, interjecting, correcting and elaborating.

THREE

Breaking the Silence

Apart from his thick German accent and a smattering of Yiddish words in his everyday speech, my father revealed virtually nothing about his European roots during my childhood in Port Elizabeth. He had left everything behind when he immigrated to South Africa, and probably assumed that nobody, especially his sons, needed to know about his past. The only other family link to his life in Germany was his younger brother Artur, who had ended up in the small Copperbelt town of Ndola. The two Robins brothers were very close, and I imagine that their profound loss and displacement cemented their relationship.

After initially struggling to make a living in Port Elizabeth, my father found employment as a salesman for a small retail clothing store. By the time he got married, nearly twenty years later, he had established his own retail business and was fairly comfortably off. His wife, Ruth Naomi Rom, was a South African–born Jewess from a family with Eastern European ancestry. I grew up with the incongruity of having an English-sounding surname, Robins, and a father with a German accent, but neither my brother nor I asked any questions about this.

The interview with my father in 1989 became my window into his life in Europe. Reading the transcript almost three decades later, I am struck by his disbelief that anyone, even his son, would be interested in his history. But with some prompting, and as the interview proceeded, he gradually began to open up about his youth:

STEVEN: Okay, Dad, could you begin by telling me a little bit about your early experiences in Strasburg, things that you remember when you were a little child, from the earliest times that you can recall?

HERBERT: That's very difficult, I mean, after all, it takes me back sixty years. Sixty years is a long time, more than sixty years, *eighty* years now as a small child, and what do I remember? It's not very much. Well I remember my elder brother Siegfried had some fights occasionally and that's it.

STEVEN: Dad, could you just talk about early memories that you recall from your youth in Strasburg? Could you tell me a bit about Siegfried, your memories of Siegfried?

HERBERT: He was two years older than I am, the same as Arthur is two years younger than I am. I am the middle of three boys. I only remember when we left Strasburg … My father had some sort of an inn in Strasburg [and] people from the countryside came, especially on Sundays after church, and they'd come there and have something to eat …

Herbert Leopold Robinski was born on 29 March 1907 in the northern Prussian town of Strasburg (now Brodnica, Poland). His grandfather, my great-grandfather, was an innkeeper and fisherman in Tatmischken, a small village within the administrative district of Rucken (also called Tilsit) in East Prussia, close to the border of what is now Lithuania. My great-grandfather had six sons, who scattered all across Europe when they left home: David, my grandfather, lived in Strasburg; his brother Isidore in Königsberg, East Prussia (now Kaliningrad, Russia); Max moved to Elbing (Elbląg) in Poland; Adolf lived in Pirmasens, Germany; Eugen immigrated to South Africa; and another son, whose name my father couldn't recall, ended up in France. My father could only remember the name of one of his father's sisters, Pauline. I am not sure if there were other sisters.

I asked my father to tell me more about Eugen as I was curious that another Robinski had lived in South Africa before him. But all he could recall was that Eugen had emigrated from Prussia in the late nineteenth century and ended up in the small Karoo town of Williston, where he became a successful businessman and hotel owner. I only discovered further details about my great-uncle much later.

As children, my parents would drag my brother and me to tea on Sunday afternoons at our aunt Evelyn Racki's home in the suburb of Summerstrand. Many years later, I learnt that Aunt Evelyn was one of Eugen's daughters from his second marriage. Also present at these occasions were two other daughters of Eugen, Lily and Laura. I can recall that Aunt Lily's husband, Ewald Nagel, spoke English with an even more pronounced German accent than my father. Eugen's three daughters were the bedrock of my father's family life in Port Elizabeth. They were also the reason that Hetty Levy – Eugen's daughter from his first marriage – could persuade my father to leave Cape Town in 1936 and move with her and her young son Harold to Port Elizabeth.

Eugen's younger brother, my grandfather David Robinski, was born on 16 May 1878 in Rucken, East Prussia. In 1904, David married my grandmother Cecilie Grünberg, who was born in Grindzaw in East Prussia on 24 November 1882. The marriage had been arranged by a *shadchen*, a traditional Jewish matchmaker or marriage agent, who sent David to the Grünberg home in Strasburg to choose a wife from one of their four marriageable daughters.

Traube and Ebraim Grünberg with their daughters Hilda, Minna, Dora, Cecilie and Frieda

After David chose Cecilie, they lived in Strasburg, where he opened an inn with a bar and grocery shop. It was in this small Prussian town, bordering Russia, that my father and his brothers were born: Siegfried in 1905, Herbert in 1907 and Artur in 1909. David ultimately became frustrated with the meagre income from the inn and moved the family to Culmsee (now Chełmża, Poland), where he owned a shoe shop called Salamander Schuhwaren. My father recalled:

> After we moved to Culmsee we had a nice flat behind the shop and there more or less we grew up. Then it didn't take very long and my father opened up a men's outfitting shop as well, but that was further

up in town. I remember it was a little dorp, not much of a town … I know when we moved into the outfitting shop in a big lorry, I fell off the lorry and my father really got mad when he saw me falling down. That I remember. He pulled me out of the street, you know, and thought I had broken my back, but nothing happened. In a short while I was quite all right again. The business went all right up until shortly before the war … I think it must have been about 1912, and my father had to give up the shop … In due course we gave up our corner shop, you know the one, we have the photograph … It's Salamander shoe shop …

My grandparents with their children outside the family's shoe store in Culmsee

Until I was in my forties, this was the only photograph I had ever seen of my grandfather. He stands on his own next to the shop's entrance, while, some distance from him, his wife stands with three of her children, who are lined up from tallest to shortest in front of the shop window. Also in the photograph is a woman in a white apron, who I assume was the family's housekeeper and saleswoman in the shop, with whom my grandfather was apparently having an affair. Next to the housekeeper stands a boy with a cap and bag; this is possibly my father's eldest brother Siegfried. The young man to the far left of the photo is probably not a family member, and other bystanders can be seen standing behind the family. The resolution is too poor to make out facial features, but for many years this was the only photograph I had of my grandfather, and it remains the only one of Siegfried.

At the start of the First World War, the towns of Strasburg and Culmsee, although still part of Prussia, were predominantly Polish-speaking. For the Robinski family, who spoke German and were Jewish, this made them outsiders in a double sense. Nevertheless, despite the frequent anti-Semitic encounters, my father recalled being quite happy there. His three sisters – Edith, Hildegard and Erika – were born in Culmsee during the war. But living conditions worsened in this time, and the family suffered financially. Tragically, my father's sister Erika died while still a baby.

David fought on the Italian front during the war, and he must have thought this patriotic act would secure his rights as a German citizen. Instead, his war experiences left him thoroughly disillusioned. On one occasion, in Culmsee while on leave from the front, he passed a young lieutenant on the street without saluting as he was carrying two suitcases. When the lieutenant insisted on being saluted, my grandfather swore at him and chased him down the street. There was widespread disillusionment in the ranks by then, and David Robinski, although not politically inclined, was fed up with the Kaiser and the military. He had been awarded an Iron Cross, but this was not enough to encourage his career as a soldier. His health had deteriorated dramatically while serving on the front, and he must have been angry about his family's hardships and devastated by his daughter Erika's death. One day, he tore off his uniform and threw it into the fireplace in disgust.

During and after the war, street riots became commonplace. Poles rose up against the unwanted imposition of German culture and the compulsory teaching of German in schools. On 8 January 1919, local Poles attacked a Prussian Grenzschutz unit and were repelled when the Germans shelled the town with artillery. On 21 January, Culmsee once again became part of Poland. Following the Treaty of Versailles, which was signed on 28 June 1919, some 2 000 German-speakers were deported from Culmsee to Germany. These factors, as well as a failing business and rising anti-Semitic and anti-German feelings, persuaded David Robinski to move westwards, to Berlin. He arrived there in 1920 and was joined after a few months by my father and some time later by the rest of the family.

When my wife Lauren and I visited Brodnica (Strasburg) and Chełmża (Culmsee) in 1999, the only evidence we found of the Robinski family having lived there were birth certificates in the town archives. In Brodnica, we met an old woman who tried to tell us something about a small, open patch of ground she was pointing to, but she spoke in Polish and broken English and I couldn't understand her. I think it might have been a Jewish cemetery, or a synagogue, or perhaps Jews had once lived there. We found no official commemorations of a Jewish presence in these two Polish towns when we visited. It was as if the Robinski family and so many other Polish Jews had never lived there. The towns were incorporated into the Third Reich in 1939 and captured by the Red Army in 1945.

During the move from Culmsee to Berlin, my grandfather had to resort to some dubious activities for money. My father recalled:

> The next thing, every five minutes he was travelling to Berlin. We didn't know then but afterwards we found that he was smuggling gold. He was buying up gold coins and took them to Germany. I still remember, I've seen my mother making sandwiches for the trip putting butter and gold on the bread and meat or cheese over that to hide the gold.

David and his eldest son Siegfried would eventually be arrested for smuggling; but they were released a week or two later with a fine.

Desperate to keep the family afloat, David managed to acquire a shoe shop in Berlin. He struggled to keep it going, however, and took to gambling to supplement its income. While he was trying to establish himself in Berlin, the rest of the family remained in Culmsee. David began an affair with his sales lady-cum-housekeeper, and regularly visited spas, ostensibly for health reasons – although my father suspected there was more to these trips away from home. Later in 1920, David decided it was time for my father to join him in Berlin. Herbert, who was twelve or thirteen at the time, recalled the journey:

> In Culmsee there were two fellows who were going to Berlin. My mother contacted them and they said, yes, they'll take me along, sure, sure. In the meantime, as soon as we came to the station, they gave me a watch, another watch, two watches and some money, some gold coins; they gave this to me to travel over the frontier. They delivered me in Berlin. By then I didn't have the watches any more, and I didn't have the coins either any more. They took them back of course. But this was a sort of easy way to get the things out of the country. There

> I came to the flat in Berlin where my father lived with that girl; she looked after the shop and she looked after the house too …

My grandfather's smuggling activities across the Polish–German border were echoed in his son Herbert's later obsession with moving money out of South Africa. In the aftermath of the Soweto uprising in 1976, Herbert, who had bank accounts in Switzerland and the United States, would successfully apply for a green card to the United States. Although there was much talk of moving to San Diego, nothing came of it. Like so many other South African Jews, my father needed an emergency exit strategy, just in case. Having lived through two world wars left its mark on him in other ways as well. In his old age he engaged in petty shoplifting episodes where he would routinely pilfer small items like batteries and razor blades from department stores – a habit inherited from the war years, when the Robinski sons were forced to steal food for their family.

Herbert couldn't get into a school in Berlin because he had not studied compulsory subjects such as Latin. Financial difficulties also contributed to his father's decision that he should abandon schooling. Three years after arriving in Berlin, at the age of sixteen, Herbert was sent to his uncle Herr Finkelstein in Gumbinnen, East Prussia, to work as an apprentice salesman. Working conditions were unpleasant and Herr Finkelstein treated him poorly: 'I was the only employee. I had full board and slept in a little storeroom next to the very small shop. I had to stay in also on Sundays when my uncle went out for drives with his family in his car. After about two and a half years I had enough. I wired the old man that I want to come back home.' Herbert returned to Berlin, where he found work as a junior salesman at a well-known Jewish-owned department store called Tietz.

Meanwhile, from 1925 onwards, David Robinski, his wife Cecilie, daughters Edith and Hildegard and their youngest son Artur were living in Wallner-Theaterstrasse 45 in Berlin's central district of Mitte. Siegfried, who owned a small button-manufacturing factory, lived in Naunynstrasse in Kreuzberg with his wife, also named Edith. David's shoe business in Berlin was always precarious because of competition, and he increasingly spent his spare time gambling and playing *skat*, his favourite card game. Given the family's bleak financial predicament, he must have thought that things couldn't get worse. That, however, was before Adolf Hitler came to power in 1933. With the rise of the Nazis, my grandfather's decision to move his family to Berlin must have weighed heavily on him.

FOUR

My Father's Flight from Hell

In 1929 my father was promoted to the position of senior salesman and manager of the linen, cotton and fabric section of the Tietz-owned department store Kaufhaus Römischer Kaiser in Erfurt, 300 kilometres south-west of Berlin. He managed a staff of about twenty and was comfortable there. 'I was on my own and I was happy,' he told me. 'I was content with my job. The turnover was good, the staff I had was all right. Then of course the Nazis came, this became a little bit more difficult.'

A few years ago, my wife Lauren found a photograph of my father and eight other men playing indoor bowls. Herbert stands in the centre of the group of men – who I imagine were his colleagues at the department store – as he is about to roll the ball for the game. All but one of the men in the photograph are wearing white shirts, ties and waistcoats, which was probably their work attire. Most are smiling or laughing, and my father is grinning widely, enjoying the camaraderie of a boys' night out. This is the only photograph, apart from those on passport and travel documents, I have of my father before he left Germany.

The photograph must have been taken soon before or after the Nazis came to power. I find it remarkable how comfortable my father looks among his colleagues, and how ordinary this scene is. When I search for hidden signs of danger in the photo, I can't find any. Like the photograph of my grandmother and her daughters in Berlin in 1937, the picture of my father playing bowls triggers in me an unsettling sense of foreboding. I look at it with the knowledge of what is about to unfold for him and his family. It is like a snapshot of the last rays of sunlight before a long, black night – before Herbert's comfortable bachelor's life in Erfurt began to unravel. At the same time, the photo also offers reassurance that my father had some good times in Germany before he had to flee.

In the late 1920s and early 1930s, Erfurt witnessed violent street battles between communists and far-right groups that later swelled the ranks of the Sturmabteilung (SA or Stormtroopers). After 1933, the Stormtroopers were granted full police powers, which allowed them to hunt down and arrest political enemies. Those who were considered to be sympathetic to the communists and social democrats were usually arrested, and then beaten, tortured and killed. In June 1933, Hitler visited Erfurt for a rally that was attended by 120 000 people, who were roused to fever pitch by the Führer's ferocious oratory about the racial superiority of the German Volk and the dangers posed to it by communists, social democrats, Jews and Roma.

My father recalls: 'At that time we Jews we hardly went out, occasionally we went out, you know, sometimes we saw the people in uniform looking at us. It scared us, then we disappeared.'

My father's life was turned upside down the year Hitler came to power. A young gentile woman who lived in the apartment above his would sometimes visit him and they would talk or listen to records or the radio. They were not romantically involved. Then one day she visited him adorned with two swastika earrings. He could not restrain himself and told her, 'Oh, it looks very lovely, put one through your nose too.' My father thought she must have told one of her Gestapo friends, because soon afterwards he was at work when the personnel chief called him and said, 'Mr Robinski, don't get frightened but here's a policeman, he wants to arrest you.' As he was escorted away by a policeman in uniform and another in plain clothes, my father asked, 'Can't the one in uniform walk behind us?'

Herbert's request that the uniformed policeman walk a little distance behind him reveals how important it was for him to retain a semblance of normality and respectability. When they arrived at the police station, however, all pretences of decorum disappeared. A policeman looked at the charge sheet, which stated that my father had ridiculed Nazi state symbols, and screamed at him, 'You bastard, you bloody Jew, you're running down our government! That is going to come to an end now. You dirty Jew! Get out!'

Herbert was taken to the Festung (military prison) where he met a prison warden from the old Weimar Republic who he could sense was not a Nazi supporter. 'Can't you shut up?' the man urged him. 'Can't you keep your bloody mouth shut? How dare you open your mouth these days? Don't you know what's going on? Don't you know you cannot fight the Nazis with words?'

My father was shaken and confused by what was happening to him and asked the warden for help. 'I can't do anything,' said the warden, 'but I'm going to put you together with one of your fellow Jews.' He opened the cell and there was a man named Samuel Tannenbaum, one of my father's salesmen, who said, '*Guten tag, Herr Robinski. Wie geht's hier?* ... Here you're welcome, but there is no such a thing as boss and salesman. It doesn't exist here. Here we are on the same level.'

In prison my father had a glimpse of Nazi brutality. One day he heard that the wife of Waldemar Schapiro, a Jewish man who had been in the adjacent cell shortly before, had arrived at the prison and accused the Nazis of murdering her husband. Schapiro had been arrested earlier for printing pamphlets for the Communist Party in Erfurt even though the party was still legal at the time. His wife was taken into custody and warned to stop making accusations or else she would face a similar fate to that of her husband. 'We know you have three children,' they told her. 'We will let you out of prison. But if you dare open your mouth about your husband you will be back in prison and it will be the end of you.' She decided to keep quiet and was released. My father never heard what happened to her.

An internet search on Schapiro reveals that he was one of the Nazis' first political victims in Erfurt. He worked as a clerk for a company that sold office machines and stationery supplies; but while he was connected to the Communist Party in Erfurt, he was not, in fact, a member. He had, however, assisted with the publication of a banned left-wing newspaper, and for this he was arrested, jailed and tortured. He was then held in the police prison in Petersberg in Erfurt for four months before being shot in the head in July 1933 by a group of SA men. Schapiro was one of thousands of communists and social democrats who were arrested, tortured and murdered in the months after Hitler came to power.

My father was released on bail after a few weeks in prison, and was told that his case was being referred to a higher court and that he could not leave Erfurt without permission. He spent the next three years secretly planning his escape. In our interview, he revealed nothing about his state of mind during this period. Such events would no doubt have scarred him deeply and shaken his sense of confidence and security as a German citizen. I suspect that what he encountered in prison went well beyond Nazi hate speech and political rhetoric, but he probably hid his feelings about this experience to protect his family. In 1937, a year after my father left for South Africa, Buchenwald concentration camp was established a mere twenty minutes' drive from Erfurt. Later, the engineers at Topf & Söhne (Topf & Sons), a company in Erfurt, would supply Auschwitz with its ovens.

I sometimes wonder what my father told his family, friends and colleagues about his experience in prison. How would they have responded to his accounts of the Nazis' treatment of enemies of the state such as Schapiro? He may have tried to protect those closest to him from the full knowledge of what was happening, or tried to convince himself that, as long as he didn't get involved in politics, the Nazis would leave him and his family alone.

* * *

Growing up in Port Elizabeth, I could always sense my father's visceral fear of officialdom and authority – a remnant of his experiences with Nazi politics and brutality in the pre-war years. In 1978, when I was eighteen and studying photography at Port Elizabeth Technikon, some of these fears began to leak into my own encounters with the apartheid government in South Africa. By then Prime Minister B.J. Vorster, a former Nazi sympathiser, had turned South Africa into a police state, although here Jews were full citizens and black people were the ones subjected to racially discriminatory laws, repression and violence.

One day, as I walked through Port Elizabeth's bustling city centre casually photographing people with my bulky Nikkormat FTN camera, I witnessed a black woman being dragged into the Baakens Street police station. She looked badly injured and was unconscious. After instinctively squeezing the shutter to capture the scene, I realised that I had better disappear from it, and quickly. But before I could get around the corner to safety, two policemen got hold of me and escorted me to the charge office, where I was bombarded with questions. Why was I photographing a police station? Did I not know that it was forbidden to photograph key-point government installations? I told them I was studying photography and that I would photograph anything of interest during my outings in the city. What they considered to be my lack of cooperation prompted them to call in one Major Philips, but I was equally stubborn and uncooperative with him. He lost patience, and demanded to talk to my parents and search my bedroom for any banned political pamphlets and literature.

When my father opened the door to the major, he was naturally horrified, and, in his desperation to mediate the situation, spluttered, 'Major, can I get you a drink? How can I help you?' Philips demanded to search my bedroom, which only intensified my father's anxiety. Seeing him in such a state made me realise that I had better make a show of cooperating.

The major found no subversive literature under my bed, but he took my camera with him when he left. He told me to come to the Port Elizabeth security police headquarters located on the sixth floor of the Sanlam Building the next day, when I would get the camera back. When I entered the security police offices the following day, I immediately sensed that I was in a place of unspeakable horror. I could smell fear and death oozing from the walls, ceilings and floorboards. Well-known anti-apartheid activists had been tortured and killed here. On 6 September 1977, barely a year earlier, Black Consciousness activist Steve Biko had been brutally beaten by security policemen in one of the rooms on the sixth floor. Biko later died as a result of these injuries.

Major Philips and another large, menacing policeman were waiting for me when I arrived. Philips played good cop and was quiet and impassive throughout my interrogation, while the brute was the bad cop who screamed accusations and abuse at me: 'What the fuck were you doing photographing a police station? You are looking for *kak* [shit] and you will find it.' And so it went on. Eventually I was given back my camera, along with the prints of all the photographs besides that of the woman who was dragged into the police station. They also kept all my negatives.

My father's encounter with Major Philips probably triggered a recollection of Erfurt in 1933, and my own brief experience with the security police caused me to inherit his fears and taught me to keep my head down from then on, below the parapet.

* * *

During a visit to Erfurt in 2009, I stood outside the three-storey red-brick building where my father had been incarcerated. The building is no longer a prison and has a plaque on it with the red triangle for Nazi political prisoners and the words 'In remembrance of Chaim Wulf Schapiro who died here on 15.07.1933'.[1] The plaque also gives the names and dates of the deaths of two other political prisoners. Standing outside the building, I tried to imagine what my father had witnessed inside these prison walls. Could this have given him a sense of foreboding about what was coming? Was this what had galvanised him into action?

Other incidents had strengthened his resolve to leave Germany. He told me about a heated argument with one of his junior salesmen at Römischer Kaiser over state-controlled prices of goods. The salesman, who also happened to be a card-carrying Nazi, informed my father, 'Herr Robinski, I warn you. If you bring up the prices, I'm going to report you.' So my father did nothing, and did not report the incident or reprimand the employee. He also recalled seeing another colleague at a Nazi rally screaming, 'Don't buy from Jews, don't buy from Jews!' even though he worked for a Jewish

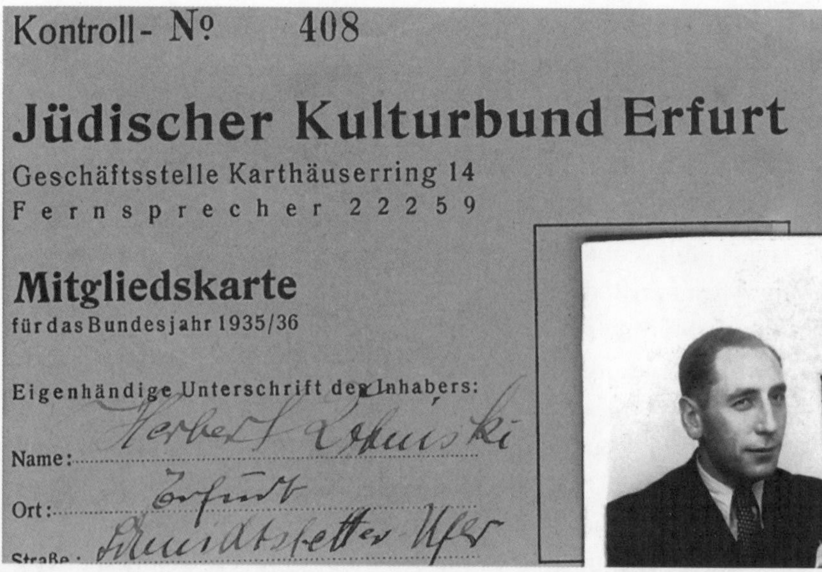
Kontroll- Nº 408

Jüdischer Kulturbund Erfurt

Geschäftsstelle Karthäuserring 14

Fernsprecher 22259

Mitgliedskarte

für das Bundesjahr 1935/36

Eigenhändige Unterschrift des Inhabers:

Name:

Ort: Erfurt

Straße:

My father's 1935/36 membership card of the Jewish Cultural Organisation in Erfurt

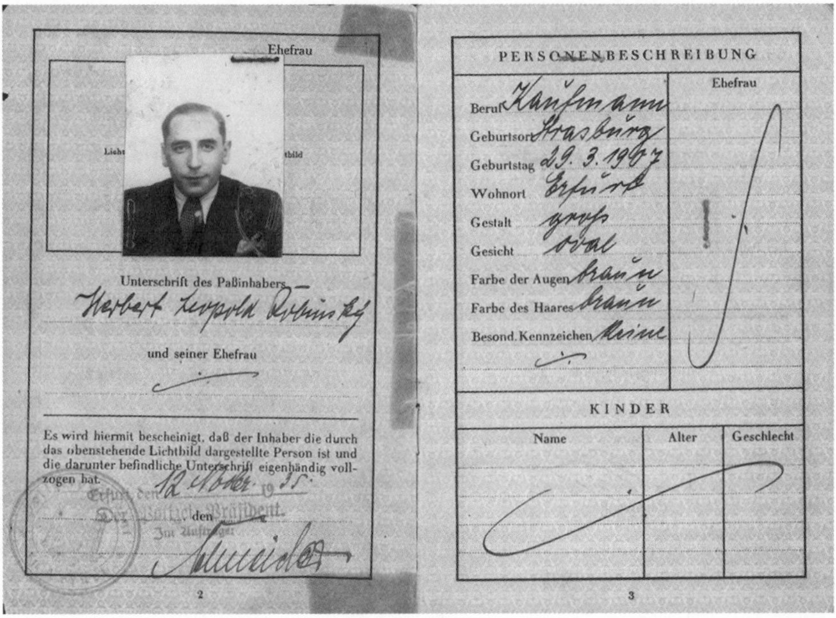

Ehefrau

Lichtbild

Unterschrift des Paßinhabers

Herbert Leopold Robinsky

und seiner Ehefrau

Es wird hiermit bescheinigt, daß der Inhaber die durch das obenstehende Lichtbild dargestellte Person ist und die darunter befindliche Unterschrift eigenhändig vollzogen hat.

Erfurt, den 12. Nov. 1935

Im Auftrage:

2

PERSONENBESCHREIBUNG

		Ehefrau
Beruf	Kaufmann	
Geburtsort	Strasburg	
Geburtstag	29. 3. 1907	
Wohnort	Erfurt	
Gestalt	groß	
Gesicht	oval	
Farbe der Augen	braun	
Farbe des Haares	braun	
Besond. Kennzeichen	keine	

KINDER

Name	Alter	Geschlecht

3

My father's German passport that he used to leave Germany in 1936

company. On Labour Day, one of the Jewish directors of the company, Siegfried Pinthus, had to make a speech lauding the accomplishments of the Third Reich. During his speech, Pinthus raised his arm in the Nazi salute, and addressed the Römischer Kaiser staff. Before him, in the front row of the audience, were about twenty uniformed Nazis.

On 15 September 1935, the Nazis passed the Nuremberg Laws, which contained the Reich Citizenship Law, declaring that only those of German or related blood were eligible to be Reich citizens, and the Law for the Protection of German Blood and German Honour, which forbade marriage and extramarital intercourse between Jews and Germans.

My father was a charming and debonair bachelor who had a number of gentile girlfriends in Erfurt. This would have been risky after the passing of the Nuremberg Laws. One of his girlfriends had managed to get a room on the fourth floor of the apartment building in which my father lived on the ground floor. They would see each other in secret, but he said he feared that the Nazis would catch them and that they would cut off all her hair. 'I don't know what else they would have done to her,' he said. 'I was very careful with my gentile girlfriends. The one who risked her life was Margaret. We still met, but secretly, at her residence; not at mine any more.'

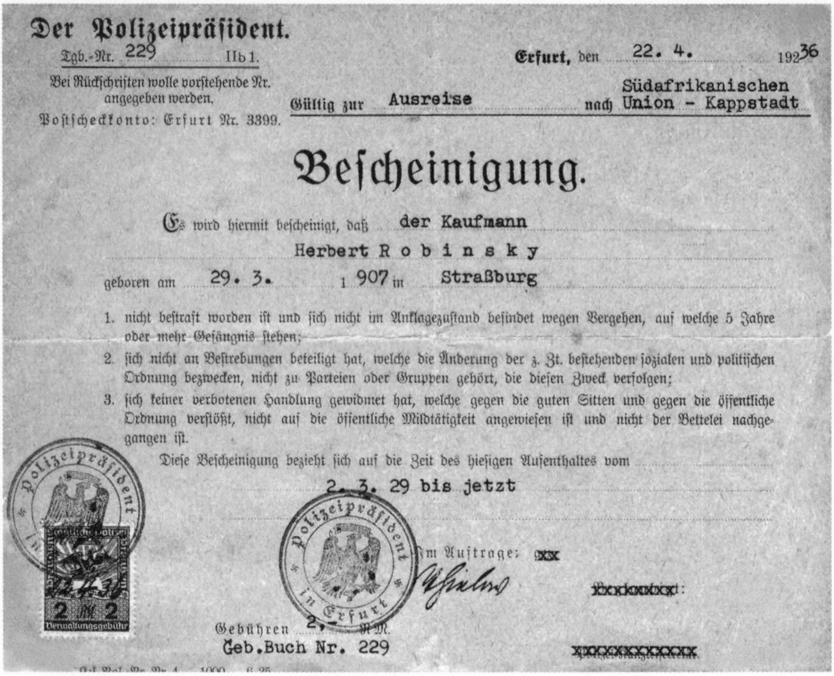

Der Polizeipräsident.
Tgb.-Nr. 229 IIb 1.
Bei Rückschriften wolle vorstehende Nr. angegeben werden.
Postscheckkonto: Erfurt Nr. 3399.

Erfurt, den 22. 4. 1936

Gültig zur Ausreise nach Südafrikanischen Union - Kappstadt

Bescheinigung.

Es wird hiermit bescheinigt, daß der Kaufmann Herbert R o b i n s k y geboren am 29. 3. 1907 in Straßburg

1. nicht bestraft worden ist und sich nicht im Anklagezustand befindet wegen Vergehen, auf welche 5 Jahre oder mehr Gefängnis stehen;
2. sich nicht an Bestrebungen beteiligt hat, welche die Änderung der z. Zt. bestehenden sozialen und politischen Ordnung bezwecken, nicht zu Parteien oder Gruppen gehört, die diesen Zweck verfolgen;
3. sich keiner verbotenen Handlung gewidmet hat, welche gegen die guten Sitten und gegen die öffentliche Ordnung verstößt, nicht auf die öffentliche Mildtätigkeit angewiesen ist und nicht der Bettelei nachgegangen ist.

Diese Bescheinigung bezieht sich auf die Zeit des hiesigen Aufenthaltes vom 2. 3. 29 bis jetzt

Im Auftrage: xxx

Gebühren 2,– RM.
Geb.Buch Nr. 229

Herbert's police clearance certificate required to leave Germany, dated 22 April 1936

Time was running out for Herbert, who had to be cautious while planning his escape from Germany since his prison release had come with conditions. He probably chose South Africa as his new home because his uncle Eugen and his children lived there. Herbert would have to obtain a passport for his trip out of the country, and then convince Nazi officials that he was only planning to go on holiday to Switzerland.

I started to make my arrangements. The first thing was to get a passport. There was a decent policeman or official and I asked him not to put down 'Strasburg, West Prussia', but just 'Strasburg'. So it could be Strasburg in Alsace-Lorraine, because there was a quota [for Eastern Europeans] in South Africa. If you came from Poland, then they wouldn't let you in. You'd fall under a quota and you had to have a special permit. But if you came from Strasburg in France, it was no difficulty… That was all I needed. I went home and said goodbye to my family and I booked for a trip to Switzerland which was popular in Germany called *Kraft durch Freude* (Power through Pleasure). I also managed to get a booking to Italy… I said goodbye to my friends. I left

in such a hurry that there were a few things I left behind ... I boarded the train with very mixed feelings. Will I get through? Will they stop me? But they did not stop me ... When we passed the Swiss frontier we all of a sudden see the Swiss railway men in uniforms, and people jumped out of the train and started dancing on the station. The others must have also been Jews, no argument. I stayed overnight at a hotel in Switzerland. Twelve o'clock at night, a knock on the door. I ask, 'Who is it?' 'Police, open.' This is Switzerland. I didn't expect anything like this. 'What are you doing, how long are you going to stay here?' I showed them my train ticket to Genoa. They said, 'Are you sure you are leaving for Genoa?' I said yes. They were satisfied and I went back to sleep. The next day I went to Genova and picked up my ticket ... When I arrived in Cape Town the immigration officer asked me where Strasburg was. I showed him Alsace-Lorraine on the map and got through ...

Herbert arrived in Cape Town on 14 May 1936, on an Italian Line ship called the *Duilio*.[2] There was little time to reflect on what he had left behind in Germany, and he had to find his feet quickly in this new and strange country.

Soon after the *Duilio*'s arrival, pro-Nazi Afrikaner nationalists and the South African Christian National Socialists, known as the Greyshirts (Gryshemde), launched their mass protests against the entry of German Jews into South Africa. The Greyshirts, a fascist organisation established in October 1933 by Louis Theodor Weichardt, a hairdresser of German descent, had been galvanising support throughout the 1930s against 'mass' Jewish immigration.[3] The year my father arrived, they planned to hold a public protest at Table Bay in October to stop the docking of the *Stuttgart*, which was carrying over 500 German Jews.

The 13 000-ton tourist liner had been chartered in late October 1936 in order to beat the impending introduction of even more restrictive immigration legislation in Germany and South Africa. The Council for German Jews in London, and the respected German Jewish leader Reverend Dr Leo Baeck, pleaded with the Jewish Board of Deputies in South Africa for support, but the board responded cautiously, fearing a public backlash that would jeopardise future Jewish immigration into the country. The board also feared that the arrival of large numbers of European Jews could intensify anti-Semitism and boost pro-Nazi support in South Africa. Following pressure from Dr Baeck, however, the board backpedalled slightly and, while refusing to accept responsibility for a rescue mission, would not oppose one either, as the law permitted those with proper papers to enter South Africa.

In spite of the concerted opposition to their arrival, on 27 October, three days before new immigration regulations were to be enforced, 537 German Jews disembarked at the Cape Town docks the morning after the planned protest by the Greyshirts. The *Stuttgart*'s captain had apparently known about the protest and wisely decided to wait a while before docking. The arrival of the refugees, predictably, generated hostile letters in the press and mass protest meetings organised by Weichardt and Hendrik Verwoerd, then professor of sociology and social work at the University of Stellenbosch.

Notwithstanding their setback with the *Stuttgart*, the Greyshirts continued to mobilise support for their cause. On 21 November 1936, a report by the Commission on the Jewish Question by Nico Diederichs was sent to the head office of the powerful Afrikaner secret society, the Afrikaner Broederbond, in Johannesburg.[4] In his covering letter, Diederichs submitted three recommendations to the leadership of the Broederbond for curbing Jewish immigration. These included the arrangement of protest meetings against Jewish immigration, sending letters about the issue to the press, and organising boycotts against Jewish businesses until the United Party government of Barry Hertzog and Jan Smuts heeded their demands. The report suggests that these acts against the Jewish population should not be carried out in a 'war-like manner' as this would be un-Christian. Afrikaners also had to be encouraged to challenge Jewish dominance in commerce; more restrictive Jewish immigration quotas were needed to protect Afrikaner business interests; decisive action against Jewish communists was necessary; and English-speakers had to be enlisted in the fight against Jewish control over commerce.

In 1937 the Hertzog government introduced the Aliens Act, which effectively closed the door to German Jewish refugees. Earlier, the 1930 Quota Act had restricted Jewish immigration from Eastern Europe. Then, with Hitler's rise to power, German Jewish immigration to South Africa spiked from 400 annually in previous years, to 596 in 1933, and peaked the following year, at 865. Although these numbers were relatively small, following the passage of the Nuremberg Laws in September 1935 there was the very real possibility that Jewish immigration would rise even further. This scenario was pre-empted by the 1936 Immigration Amendment Act. From then on, bonds or guarantees were no longer acceptable under South African law, and immigrants had to make a cash deposit of £100 for an adult and £50 for a child. Since the Nazi government did not allow refugees to leave with much more than RM10 (less than £1), from November 1936 onwards it became practically impossible for German Jewish refugees to get into South Africa.[5] Weichardt's far-right organisation, which had about 2 000 members at its zenith, was also in the process of setting up a paramilitary unit modelled on the Nazis' brown-shirted Sturmabteilung. With the support of National Party leaders such as Verwoerd and Malan, the Greyshirts would ensure that, between 1933 and the start of World War II in 1939, only 6 000 German Jewish refugees entered South Africa. This was a tiny fraction of the quarter of a million German Jews who fled Nazism.[6]

It was into this maelstrom of pro-Nazi political mobilisation that my father arrived in Cape Town in 1936, having managed to scrape in just before the most restrictive immigration laws had taken effect. He was soon to relocate to Port Elizabeth, the headquarters of the Greyshirts. The task that lay before him was to attempt the miraculous rescue of the rest of his family in Germany.

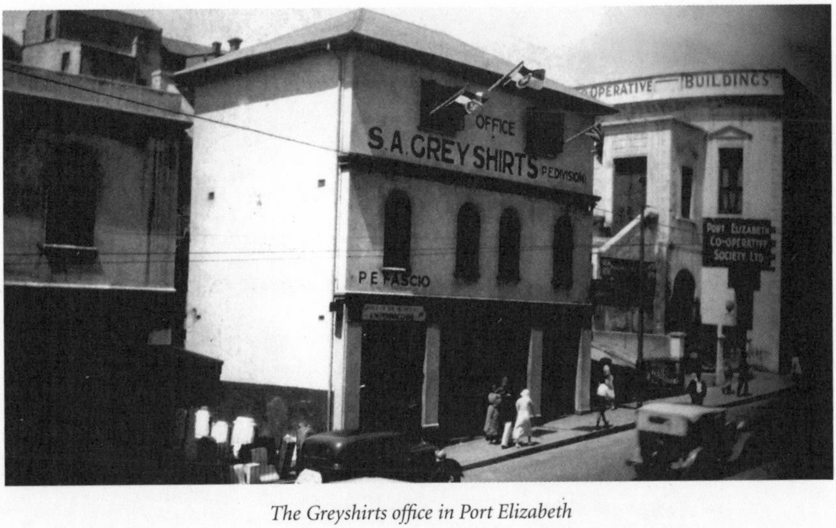

The Greyshirts office in Port Elizabeth

FIVE

My Eyes Open

A year after my interview with my father, I received a call from my cousin Cecilia informing me that he was very ill. I had recently arrived in Harare, and was about to embark on two years of rural fieldwork in Zimbabwe for my doctoral thesis. I also spoke to my mother, who tried to downplay the seriousness of the situation, but, having heard the urgency in Cecilia's voice, I flew to Cape Town a few days later. My father was in good spirits despite the hopeless cancer prognosis, and had come to terms with his diagnosis. 'It's enough already. It's time to go,' he said to me. I spent ten precious days with him before returning to Zimbabwe. A few months later, at my fieldwork site in Matabeleland South Province, I received news from home that my father's condition was critical. I arrived at the hospital just in time to say goodbye to him.

He was heavily sedated on morphine, but I was sure he could hear me as I spoke to him and stroked his head. As his life ebbed away, his eyes stared into mine, and it was as if he was trying to tell me something important. A nurse who saw me caressing his head remarked, 'They still have feeling, even after the pulse stops.' There was so much more I would have wanted to ask him. There was so much between us that was left unsaid.

* * *

My father had lived long enough to see an extraordinary change come to South Africa.

In February 1990, President F.W. de Klerk had announced that Nelson Mandela would be released after twenty-seven years in prison, and that this would be followed by negotiations between the apartheid government and the ANC. Mass euphoria greeted this astonishing announcement.

On the day of Mandela's release a week later, I found myself standing with tens of thousands of revellers who had waited in the scorching sun for hours to hear his historic speech. Soon afterwards, I packed my Toyota bakkie and, with my partner Julia, began the long journey to Zimbabwe.

It was a difficult period to be away from my country, and I'd had little time to properly mourn the loss of my father.

From 1990 to 1992, I lived in Sengezane village in Matabeleland South. It was my first experience of long-term rural fieldwork, and I had to learn to cope with unbearably hot Lowveld summers, scorpions and snakes, as well as live without electricity or running water. I had little privacy in the village and was unprepared for the constant observation and surveillance of my every move by residents. I can vividly recall the good-natured laughter of the villagers as I made a dash for the pit-drop latrine after my first encounter with rather uncooked, traditionally brewed beer. For a nice Jewish boy from the middle-class suburbs of Port Elizabeth, these kinds of fieldwork experiences were a rude awakening to the rigours of daily life on the rural periphery.

At the homestead of Mr F. Sibanda (seated), Sengezane village, Gwanda District, Matabeleland South Province, Zimbabwe, c. 1991

I had decided to do fieldwork in Zimbabwe because I assumed that the country's land-reform programme was democratic, socialist and progressive. I also believed Zimbabwe's democratic transition could have positive implications for a future post-apartheid South Africa. A couple of months into my research, I discovered just how naïve my assumptions had been. Villagers informed me of the state terror that had persisted in Matabeleland even after independence. In the 1980s, an estimated 20 000 Ndebele-speaking people, accused of being political dissidents by President Robert Mugabe, were killed by his North Korean–trained Fifth Brigade soldiers, in a campaign called Gukurahundi ('the early rain that washes away the chaff'). My romantic visions of Zimbabwe's brand of African socialism took a beating as well when I realised that millions of peasants still struggled to make a living off the land in spite of the change in government. Facts like these proved an antidote to my idealism, and I left Zimbabwe in December 1993 thoroughly disillusioned by the grim realities of state corruption, authoritarianism and political repression.

The early 1990s in South Africa, by contrast, was a period of great hope. After the unbanning of the liberation movements and the release of Mandela and other political prisoners, the negotiation process between President de Klerk's National Party and the ANC leadership began in earnest. Despite a string of bombings by the far right-wing and the Azanian People's Organisation's military wing, as well as bloody battles between the Zulu cultural nationalists of Inkatha and ANC cadres, the country's first democratic elections took place peacefully in April 1994, with millions of black South Africans voting for the first time in their lives. The ANC assumed power in the government and Mandela became South Africa's first democratically elected president.

When I completed my doctoral dissertation in 1995, I was desperate to turn my back on Robert Mugabe's tyrannical regime and return to the dynamic and promising new democracy of South Africa with Mandela at the helm. I got a position at the University of Cape Town (UCT) as a researcher with the Kaplan Centre for Jewish Studies, where my work involved interviewing South African Jews on their sense of belonging and identity during the transition to democracy – a project over which I felt a deep ambivalence. Having spent the past decade or more running away from my Jewishness, how was I going to research such a discomforting topic? I was taken by surprise, however, when I found the interviews revitalising my interest in my Jewish identity.

Some of my research for the centre involved speaking to Jewish radicals who had joined the ANC and Communist Party, and who were now returning triumphantly to the new South Africa after decades of exile in London, Maputo, Dar es Salaam and Lusaka. I also interviewed feisty Jewish trade unionists and communist stalwarts like Ray Alexander, who had fought courageous battles on factory floors and come out on the winning side. After having been ignored and ostracised by the conservative Jewish community during apartheid, these radicals were now being lauded by the same establishment that had shunned them. None of this, however, could sweep away the fact that most Jews were bystanders in the apartheid struggle, and a few had openly colluded with the apartheid state. The most notorious of these collaborators was Percy Yutar, the first Jewish attorney-general in apartheid South Africa, who had zealously secured Mandela's conviction of life imprisonment on Robben Island. I got to interview Jews who operated on the social margins as well, such as gay and lesbian activists who challenged conventional Judaism in their quest for sexual equality and social and religious acceptance. After six months of interviewing Jews across the political spectrum, I felt my submerged Jewishness begin to rise to the surface.

In 1995 I left UCT's Kaplan Centre and joined the Department of Anthropology at the University of the Western Cape. A year later I was researching the Truth and Reconciliation Commission (TRC) and writing articles in the press about this extraordinary process. I attended numerous TRC public hearings during the mid-1990s, where I was exposed to the emotionally raw testimonies of victims of political violence. I heard relatives of murdered anti-apartheid activists demand the truth about their deaths and the locations of their remains from former members of apartheid's security forces. Soon I would begin to ask similar questions about my own family, and it was not long before I started getting some answers.

* * *

In 1996, while attending an American Anthropology Association conference in Washington DC, I took time out from sessions to visit the US Holocaust Memorial Museum. The exhibits, which featured massive piles of shoes, spectacles and suitcases from the death camps, shocked and unsettled me. Other exhibits revealed the complicity of big business and science, and physical anthropology in particular, in the genocide. In one exhibit, prominence was given to German anatomist and physical anthropologist Dr Eugen Fischer, a Nazi scientist whose footprint I would again stumble across many years later. It was Fischer's scientific work that led directly to Nazi policy decisions regarding racial classification, and created the conditions for the mass murder of Roma, Sinti and Jews. Another German scientist featured in the exhibition was psychiatrist and physician Robert Ritter, who wrote a report that led the Reich Interior Ministry to issue guidelines in 1936 'On Combatting the Gypsy Plague'. The same year, Ritter was appointed to head the newly created Eugenic and Population Biological Research Station of the Reich Health and Sanitation Office. By 1941, Ritter's research and policy guidelines mandated the photographic surveillance and fingerprinting of Roma, thus setting in motion the processes for extermination.

The museum also provided information about Operation T4 (the Nazi euthanasia programme), the use of slave labour at the camps by the Bavarian Motor Works (BMW), the role of IBM in Nazi racial-classification systems, and the fact that more than half of the participants at the 1942 Wannsee Conference, which decided on the Final Solution, had doctoral degrees. It was ultimately German scientists and engineers who volunteered their expertise towards the design and construction of the machinery for mass murder, while businessmen from IBM and pharmaceutical and chemicals company IG Farben were the capitalist cogs in this catastrophe.

Mieczysław Stobierski's model of Crematorium II at Auschwitz-Birkenau at the museum made this modern, industrial-scale mass killing machine more concrete in my imagination. The model reconstruction of the gas chambers contained small clay figures sculptured with frightening realism, and I tried to imagine the terror and the screams as the gas was released. Were the victims aware of what was about to happen to them? They would have had to stand naked in front of Josef Mengele and his selection team before being sent to this terrifying death. Adolf Eichmann, Reinhard Heydrich and countless other Nazi officers and foot soldiers set in motion a series of bureaucratic procedures – including racial classifications and ordinances that stripped Jews of citizenship, the confiscation of their property, and slave labour, deportation and selection – that culminated in the murder of my father's family.

The exhibition left me in a state of stupefaction, and I was relieved when I happened upon the museum's library and resource centre. I needed to speak to someone about what I had just experienced, and found a museum staff member, who listened as I told him how disorienting I had found the exhibition. When I mentioned that my father's family had perished in the Holocaust, he looked for their name in a bulky black book called the *Berliner Gedenkbuch* (its full title is *The Memorial Book of the Federal Archives for the Victims of the Persecution of Jews in Germany (1933–1945)*), searching among the pages with surnames that began with the letter R: Reich, Rosen, Rubinstein ... Paging back, he stopped at the names of the six Robinski family members: Cecilie, David, Edith, Hildegard, Siegfried and another Edith (Siegfried's wife). Next to their names were their addresses in Berlin, dates and places of birth, and dates and places of deportation. My grandparents were the first members of the Robinski family to be deported, on the 21st Transport to Riga, on 19 October 1942. Hildegard was deported to Auschwitz on 19 February 1943, and, shortly thereafter, on 1 March 1943, my uncle Siegfried was sent there on the 31st Transport. Their sister Edith was deported to Auschwitz five months later.

Upon discovering this information, I felt like a detective stumbling across the first hard evidence that ties a murderer to a crime scene. What had once been vague and abstract knowledge about the fate of my father's family now took on a concreteness in form. The discovery, to me, seemed similar to those made by members of the TRC when they unearthed the brutal secrets of the apartheid regime. I remember the confusion on the museum worker's face as he witnessed the satisfaction and relief that passed over me after learning the truth about my family. Perhaps my expression should have revealed shock and sorrow instead. In my mind, however, the terrifyingly mundane, officious details about the Robinski family's deportation and their final destinations gave substance to their existence. It meant that the memory of my father's family had not been completely erased off the face of the earth.

The preface of the *Berliner Gedenkbuch*, written by then federal president of Germany Horst Köhler, comes close to capturing what I was experiencing in that moment: 'This Memorial Book gives those murdered their names and dignity back. It is a memorial and at the same time a reminder that every single life has a name and its own truly unique tragic story.' The knowledge the book imparted would forever change my life, but I could never have imagined at that point where it would lead me. As I left the museum I was acutely aware that I carried with me information that had been buried for decades in the black hole of silence in my father's house. That silence had finally been broken.

I wondered how my father would have responded to this exhibition. I wasn't sure if he had ever gone to Holocaust museums and exhibitions. In the days after my visit, I struggled with unsettling questions about my own relationship to this devastating past. To what degree was it my past too, or was I intruding upon, and perhaps even cannibalising, my father's memories and experiences? I tried to understand why he had been so silent and realised it would have been difficult for him to have spoken about his family's fate and that he probably knew very little about it himself.

The museum visit had opened a portal into my family's past that I might never be able to close, and I had no choice but to cautiously peer in. I decided I needed to go to Germany, to Berlin, the quintessential city of ghosts. But did the ghosts even want visitors? Would my father have approved of what I was doing, or would he have implored me to firmly close the lid of this dreaded black box of memories?

At the time, a debate was raging about the Third Reich after the publication of *Hitler's Willing Executioners: Ordinary Germans and the Holocaust*, by Daniel Goldhagen.[1] In this book, Goldhagen makes sweeping claims about what he describes as a universal, innate hatred of Jews by all Germans – that the vast majority of ordinary Germans were 'willing executioners' in the genocide because of a unique and virulent 'eliminationist anti-Semitism' deeply embedded within German political culture and identity, which has its origin in the religious ideas of medieval Europe. For Goldhagen, all Germans should be held accountable for the Holocaust, and not just card-carrying Nazis and the SS.

Goldhagen's argument challenges American historian Christopher Browning's 1992 book *Ordinary Men*, which analyses the Reserve Police Battalion 101 of 1942 that massacred and rounded up Jews for deportation to death camps in Poland. Browning's startling conclusion, which was strongly influenced by the famous Milgram experiment on compliance, was that the men of Unit 101 were not fanatical anti-Semites but ordinary working-class men from Hamburg, who had been drafted but found to be unfit for military action. Goldhagen, however, insists that these massacres of Jews were not the outcome of the sociological phenomenon of compliance to authority, but that the members of Unit 101 were part of an extraordinarily barbaric German political culture that promoted an irrational, genocidal hatred of Jews.

Goldhagen's book became a publishing phenomenon, even though it received scathing reviews. In the words of the illustrious Holocaust historian Raul Hilberg, the book was 'totally wrong about everything' and 'worthless'.

In the German capital I made my way to the state archive, the Landesarchiv Berlin, a large, imposing red-brick structure near the Eichborndamm S-Bahn station. The Landesarchiv building, which was once a weapons and ammunition factory, has holdings that range from tax files documenting the confiscation of Jews' property to the over 800 000 case files of the Berlin Restitution Offices. I was struck by how user-friendly it was for visitors searching for information about relatives. An affable librarian approached me when I arrived and, instantly assessing what I wanted, asked for the family name in which I was interested. About twenty minutes later, after searching the archive, she provided me with photocopies of about 100 pages of official documentation concerning the last days of the Robinski family. The documents were in German, however, so I could not read them. To this day, I have only translated a small fraction of the pages from the Robinski file.

An enormous amount of methodical labour went into the racial classification of Jews and Roma, as well as the documentation of the expropriated property of Jews and their deportation and extermination. Now, as an act of recompense, post-Holocaust German state archives and libraries make this information available to the families of the Nazis' victims.

As I worked my way through my own family's file, I observed the impersonal bureaucratic rationality of the Nazis in their documentation of their victims' identities and belongings – what the German Jewish political theorist Hannah Arendt referred to as the banality of evil.[2] All information was systematically recorded, including the exact details of the Robinskis' confiscated property and their value. From having nothing but a single photograph of Edith, her mother and her sister, I now possessed their official records, and I could begin the process of piecing together the story behind these bare facts.

On 16 October 1942, a sixteen-page *Vermögenserklärung* (declaration of assets) was filled in for each of my grandparents. My grandfather's form began:

Name and surname: *David Isr. Robinski*
Profession: ——
Jew?: *Yes*

Last occupation: —
Residence (city, area, street and house number, since when?):
1925, 62 Wallnertheaterstrasse 45 II

The form asks for the 'Name, address and possible Jewish race of house owner', and the 'name, address, and possible Jewish race of subletter'.

Size of apartment (number of rooms and type of rooms, toilet, hot water, steam or hot-water heating, balcony, floor, elevator, garden, other rooms as hall, bathroom, maiden room, cellar, attic ... exact details): *4 rooms, kitchen*
Amount of monthly or quarterly rent (add lease agreement):
RM 90 per month
Is the rent paid, to whom and up to when? *Up to the 31.10.42*
Do you have subtenants (if so, name address and possible Jewish race of subtenant as well as number and size of sublet rooms and amount of daily, weekly, monthly rent? Up to when is rent paid and till when the agreement can be cancelled? Attach subletting agreements. Are these subtenants emigrating?:
Paula Sara Karriel – 1 room – RM 21; Vera Sara Karriel – 1 room – RM 21
Registration card (place and number): *Berlin A023055*
Born: *10.5.78 in Rucken/Tilsit*
Nationality: *German*
Marital status: *Married*
My household consists of – *4* – people, and these are: *my wife and 2 daughters and me*
Wife/husband (name, former names, possible Jewish race and date of birth): *Cäcilie Sara Robinski, born Grünberg, born 24.11.82*
Children (also the ones over 21 years old):
a) living in the household (name, date of birth, possible Jewish race):
Edith Sara Robinski 26.1.15; Hildegard Sara Robinski 15.5.17
b) living outside the household (personalia, address, possible Jewish race):
Siegfried Isr. Robinski – Naunystraße 46/48
Which of the children have own income, how much?: —
Which of the family members are migrating with you?: *My wife*
Which family members already migrated and where to?: *2 sons to Africa*

Three days after this form was filled in, my grandparents were deported to Riga.

From October 1942 until February 1943, Hildegard and her sister Edith were without their parents, and, along with Siegfried, all three siblings were working as slave labourers (*Zwangsarbeit*) during this time. They would have been severely distraught and disoriented once their parents were deported.

Hildegard was working in a laundry company called Max Burmann & Co. at Herzbergstr 68–70 when she was arrested by the Gestapo and sent to their headquarters in Berlin on 17 February 1943. A form filled in on that day states that 'On the basis of section 1 of the law on the confiscation of communist assets on 26 May 1933 ... in conjunction with the law on the seizure of unpatriotic and anti-state assets on 14 July 1933 ... in conjunction with the decree of the Fuhrer and Chancellor on the realisation of confiscated assets of enemies of the state on 29 May 1941 ... all assets of Hildegard Sara Robinski ... will be confiscated in favour of the German Reich'.

Another document is a 'proof of delivery' notice.

> **Proof of delivery**
> One copy of the attached document on behalf of the Gestapo, Gestapo headquarters Berlin, for the purpose of delivery of
> Hildegard Sara Robinski
> I handed over today to the recipient himself at Berlin N 4, Grosse Hamburger Street, Berlin ... 17 Feb. 1943
> Chief Executor in Berlin

Hildegard's 'delivery' evokes the now routine reduction of Jews to property, to mere things. It was not enough to dispossess them of their belongings, livelihoods and dignity, and then to enslave them. Their very identities, the idea of a Jew as a person, had to be stripped away completely, to a state of nothingness. Hildegard was deported to Auschwitz two days later.

Siegfried worked with his sister Edith in Berlin-Zehlendorf at the Zeiss Ikon factory, which manufactured lenses for military equipment, until 27 February 1943, the day of the notorious *Fabrikaktion*, when Jewish slave labourers were replaced with prisoners of war and deported to the east. Siegfried was deported to Auschwitz on 1 March, and his wife Edith followed on 6 March. His sister Edith was arrested five months later, on 29 July, and held in detention at the Jewish Senior Centre (das Jüdische Altersheim) at Grosse Hamburgerstr 26. On 4 August, she was deported on the 40th Transport to Auschwitz.

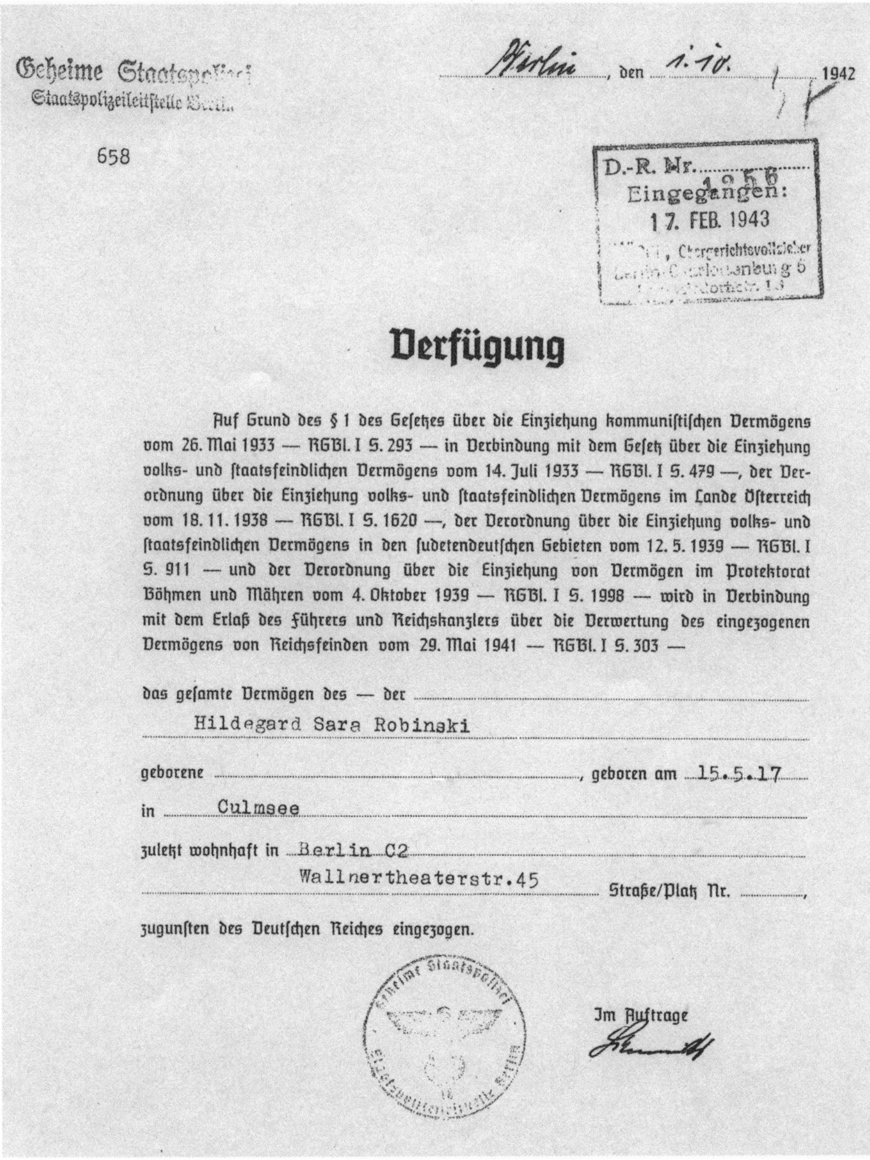

Geheime Staatspolizei
Staatspolizeileitstelle Berlin

658

Berlin, den 1.10. 1942

D.-R. Nr. 1956
Eingegangen:
17. FEB. 1943

Verfügung

Auf Grund des § 1 des Gesetzes über die Einziehung kommunistischen Vermögens vom 26. Mai 1933 — RGBl. I S. 293 — in Verbindung mit dem Gesetz über die Einziehung volks- und staatsfeindlichen Vermögens vom 14. Juli 1933 — RGBl. I S. 479 —, der Verordnung über die Einziehung volks- und staatsfeindlichen Vermögens im Lande Österreich vom 18. 11. 1938 — RGBl. I S. 1620 —, der Verordnung über die Einziehung volks- und staatsfeindlichen Vermögens in den sudetendeutschen Gebieten vom 12. 5. 1939 — RGBl. I S. 911 — und der Verordnung über die Einziehung von Vermögen im Protektorat Böhmen und Mähren vom 4. Oktober 1939 — RGBl. I S. 1998 — wird in Verbindung mit dem Erlaß des Führers und Reichskanzlers über die Verwertung des eingezogenen Vermögens von Reichsfeinden vom 29. Mai 1941 — RGBl. I S. 303 —

das gesamte Vermögen des — der
Hildegard Sara Robinski

geborene ...., geboren am 15.5.17

in Culmsee

zuletzt wohnhaft in Berlin C2
Wallnertheaterstr.45 Straße/Platz Nr. ....,

zugunsten des Deutschen Reiches eingezogen.

Im Auftrage

A form authorising the confiscation of Hildegard's property

One of the documents in the file was an inventory of Siegfried and his wife's belongings, created a month after their deportation but meticulously recorded by the Nazis despite how little the items were worth.

Special order: Inventory and evaluation

List every room separately and with heading (e.g. 'bedroom'). Only related things can be evaluated together – small things have to be listed under collective items

		Value in RM
1.	1 metal bed base with mattress	20
2.	1 day bed	no value
3.	beds	25
4.	1 wardrobe	20
5.	1 small table	
6.	4 chairs	30
7.	2 wicker tables	
8.	2 wicker chairs	10
9.	1 lamp	20
10.	2 shelves	10
11.	curtains	10
12.	2 bed bases	15
13.	1 kitchen furniture, 6 pieces	35
14.	cooking vessels and other household utensils	10
		205
	cost of evaluation	7
		212

cost calculation:	
tax fee:	5
writing fee for 4 pages:	1
travelling expenses:	1
total:	7

Berlin, 3rd April 1943

thoroughly and conscientiously evaluated.

estimated at	205 RM
off 10%	20,50 RM
remaining	184,50 RM

The Bailor.
(signed)

Zur Beachtung! 45/26555

Zwischen dem Oberfinanzpräsidenten Berlin-Brandenburg und dem Oberbürgermeister der Reichshauptstadt Berlin ist vereinbart worden, daß bei der Bewertung der zu schätzenden Sachen ein **vernünftiger mittlerer Preis** auf der Grundlage des Vorkriegspreisniveaus, und zwar unter Berücksichtigung des allgemeinen Vorkriegsverkehrswertes der Sachen gelten soll.

Akt.-Z. d. OFP lt. Straßenliste Erm. 3043

Schätzungsblatt Nr. 1

(Gehören zu einer Wohnung mehrere Schätzungsblätter, so sind diese laufend zu numerieren.)

Berlin- S.O.36 Straße: Naunystr. Nr. 46 Lage: v. IV.

Früherer Mieter bzw. Untermieter: Robinski, Siegfried u.Edith
(Früherer Eigentümer der Gegenstände)

Ungezieferfrei! — Nicht ungezieferfrei!
(Nichtzutreffendes bitte zu streichen!)

Schlüssel sind abgegeben bei: Reinerz, v. III.

Sonderauftrag

Inventar und Bewertung

Jeden Raum gesondert aufführen und mit Überschrift versehen (z. B. Schlafzimmer).
Nur zusammengehörige Sachen gemeinsam bewerten. — Kleinigkeiten als Sammelposten aufführen.

lfd. Nr.	Stück	Gegenstand	Nähere Kennzeichnung	Bewertung in RM	Bemerkungen
1	1	Metallbettstelle m.Aufl.		20.-	
~~2~~	~~1~~	~~Ruhebett~~	wertlos	------	
3		Betten		25.-	
~~4~~	~~1~~	~~Kleiderschrank~~		~~20.-~~	
5	1	Pilztisch)			
6	4	Stühle)		30.-	
7	2	Korbtische)			
8	2	Korbstühle)		10.-	
9	1	Lampe		20.-	
10	2	Regale		10.-	
11		Gardinen		10.-	
12	2	Bettstellen		15.-	
~~13~~	~~1~~	~~Kücheneinrichtung~~	~~6 teilig~~	~~35.-~~	
14		Küchengeschirr u.Hausrat		10.-	
				205.-	
			Schätzungskosten	7.-	
				212.-	

Kostenrechnung:
Taxgebühr 5.- RM.
Schreibgebühr 4 S. 1.- "
Fuhrkosten 1.- "
7.- "

Berlin, den 3.April 1943
Gewissenhaft aufgenommen und bewertet.

Hoffmann
Gerichtsvollzieher.

Geschätzt auf 205 RM.
ab 10 % 20.50
bleiben 184.50 RM.

zu übertragen Seitensumme: RM

Inventory and evaluation, Naunynstrasse 46, Berlin,
Apartment Siegfried and Edith Robinski, 3 April 1943

This inventory exposes the perversity of Nazi bureaucracy in its careful evaluation of everyday and often worthless items, while giving away nothing about the people who once owned this property. Trivial household articles, such as curtains – estimated to be worth 10 Reichsmark – are attributed value, but Siegfried and his wife Edith are not; they are soon to be reduced to ashes.

The Robinski file also contained a letter that was sent on 13 August 1943 on behalf of Herr Eugen Fluss, the owner of Kuchen Kaiser Café and the apartment that Siegfried and Edith occupied before they were deported, to the finance president of the Berlin Municipality. Following their departure, the flat was allocated to the family of Adolf Eichler, who were victims of air raids, and who had started paying rent from 1 August. The letter concludes:

> I ask you now kindly to provide the rent for the months of April, May, June and July to a total amount of 168 RM, as I am extremely reliant on the money. If the matter were resolved quickly I would be grateful.
>
> Heil Hitler!
> on behalf of Mr Fluss
> Caretaker

I later found a document revealing that in February 1955, shortly before his marriage, my father received a letter from the Joint American, British and French Military Administration of Berlin informing him that his parents had been deported to Riga on the 21st Ost (Eastern) Transport on 19 October 1942. He probably already knew that they had been sent to the east, but now he had confirmation of the precise date and destination.

* * *

A few days after my discoveries in the Berlin Landesarchiv, I found more traces of my father's family in Berlin. On a bitterly cold night in December 1996, I set out with German historian Jan-Georg Deutsch to try to locate Naunynstrasse 46 in Kreuzberg where Siegfried had lived with his wife Edith prior to their deportation. This was a part of Berlin that had miraculously remained unscathed by the bombings. I don't know what I expected to find when I began my search, but I felt some satisfaction after coming face to face with the remains of the world my uncle and his wife once inhabited. Berlin was becoming for me more than a repository of bureaucratic facts and paper trails.

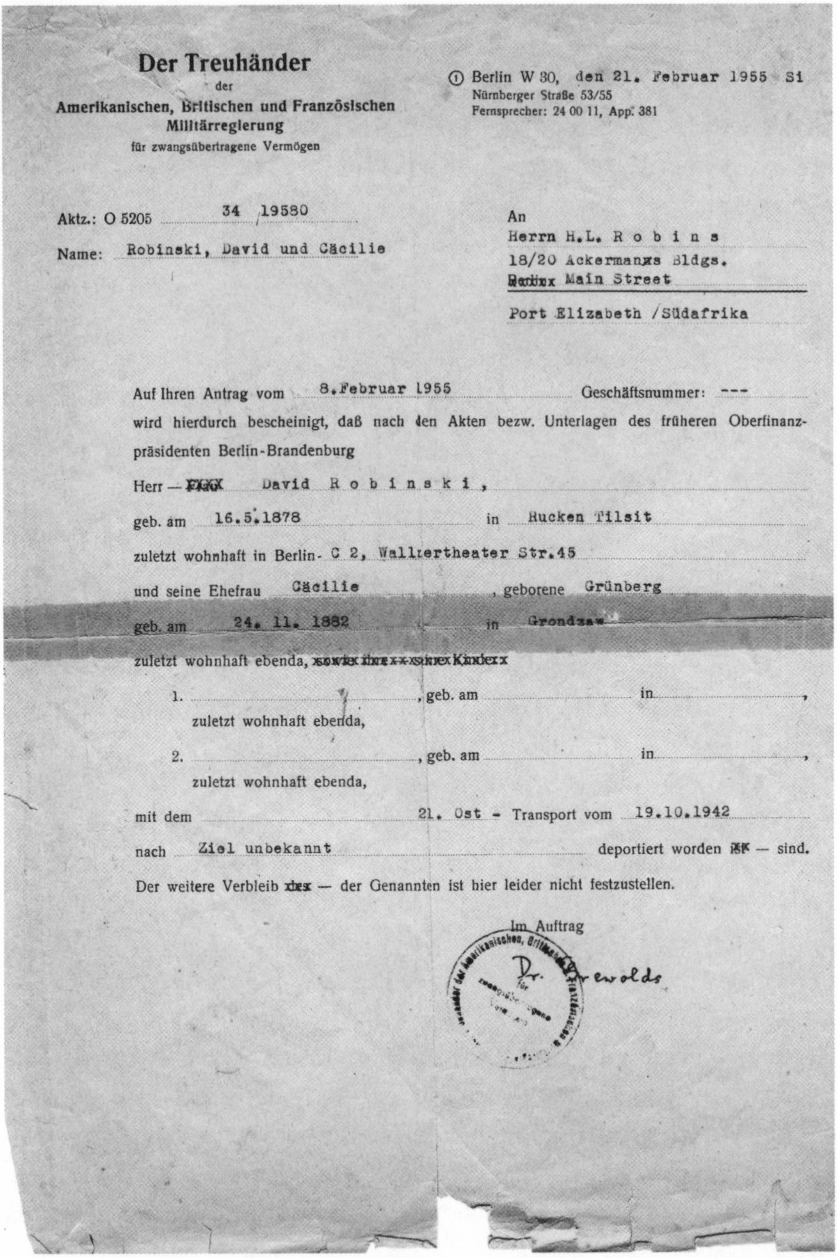

Der Treuhänder
der
Amerikanischen, Britischen und Französischen Militärregierung
für zwangsübertragene Vermögen

① Berlin W 30, den 21. Februar 1955 Si
Nürnberger Straße 53/55
Fernsprecher: 24 00 11, App. 381

Aktz.: O 5205 34 / 19580

Name: Robinski, David und Cäcilie

An
Herrn H.L. R o b i n s
18/20 Ackermanxs Bldgs.
Bedixx Main Street

Port Elizabeth /Südafrika

Auf Ihren Antrag vom 8.Februar 1955 Geschäftsnummer: ---
wird hierdurch bescheinigt, daß nach den Akten bezw. Unterlagen des früheren Oberfinanzpräsidenten Berlin-Brandenburg

Herr — FXXX David R o b i n s k i ,

geb. am 16.5.1878 in Rucken Tilsit

zuletzt wohnhaft in Berlin- C 2, Wallnertheater Str.45

und seine Ehefrau Cäcilie , geborene Grünberg

geb. am 24. 11. 1882 in Grondzaw

zuletzt wohnhaft ebenda, sowie ihre Kinder (typed over with x)

1. ......, geb. am ...... in ......,
zuletzt wohnhaft ebenda,

2. ......, geb. am ...... in ......,
zuletzt wohnhaft ebenda,

mit dem 21. Ost - Transport vom 19.10.1942

nach Ziel unbekannt deportiert worden ist — sind.

Der weitere Verbleib des — der Genannten ist hier leider nicht festzustellen.

Im Auftrag
Dr. Drewolds

The letter sent to my father from the Joint American, British and French Military Administration of Berlin informing him that his parents were deported on the 21st East Transport on 19 October 1942

Herr Ulrich Fluss Jr, standing outside Naunynstrasse 46 and Kuchen Kaiser in Kreuzberg

During a later visit to Naunynstrasse 46, I met Herr Hans-Ulrich Fluss, the son of Siegfried's landlord and the former owner of the Kuchen Kaiser bakery. Both the bakery and the apartment building had been owned by the Fluss family since the early decades of the twentieth century. Siegfried and Edith rented the small garden flat in the courtyard of the apartment building and were given the cheaper and smaller accommodation because they were poor Jews from Poland. Fluss said he couldn't find any evidence of their stay in his father's building, but he did try to arrange a meeting for me with an elderly woman who lived in the building in the 1930s and 40s. She refused to meet with me, however, claiming that she remembered nothing about the couple. Herr Fluss also showed me dozens of photographs of Oranienplatz taken from his living-room window over the course of the past century. The photographs of the square included scenes of worker protests, Nazi rallies, Kurdish religious ceremonies, squatter demonstrations and protests by Kreuzberg anarchists, Marxists, and ethnic and religious minorities.

Herr Fluss told me that his father employed Jews at his bakery, and that he assisted some of their escapes to South America using his Spanish fascist contacts. His father had also assisted a wealthy Jewish business associate whose rescue mission involved a sizeable financial transaction.

View of Kreuzberg's Oranienplatz looking onto the Kuchen Kaiser building where Siegfried and Edith Robinski lived in a garden flat in the 1930s, and which also housed the bakery and café called Kuchen Kaiser

Given that Siegfried and Edith were poor, Fluss Sr was unlikely to have gone out of his way to help them. Herr Fluss Jr portrayed his father as an enterprising and opportunistic man who wanted to join the Nazi Party so he could have access to government contracts. Proof of racial purity and Nazi Party membership would have been a sure ticket to lucrative tenders. To become a member, Fluss had to obtain a family genealogy and certificate of descent to prove his pure Aryan ancestry. Fluss had a large nose and 'looked Jewish', and Herr Fluss Jr told me his father was convinced that there was 'Jewish blood' in the family.

I later learnt that staff members at Eugen Fischer's Berlin-based Kaiser Wilhelm Institute for Anthropology, Human Heredity and Eugenics rou-

Kuchen Kaiser kitchen, 9 March 1932

Kuchen Kaiser delivery driver, 1938

tinely investigated such descent claims, and submitted 'genetic and race science certificates of descent' to the Reich Ancestry Office in the Reich Ministry of the Interior. With the passing of the Aryan Clause in the Law for the Restoration of Career Civil Service of 1933 and the Nuremberg Laws of 1935, proof of descent became even more important for the Nazis.[3] Only people with German or related blood could be Reich citizens; the rest were classified as state subjects with no citizenship rights. It is unclear whether Herr Fluss Sr obtained the Small Certificate of Descent that traced one's ancestors to the grandparents, or the Large Certificate of Descent, which went further back to 1800.

A 1930s map of the area near Wallner-Theaterstrasse in Berlin-Mitte where the Robinskis lived from 1925

Having found the intact Kreuzberg building where Siegfried and his wife lived, Jan-Georg Deutsch and I now turned our attention to searching for my grandparents' former home. Jan-Georg used a 1930s telephone book and map of Berlin to locate the building Cecilie and David occupied in Wallner-Theaterstrasse 45 in Berlin-Mitte with their daughters Edith and Hildegard. But, as he suspected, the building had been completely destroyed by Allied bombs. After the war, nearly all of the buildings in Mitte that were damaged by the carpet-bombing were replaced with modern, high-rise apartment blocks called *Plattenbauten*. Made from prefabricated concrete slabs, and considered to be a typically East German style of high-modernist architecture, *Plattenbauten* were constructed throughout East Germany in the 1960s. The night of our search, Jan-Georg and I wandered through a disorienting maze of tall buildings trying to figure out where Wallner-Theaterstrasse 45 must have been, but we couldn't identify the spot with any certainty. My grandparents' presence had been completely erased from Berlin's urban landscape.

A few days later, on 30 December 1996, I met Klaus, a Berlin-based architect who had lived in Cape Town for a number of years. We did not discuss socialist architecture in the former East Berlin; instead, Klaus raged for an hour about Germany's Holocaust memory culture and its unhealthy obsession with the dozen-year reign of the Third Reich. He also railed against Goldhagen's book *Hitler's Willing Executioners* for implying that Germans were genetically hardwired to genocidal anti-Semitism. Klaus wanted contemporary Germany to become a more future-oriented society, and he denounced the country's excessive and morbid preoccupation with what he referred to as a short catastrophic aberration in the country's long and illustrious history. In his opinion, Berlin had to escape the memory of the brief but disastrous Nazi era. I returned to South Africa a few days later, exhausted after this brief but intense encounter.

It was this same culture of memory that Berlin fostered, and to which Klaus was so opposed, that had allowed me to learn about my family's final days in Germany. But I still knew very little about their daily, domestic existence – their fears, desires and dreams. There remained glaring gaps and stony silences about their lives.

* * *

Shortly after returning from Berlin, I wrote an essay titled 'Silence in My Father's House',[4] which examined questions of violence, loss, memory and identity in relation to the Truth and Reconciliation Commission, indigenous land claims and my recent search for traces of my father's past in Berlin. I decided to use the photograph of Edith, Cecilie and Hildegard in the essay, and took it to the publisher's office to be scanned. When I removed the photo from its small metal frame I discovered a date written in neat Gothic script at the back of the photo: '*20/12 1937*'. Next to this, in black print, were further details about the photograph: '*Photogr. Atelier,* SELMAN BERLIN, KÖNIGSTRASSE *im Wertheimhaus*'.

Then came a startling revelation. Concealed behind the portrait of my grandmother and her daughters was another postcard-size photograph –

one I had never seen before. My grandparents David and Cecilie appear in it, and, at the back, in the same tidy, handwritten script was the inscription *Berlin 10.11.38*, which I assume means 10 February 1938. The names of the photographer and studio were the same as on the photo of Cecilie and my aunts.

Cecilie and David Robinski, Berlin 1938

This photo was the only portrait I had ever seen of my grandfather. My grandmother's hair looks greyer and she seems older and wearier than in the photograph taken only a couple of months earlier. Both photographs must have been sent to my father by his family in Berlin when he was in Port Elizabeth. Perhaps they were sent to him together with a letter from his mother. Or maybe Artur brought them with him when he came to South Africa in 1938. I have never found out why the portrait of my grandparents was hidden for so long behind that of the three sombre women that stood on a table in my childhood home.

SIX

Stumbling Stones

In 1998 I returned to Berlin for three months as a visiting scholar at Humboldt University Law School near Unter den Linden Strasse. I was given an office looking directly onto Bebelplatz Square, where, on 10 May 1933, the Nazis burnt 'un-German' books by authors such as Heinrich Mann, Heinrich Heine, Rosa Luxemburg, Sigmund Freud and Karl Marx. In the centre of the square, a glass plate embedded in the pavement, designed by Israeli artist Micha Ullman, memorialises this event. Called *Library*, this glass structure provides a view of something resembling a library when you peer through it, but which is actually a subterranean room full of empty bookshelves that can hold around 20 000 books – the estimated number burnt by the Nazis. On one of the two bronze plaques next to the glass plate is inscribed the famous Heinrich Heine quote:

> That was only a prelude,
> there where they burn books,
> they burn in the end people.
> – Heinrich Heine, 1820

During my stay in the city, I was mesmerised by Berlin's spectral urbanscape as I stumbled upon traces of its extraordinary history with nearly every step I took. Berlin is swamped with memorials, monuments, museums, plaques, commemorating artwork and installations, and old buildings with tragic and terrifying histories. Walking through the Kreuzberg district I saw numerous brass plaques nested among the paving stones of building entrances. Engraved on the plaques were the names of victims of the Holocaust as well as the dates of their deportations. Curious about the origin of these plaques, I found out from Martin Düspohl, the director of the Friedrichshain-Kreuzberg Museum, that they were known as *Stolpersteine* (stumbling stones), and were made by a Berlin-born artist named Gunter Demnig. Without seeking permission from municipal authorities, Demnig had clandestinely placed dozens of these *Stolpersteine* in public areas in Kreuzberg. In 1996, as part of the project 'Artists search for Auschwitz', he installed the first fifty *Stolpersteine* at the entrances of buildings in Oranienstrasse from which Jews were deported.

In 1998, with Martin's help, I met the artist, and a few days later we began the lengthy process of obtaining official permission to place two stones in front of the Kreuzberg building from which Siegfried and Edith Robinski were deported. The support of the district assembly, the Kreuzberg Commemorative Plaque Commission, city-council members and the mayor were required. We also had to overcome stiff opposition from the public-works department, which opposed the *Stolpersteine* project because Demnig's first fifty stones had been laid illegally. After many meetings and much paperwork, we were finally given the official go-ahead to place two *Stolpersteine* outside Siegfried and Edith's building.

Stolpersteine *outside Siegfried and Edith Robinski's building in Kreuzberg, Berlin*

These days, the *Stolpersteine* commemorative project is quite formalised. Finding individuals to commemorate usually begins with research by students, youth groups, relatives of victims and neighbourhood organisations, who often rely on the Yad Vashem database in Jerusalem. Demnig then makes a concrete block of ten by ten centimetres, which he covers with a sheet of brass, upon which he inscribes the details of a victim of the Nazis. The inscription starts with: '*Hier wohnte*' (Here lived), followed by the individual's name, year of birth, date of deportation, and place and date of death. The stone is then set into the pavement next to the building where the victim last lived.[1]

Demnig mostly uses these stones to commemorate Jewish victims, but he has also included other victims of the Nazis in the project, including Roma, homosexuals, Jehovah's Witnesses, black people, Christians opposed to the Nazis, communists, military deserters and resistance fighters, as well as the physically and mentally disabled. In May 2004, six stones were laid for patients who were murdered as a result of Nazi euthanasia programmes at Berlin's Municipal Mental Hospital for Children. Nine years later, on 7 June 2013, the 5 000th stumbling stone was dedicated in Berlin's Reinickendorf district to Paul Hohlmann, a child who was euthanised by the Nazis. Paul, a fourteen-year-old boy who had been diagnosed by doctors with 'mongolism' and 'idiocy', died in August 1942 after medical experiments were conducted on him and doctors denied him medical care because of his 'developmental disorder'. My own discipline of anthropology was intimately involved in these Nazi euthanasia and eugenics programmes.

There are suggestions that the *Stolpersteine* were inspired by a custom in Germany from the period before the Shoah, when, after tripping over a protruding stone, a non-Jew would say, 'There must be a Jew buried here.'[2] The official *Stolpersteine* website[3] traces the concept to 16 December 1992, a day that marks fifty years since Heinrich Himmler signed a decree to deport Cologne's Roma and Sinti to death camps. Demnig commemorated this day by engraving the decree's first sentence onto a stone block which was laid in front of Cologne's town hall. At the time he laid the stone, there were contentious public debates about granting Roma, who were from the former Yugoslavia, the right of residence in Germany. Demnig also met a Cologne resident who insisted with absolute conviction that no Roma or Sinti had ever lived in her neighbourhood – a denial that prompted Demnig to conceive of the *Stolpersteine* as a symbolic return of Nazi victims to their neighbourhoods, and to their last places of residence. In 1994, in commemoration of murdered Roma and Sinti, he laid some 250 of these engraved brass plaques into Cologne's pavements. This was followed by fifty *Stolpersteine* in Berlin two years later. A decade later, tens of thousands of these stones could be found throughout Germany and European cities. Walking over one, you literally stumble over a material remnant of a history that was meant to be entirely erased.

With Gunter Demnig (middle) and Kreuzberg Councillor Minz (right) at the Stolpersteine *ceremony outside Siegfried and Edith Robinski's last residence in Naunynstrasse 46, Kreuzberg, in 2000*

Demnig comes across as a quirky character in his Stetson and leather waistcoat. He insists on both making and installing the *Stolpersteine* himself, which inevitably slows down their production. He is adamant that the process not become part of a factory production line, even though he knows he could never produce enough stones to honour every one of the Nazis' victims. However, he believes that if they can inspire discussions about some of these victims and their suffering during the Holocaust, then he's achieved something. 'The stones prevent forgetting,' he says. 'They bring back the name of each individual victim.' For Demnig, the stones have become a means of remembering people whose rights were systematically stripped away until they were taken to 'Jew houses', or deported and forced to leave the country of their birth.[4] Remembering the name of an individual victim forms the heart of the *Stolpersteine* practice. The stones can create spaces for memories of those, like my father's family, who do not have gravestones to remember them by. When a stone is laid before the home of a former Holocaust victim, it forces its current residents, and those who live nearby, to think about what might have happened to the individual. By 2015, there were over 50 000 *Stolpersteine* in the cities of eighteen countries in Europe, making this the world's largest memorial project.

Demnig courts controversy as well. He provoked contentious debate in 1990 when he marked in chalk the route taken by Cologne's Roma and Sinti when they were deported in 1940. In Munich and Leipzig, homeowners tried to prevent his stones from being placed in front of the doors of their buildings. Munich ultimately rejected *Stolpersteine* following objections from the city's Jewish community. In Krefeld, a local Jewish community leader compared Demnig's memorials to the Nazis' use of Jewish gravestones as slabs for sidewalks. Some of his critics even claim that placing plaques on the street so that people can walk all over them is disrespectful towards both the dead and their living descendants. A compromise was eventually reached whereby a *Stolperstein* is only installed once both a building's owner and, if possible, a relative of the victim consents to the process.

I see the Robinski *Stolpersteine* as a physical embodiment of my family's formerly erased presence in Berlin. They are a way of refusing to forget their names and their fates. Every time I visit Berlin, I place flowers by these tiny stones and pay my respects to my ancestors.

* * *

In 1999, the year after commissioning the *Stolpersteine* for my family, my wife Lauren and I embarked on a journey to Auschwitz, where Edith, Hildegard, Siegfried and his wife Edith were killed. When our bus entered the small Polish town called Oświęcim, we were both taken aback by its grey, drab ordinariness. We drove past suburban houses with neatly trimmed gardens before arriving at the camp entrance with its infamous sign: '*Arbeit Macht Frei*'. As we walked into the former death camp, we were shocked and dismayed at the sight of visitors eating in a restaurant on the premises. How could anyone actually enjoy a meal in such a place? It seemed obscene. However, before we left hours later, we too sat down and had something to eat there.

During our visit to Auschwitz, we joined a tour group with an elderly guide – a short, stocky Polish man whose family had been interned at the camp. They were not Jewish, and I had learnt only recently the extent to which non-Jewish Poles were also victims of the Nazis. On the train journey from Berlin to Warsaw, Lauren and I had met a young Polish filmmaker who told us that almost every family in Poland had lost relatives in the Second World War. Polish intellectuals, officers and nationalists had been rounded up and killed in their hundreds of thousands, while a further six million Poles died during the war – three million of whom were Jews. Warsaw was completely flattened, and Poland was forever contaminated by the death camps constructed on its soil.

I had not viewed the Poland of the Second World War in this way before and always assumed that the country was a willing accomplice in the extermination of Jews. I had read stories about Poles who attacked and chased away Jews who came back to their villages after the war, but the story was clearly far more complicated than I thought. A straightforward account of Polish anti-Semitism obscures the centuries-long, entangled history of the peaceful coexistence of gentiles and Jews in Poland. It also ignores the overwhelming suffering and loss of life during Poland's nationalist resistance to both the Nazis and the Soviets.

Although I had always thought of my father as German, the Robinskis were in fact born in what is now Poland. They were German-speaking Jews who lived in an area in Prussia that Poles regarded as historically part of their own country. After the First World War, when this territory was returned to Poland, rising anti-German and anti-Jewish sentiment in the country convinced my grandfather to move westwards, to cosmopolitan Berlin. There is a cruel irony in the fact that his children – my aunts and uncle – were later deported back to Poland and killed there.

Throughout my visit to Auschwitz, my video camera was firmly glued to my forehead like a prosthetic third eye, creating a protective barrier between myself and the former concentration camp. I have tried to watch the video footage but haven't been able to make much sense of it. The filming is shaky, the footage flitting from one scene to the next in my mad, neurotic bid to capture everything on film, and I feel dizzy and disoriented whenever I try to view it. While I had filmed everything that unfolded in front of me, I clearly did not absorb or understand what I was seeing and hearing. Perhaps I didn't want to – or maybe I simply couldn't. Filming in this way probably allowed me to switch off my emotional register and dissociate myself from the truth of what I was witnessing. Reflecting back on the visit, I am not sure what more I could have grasped, even if the camera had not been stuck to my forehead. This was a place beyond comprehension, and I walked about like a man stumbling blindly in a thick, black fog.

* * *

A year later, I returned to Berlin to attend a public ceremony for the inauguration of Siegfried and Edith Robinski's *Stolpersteine* in Kreuzberg. These were the first official *Stolpersteine* to be laid in Germany and the Berlin media was there in full force. In my speech at the ceremony, I spoke about how you can walk over the *Stolpersteine* for years without noticing them until the day that your eye or shoe happens to stumble over them. Suddenly you are confronted with physical evidence of a named Holocaust victim who once lived in your neighbourhood.

The Stolpersteine *for Siegfried and Edith Robinski in Kreuzberg*

During my visit I also participated in an event at which schoolchildren from the largely Muslim Turkish-German community of Kreuzberg presented research on Nazi victims who once lived in their neighbourhoods. Residents can also pay an amount of 120 euros to adopt *Stolpersteine* in memory of victims who had lived in their buildings. Unlike the anonymous mega-monuments imposed on the Berlin cityscape by architects, politicians and city officials to commemorate huge numbers of Holocaust victims, the stumbling stones operate on an intimate, human scale.

A few years after the *Stolpersteine* ceremony for Siegfried and Edith in Kreuzberg, Demnig laid four stones in Mitte in the area where my grandparents' Wallner-Theaterstrasse 45 apartment once stood. Unlike the ceremony in Kreuzberg, there was no media and little public interest at this event. The residents I initially encountered while placing flowers by the stones seemed embarrassed by what I was doing and avoided my gaze. In more recent years, however, they seem to have grown accustomed to our visits, and there are now many more such memorial stones in the neighbourhood.

My son Joshua and the Stolpersteine *for my grandparents and aunts in Berlin-Mitte*

Once the Robinski *Stolpersteine* were in place, I believed it was time to finally close this chapter on my family's tragic past. I felt I had got as far as I could on this journey. I now had two photographs: one of my grandmother and aunts, and another of my grandparents taken in Berlin in 1938. The rest of my family archive consisted of documents recording births, deaths and deportation dates and destinations. The silence and gaps in my knowledge about my father's family seemed insurmountable, and I had a strong need to get on with my life, to focus on my work on the pressing political realities facing post-apartheid South Africa. Dwelling among Berlin's ghosts would simply prolong the unsettling state of melancholia I had been experiencing since I started this process of remembering. I would soon learn, however, that this determination to return to worldlier, present-day matters was merely a futile desire on my part. The otherworldly spectres of Berlin had different plans for me, and I was not going to be able to turn away so easily.

SEVEN

In Search of Eugen Robinski

In the years that followed, I discovered I still had unfinished business with my family history. While I had gone as far as I could in the search for my ancestors in Berlin, I found myself drawn towards investigating the life of another Robinski forebear: my great-uncle Eugen Robinski, my grandfather's elder brother who had immigrated to South Africa in the late nineteenth century and settled in the dry Karoo town of Williston. He died in the town in 1931, five years before my father arrived in the country. When my father left Germany in 1936, he must have known that he had relatives in South Africa, but he probably didn't know where they lived.

Shortly after his arrival in Cape Town, my father visited a friend he had met on the ship during the voyage to South Africa. His friend introduced my father to his landlady, whose name (as far as my father could recall in 1989) was Shapiro. This meeting would change the course of my father's life in his new home.

'Mrs Shapiro, meet Mr Robinski, he came on the same boat with me.'

'Robinski, Robinski, I know the name Robinski,' she replied. 'Have you got *mishpoche* [family] here?'

'Yes,' said my father, 'I know an uncle of mine immigrated to South Africa, but I'm not in touch with him.'

The woman then told him she knew the daughter of a Robinski who was married to a lawyer in Cape Town, and suggested my father meet her.

My father took up the suggestion and went to see the lawyer, Joe Levy, telling him that he was possibly related to his wife.

'Oh, what's your name?' asked the lawyer.

'Robinski,' said my father.

'Are you sure you've got relatives here?'

'Yes, my uncle.'

'What's his name?'

'Eugen,' said my father.

Joe Levy phoned his wife Hetty and said to her, 'Well, Hetty, there's a German refugee here; he claims relationship with you, his name is Robinski, Herbert Leopold ... he comes from Erfurt.'

Levy told my father to come back later that afternoon, and when he did, Hetty and her brother Max, two of Eugen Robinski's children, were there to meet him.

Herbert on the left with Hetty Levy. Kneeling in front is Hetty's son Harold and her husband Joe Levy. The man on the right of Hetty might be her brother Max. This photograph was probably taken at Cape Town harbour when Herbert left with Hetty and Harold for Port Elizabeth in 1936

Hetty was in the process of separating from Joe and had decided to move with her son Harold to Port Elizabeth, where she planned to open a small clothing business. Soon after they met, she persuaded my father to relocate with her, convincing him there were better opportunities for them both in Port Elizabeth. At the time, my father was struggling to find work in Cape Town, so the plan made sense. Hetty's half-sisters Evelyn, Laura and Lily, Eugen's daughters from his second wife, lived there, too.

Harold told me that my father was afraid about moving to Port Elizabeth, which I assume was due to the presence of the pro-Nazi Greyshirts, who were very active there in the mid-1930s. By moving there, however, he gained entry into the intimate family circle of Eugen's four daughters.

Harold told me stories about Eugen Robinski's larger-than-life presence in Williston, where he owned a hotel and was mayor at one point. Intrigued, I dragged my family along with me on a road trip to this small Karoo town in July 2010. From Cape Town, we drove north and east past rural towns such as Piketberg, Citrusdal, Clanwilliam, Vanrhynsdorp, Nieuwoudtville and Calvinia. This journey transported us to another world – a dry and barren landscape full of vast, empty spaces and stony silence.

After crossing a small bridge over a dried-up river, we came to a large hill that had the name 'WILLISTON' marked on it with white stones. Entering the town, we approached the Dutch Reformed church, an imposing stone structure that dwarfs the surrounding buildings, as in so many small Karoo towns. Next to the church we found, remarkably, Robinsky Street, which runs the length of the town, and is named after my great-uncle, probably in recognition of his role as a mayor and as a generous donor to the church. A little further along the main road is the run-down Williston Hotel and bottle store, which were once owned by Eugen. The main road also has a few general-dealer stores and a museum, where I found a Victorian-style portrait of Eugen who, with his well-pressed white-collar shirt, tie, waistcoat and suit jacket, has the comportment of a distinguished town elder.

The large footprint Eugen left in this town differed vastly from the absence of traces of my father's family in Berlin, or of the millions of other Jews whose existence was erased by the Nazis. With the help of local amateur historian Elsa van Schalkwyk, I found press clippings and official records detailing Eugen's achievements, as well as his large marble tombstone in the Jewish section of the Williston cemetery. Eugen's presence also survives in local folklore and in the memories of his descendants.

A mystique surrounds Eugen's life, and the stories I heard about him had a mythic quality. Elsa told me how, during the South African War (1899–1902), Robinski's pub had apparently been the venue for a raucous gathering of Boer soldiers and a small group of British soldiers they had captured. The party racked up a massive bill, and it was agreed that whoever won the war would have to pay up. When the war ended, the British ended up paying Eugen for the expenses incurred. When his hotel was built in 1903, it was the only double-storey building in the entire Karoo. Once completed, however, it was discovered that the builders had forgotten to put in stairs!

A paragraph about Eugen appears in a 1991 manuscript titled *Memories of Williston: A Tribute to Leonard Oddes on his 70th Birthday*, which celebrates the life of Eugen's grandson, who took over ownership of the

The Williston Hotel with Eugen Robinski in the middle in the front row

Williston Hotel from Eugen's son Isidore: 'Our great grandfather, Isaac Eugen Robinski, came to Williston from Lithuania some time towards the end of the 19th century. He was a *smous*, a travelling salesman, who bought two farms in Williston and so became a farmer. Later he became the first mayor of Williston, and there is a street named after him.' But only the bare facts about Eugen are remembered; his interior, psychic world remains a mystery.

Eugen was mayor of Williston from 1911 to 1913, and he played a large role in the running of the town until his death in 1931. I was intrigued by how a Jewish immigrant could rise to such prominence in this rough, predominantly Afrikaans farming community.

In 2012 I returned to the town, this time with documentary filmmaker Mark Kaplan and a Stellenbosch University anthropology colleague, Kees van der Waal, with the aim of making a documentary about my family history. These visits, along with my searches in the National Archives in Cape Town, helped me to discover more about my great-uncle.

* * *

Eugen Robinski arrived in South Africa in 1888 after fleeing from Königsberg, the capital of East Prussia.[1] Whenever I asked family members why he left Prussia, I was given conflicting accounts. Some claim that Eugen, a physically robust man with a combustible temper, had beaten up and 'bounced' a drunken customer from his father's pub, and that the man, referred to in some accounts as a Cossack, was found dead the following morning. Others believe Eugen killed the man by mistake, while some imply that he died of exposure or was robbed and murdered by someone else after Eugen threw him out of the pub. Most accounts agree on one thing: that Eugen was arrested and imprisoned in a Königsberg jail from which he managed to escape.

My brother Michael heard yet another version of the story. In his account, Eugen is on a horse galloping towards a guard at the border between Prussia and Russia. At the border post, Eugen gets into an argument with the guard and knocks him down with a powerful punch. The guard is badly injured and taken to hospital, where he dies. Fearful of being arrested, Eugen decides to flee Prussia for South Africa. Michael's son Isaac produced a somewhat different account of this incident in an illustration for a student project.

Isaac Robins' illustration of Eugen's dramatic flight from Prussia

Fearing he had Killed the man he fled with his family...
And ended up on a boat to South Africa
Decades later in the 1930s my grandfather also ended up on a boat to south Africa
Ah! they were meant to send me to Sweden not Switzerland!
in an attempt to escape Nazi Germany, he had Charmed his way across Europe
he didn't even know where the boat was going
he soon met Eugen, who had changed his name to Robins, after the incident with the border guard.
But all the other Robinskys who had made it to South Africa had also changed their last names in order to be recognised as a member of the family, he also had to change his name.
BINS

There are also differing accounts of Eugen's flight from prison in Königsberg. His father might have bribed the warden to help him escape or was owed a favour by this warden, whose church had received generous donations from the Robinski family. Another possibility is that Eugen was given the day off from prison for Yom Kippur, and that he used the opportunity to escape. Whatever the truth, he arrived in Cape Town in 1888, and soon thereafter undertook the gruelling 600-kilometre journey northwards into the dry hinterland. He had left Europe and city life behind forever.

Located on the Sak River, Williston was named in 1883 in honour of the former British Cape colonial secretary Hampden Willis. Before that it was known as Amandelboom (almond tree), after a tree planted there by a Dutch settler. A German Rhenish mission station was established in 1845 by Johann Heinrich Lutz to minister to the semi-nomadic Baster people, who were the offspring of white Boer fathers and 'Hottentot' (Khoikhoi) mothers.

This was a violent frontier world, where colonial brutality led to the virtual extermination of the 'Bushmen' (San)[2] from the area following bloody skirmishes in the 1860s with the joint forces of the Basters and Afrikaner trekboers. The Basters then lost their land to the trekboers, and were pushed northwards. By the time Eugen arrived, there were few signs of the Bushmen and Basters in Williston, and today their existence is barely visible in the museum or in local town histories. It is a forgotten past whose only contemporary traces are in the beaten faces of the Williston poor.

When Eugen arrived, it was still relatively easy for Eastern European Jews to immigrate to South Africa. But anti-Semitism in the country was intensifying, finding regular expression in the local press, where cartoons caricatured Jews as hook-nosed, dirty and shifty traders, or as rapacious capitalists like the popular cartoon character Hoggenheimer.[3] If they were not miserly country *smouse* (itinerant traders), then they were dangerous Bolsheviks. Only Anglo-German middle-class Jews had been able to assimilate into the white settler population; the dishevelled, bearded, Yiddish-speaking working-class Jews from Eastern Europe found fitting in more difficult, and were viewed as pedlars, pariahs, shirkers and outsiders. The majority of this latter group, about 80 per cent, were 'Litvaks' from present-day Lithuania, Belarus, Ukraine, Latvia and Poland, who arrived in South Africa between the 1880s and 1914 – and even their status as whites and Europeans was questioned by the South African Parliament, with debates focusing on whether Yiddish could be considered a European language or not. Yet, as the mining and industrial economy continued to grow, European immigrants, even Eastern European Jews, were seen as useful recruits into the white settler population. This enabled Eastern European Jews to make their way to Cape Town or travel by ox wagon to small rural towns where they quickly established themselves as successful traders. Most made a decent living selling their wares to white farmers scattered across the vast, desolate Northern Cape countryside.

I imagine that twenty-one-year-old Eugen was welcomed by the German-speakers from the Rhenish mission station who, along with local white farmers, would have been impressed by his literacy, knowledge of commerce and his sophisticated European manners.

Eugen acquired a bottle store, two general trading stores and two sheep farms, and successfully reinvented himself as a businessman and *Boerejood.* Adopting the name Isaac, while also answering to the Afrikaans Izak, he applied for citizenship in 1893 at the magistrate's office in Carnarvon in the Northern Cape. To the magistrate's question: 'Have you ever been convicted and sentenced to any of the following crimes: Treason, Murder, Culpable Homicide, Rape, Theft, Fraud, Perjury or Forgery', Eugen answered 'No'. Transforming himself from fugitive to patriarch, he made his mark in the Karoo and established his lineage.

Dora Gordon with her daughter Ellen

When he fled Prussia, Eugen had left a wife behind, a woman named Dora Gordon whom he had married at fifteen, apparently to avoid conscription into the Prussian army. A few years after his immigration to South Africa, Dora joined him in Williston, and the couple had five children: Isidore, David, Ellen, Max and Hetty. Dora died in 1904, and Eugen married Ray Elsie, who gave him four daughters: Evelyn, Lily, Esther and Laura. Ray Elsie, a delicate, prim and petite woman from England, had apparently hoped to marry another man there, but when this relationship fell apart, she travelled to South Africa to find a successful Jewish trader for a husband. The urbane Ray Elsie could not have anticipated what she would encounter in the harsh, arid hinterland of the north-west Cape, nor could she have known that she was marrying a taciturn, hardened frontiersman with whom she had very little in common. Jeffrey Racki, one of Eugen's grandsons, told me that Ray Elsie never used Eugen's first name and always referred to him as 'Robinski'. There was nothing tender or endearing about him and they had a troubled relationship. Eugen became ever more withdrawn.

During my 2012 visit to Williston, I discovered that Eugen had not confined his sexual relations to his two wives. An Afrikaans-speaking Williston man in his early seventies confided to me that his grandmother had had an affair with Eugen, and that his mother was the result of this relationship. I shook his hand and said, 'Welcome. We're relatives.' This made him laugh, and he seemed relieved to have unburdened himself of this family secret. With his two wives and his mistress, Eugen had at least ten children: he was clearly a prolific and virile man. I find it strangely comforting that another Robinski survived and planted his seed so widely in the Karoo.

Eugen was a heavy drinker and was prone to violent outbursts. Jeffrey Racki's mother Evelyn told him that his grandfather had once punched a farmworker in a fit of blind fury, sending him flying across the floor of his garage. Evelyn also mentioned that some of Eugen's children had to turn to the courts to prevent him from squandering their late mother's estate on drink and bad business deals. Eugen had even taken a Bushman girl into his household after her mother came to his home begging to exchange her for medicine and food. The child, renamed Bushy, became my aunt Evelyn's friend, which Jeffrey believes was the result of them both being marginal figures – as a child, Evelyn was teased for being Jewish and a 'cripple' (she had a clubfoot). The Bushman girl and the Jewish girl apparently maintained contact well into adulthood.

This fraught and ambiguous story of a childhood friendship exposes the extraordinary violence to which Bushmen were subjected in the colonial frontier. It echoes a story told to me by historian Aubrey Herbst, a professor at the Nelson Mandela Metropolitan University in Port Elizabeth, who was born in Williston. Aubrey spent months in the Rhenish Mission Archives in Wuppertal in Germany paging through the diaries of missionaries who had been stationed at Amandelboom. One entry, written by the missionary Johann Heidmann in 1847, mentions an unnerving interaction he had with Paul Diergaardt, a prominent Baster leader in Amandelboom. During their meeting, Diergaardt presented the missionary with a one-year-old Bushman child who had been captured during a Bushman and springbok hunt. Diergaardt, who was part of a combined Baster and Boer commando, reported to Heidmann that his men shot and killed about forty-six Bushmen, including twenty-one males, and captured three women and twelve children. The diary reveals that the Basters routinely joined Boers in these brutal Bushmen massacres.

Diergaardt's story captures the tragic ironies and ethical grey zones of everyday life in this violent frontier, where the Basters were both victims and perpetrators. After he handed over the child to Heidmann, the missionary had her washed and her hair shaved, after which she was given new clothes and absorbed into his household as a servant. This ritual of cleansing and conversion was a common practice at the missions which, through its own form of symbolic violence, inscribed this Christian 'civilising process' on the bodies of converts. This was a world of complicated complicities.

I wonder what Eugen made of this world, and whether he eventually acquired the brutal customs of colonialism. Whatever his methods, he managed to successfully insinuate himself into the colonial social order.

Eugen's elevated social position in Williston is portrayed in a photograph of him and a group of white town elders taken in 1896, which Elsa found in a wooden cabinet in a municipal building. Eleven sombre men stare at the camera: the *dominee*, the prosecutor, the magistrate, a handful of businessmen and the town's doctor. Eugen sits on the far left of the portrait, leaning forward with a forceful expression on his face, as if he is bracing himself for a struggle – perhaps to secure his place in this world. Eugen seems to me the most earnest of these men, his penetrating eyes and tough physique the outward signs of a hardy frontiersman who, unlike the other men in the photo, is ready to get on with things. To me, he also comes across as someone fleeing a troubled past.

There is another story embedded in the photograph. The elderly, bearded man on the far right is Aubrey Herbst's great-grandfather, the local homeopath Dr Robert Otto Herbst. Aubrey was in fact named Robert Otto Herbst after this man, but he made the decision as an adult to reject this name and everything else associated with his family's past, particularly his absent alcoholic father. His shame at having grown up in a 'dysfunctional' poor white family had left lifelong scars, so when he went off to study history at Stellenbosch University after high school, he

Agter (vlnr) Eerw. Middelton, ds. Kühn, mnr. W.F. Johnson, landros of
dr. Fowles? mnr Göts, mnr Curtis . mnr G. Müller
Voor (vlnr) Mnr Robinsky mnr Daiyson (prokureur) mnr. Syms mnr Robert Herbst
± 1896

Eugen Robinski is seated on the left, and Dr Robert Otto Herbst is seated on the right. The photograph was taken in Williston, c. 1896, eight years after Eugen arrived in the town

didn't return to Williston until two decades later. It was after exchanging a few calls and emails with me about the history of the Basters and Eugen Robinski that he decided, in spite of his struggles with his history, to drive a thousand kilometres from Port Elizabeth to meet me in the town. He told me he had managed to run away from his past before I came along, but was now reliving his romance with what he called 'my Basters'. He would become our documentary's narrator on the Basters at the Amandelboom Rhenish mission station in the mid-nineteenth century.

Aubrey has written about the escalation in conflict between Baster pastoralists and the trekboers in Amandelboom in the 1860s. Both the Basters and trekboers were largely livestock farmers who increasingly found themselves competing with wealthier white wool farmers for land and water. These farmers persuaded the Cape colonial government to enforce land laws that established freehold title and privatised the commons, which culminated in the passing of the Land Beacons Act in 1865. Thereafter, landowners were required to have proof of legal ownership of land in the form of title deeds, marking the end of the semi-nomadic way of life for the Baster pastoralists. Losing access to their grazing lands, many Basters had to move northwards, eventually settling in Rehoboth in South West Africa, in 1870. Their departure created business opportunities for Jewish merchants such as Eugen Robinski, who bought up a number of Baster town and farm properties in the wake of the Basters' dispossession.

At this point the story takes a stranger turn.

In 1908, German anthropologist Eugen Fischer arrived in Rehoboth to study the effects of miscegenation in the mixed-race Basters. He had come to German South West Africa a year after the brutal suppression of the Herero and Nama rebellion, which resulted in the deaths of tens of thousands of people. Fischer's study, conducted in the shadow of this first genocide of the twentieth century, was a catalyst for many of the horrors that would be suffered by European Jews, including a branch of the Robinski family trapped in Berlin.

Some of the Rehoboth Basters that Fischer met and studied would have been the same people who were forced out of Amandelboom in the 1860s, two decades before Eugen Robinski arrived in the Karoo and four decades before Fischer came to Rehoboth. The publication in 1913 of Fischer's ethnography of the Basters[4] received considerable international acclaim and ignited an illustrious academic career. By the late 1920s, Fischer was a leading scientist in Europe and a key figure in the international eugenics movement. By then, eugenics – a word derived from the Greek *eugenēs* meaning 'well born' – was recognised worldwide as a respectable and promising science for improving populations through 'controlled breeding', a method that would increase their ability to produce desirable heritable characteristics. By the early 1930s, Fischer was one of the Nazis' most senior racial scientists.

I learnt more about Fischer and the Basters from Ute Ben Yosef, an art historian and former director of the Jacob Gitlin Library in the Cape Town Holocaust Centre. Ute had worked at the South West African Scientific Society in Windhoek in the mid-1960s and was knowledgeable about Fischer. In March 2013 I sent her an email asking to interview her about the German scientist, to which she replied:

> Dear Steven
> It is strange that you contact me. I was born in Rehoboth Namibia and my family farm was on the border of the 'Baster Land'. For some reason

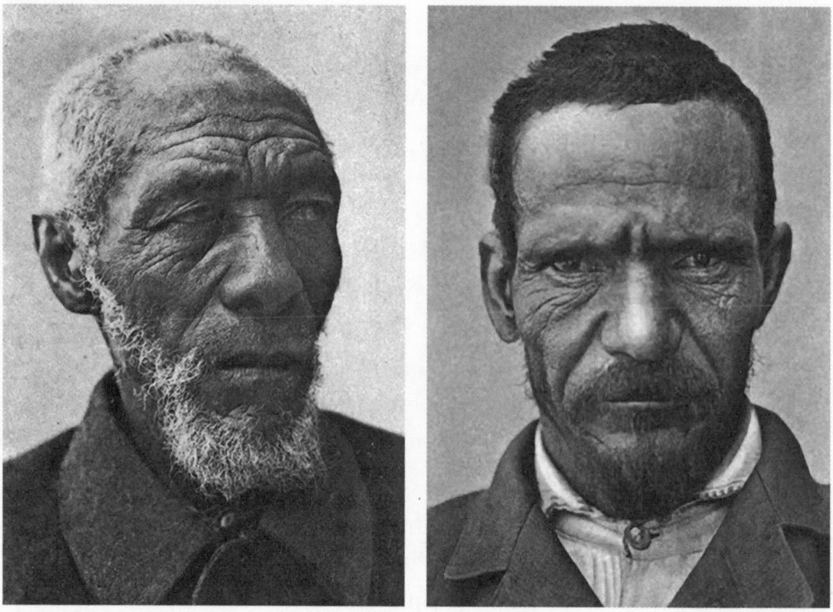

Photographs from Fischer's Die Rehobother Bastards*: Josef Claasen, Matheus Diergaart,*

> I was confronted with the issue you are dealing with, without knowing consciously, anything about it. I worked for the 'Wissenschaftliche Gesellschaft' [Scientific Society] in Windhoek under a Dr. R and he dictated letters to me to Eugen Fischer, whose friend and admirer he seemed to have been. I did not know about Eugen Fischer, or Nazis. But later I found out that Dr R. was a Nazi – and you know about Eugen Fischer. He was the spiritual father of [Josef] Mengele, one may say ... Of course I would love to speak to you about this topic. But I don't know whether I could help you ... Sorry. I have such scant knowledge about it all and much emotion.

We met afterwards at the Holocaust Centre's café, where Ute told me about her background. She had not been born Jewish, but had converted when she married a Jewish man. She came from a German-speaking white South West African family, and recalls that during her childhood in the post-war years, any talk of Hitler and the Nazis was strictly taboo. A pact of silence seemed to exist among this section of the country's white population about their support of the Nazis, which had resulted, during the 1930s and 1940s, in South West Africa becoming the biggest bastion of Nazism outside of Europe.

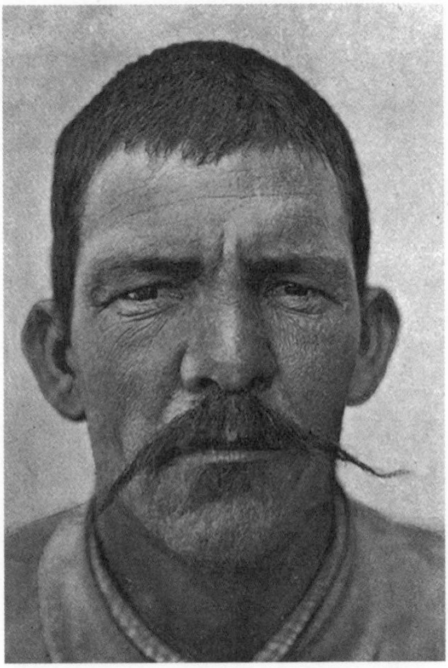
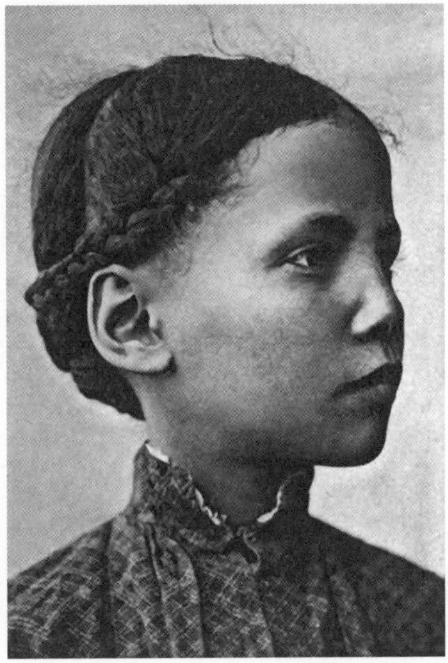

Charles MacNap and Hanna Sch.

The country had even come close to being a Nazi state. On 19 April 1939, the day before Hitler's birthday, a contingent of 300 South African police officers travelled to South West Africa with the sole purpose of abolishing the country's police force. The South Africans had uncovered plans for a Nazi overthrow of the country, which was to be given to Hitler as a birthday present. Robert Gordon, an anthropologist who grew up in Keetmanshoop in southern Namibia, where his Jewish father was mayor, also remembers the strong Nazi presence in the district, and how his father would be greeted with 'Heil Hitler' salutes whenever he visited small towns in the area in the years before and during World War II.

Between 1966 and 1968, when she was in her twenties, Ute worked as a secretary to Dr H.J. Rust, director of the Scientific Society in Windhoek. Ute would type Dr Rust's letters, some of which were to his dear friend Dr Eugen Fischer in Freiburg, West Germany, a correspondence that continued until Fischer died in his mid-nineties in 1967. Ute always thought of Fischer as a harmless and kind old man, and it was only three decades later that she learnt about his study of the Rehoboth Basters, and how he used these findings for Nazi racial science.

Ute left her job at the Scientific Society in the late 1960s and began her doctoral studies in art history in Pretoria. It was while she was studying there that she fell in love with an Israeli lecturer in Jewish studies at the University of South Africa (UNISA). They wanted to get married, so Ute converted to Judaism – a decision that greatly disappointed her parents. Ute's husband went on to become an influential, progressive rabbi in the South African Reform movement and, some years later, got a job in Switzerland, where Ute 'moonlighted' as an art critic, often writing about Jewish and Holocaust survivor artists. Ute and her husband eventually returned to South Africa and settled in Cape Town, and she began working at the Holocaust Centre.

It was there that she heard a lecture by Dr Annegret Ehmann, a former director of the Wannsee Museum, about Fischer's research of the Rehoboth Basters. After the talk, Ute mentioned to Dr Ehmann that she was actually born on a farm next to Rehoboth, so Dr Ehmann recommended she read Fischer's 1913 Rehoboth ethnography. But the book contained nothing controversial or untoward when Ute read it, and was packed with what seemed to her to be dull scientific data and measurements of Baster bodies. Ute, however, had been reading the second edition of Fischer's book, printed in 1961, which had been sanitised. 'It gives the stories of each of the families,' Ute told me, 'but it omits what it said in the first edition, namely that his research on the Rehoboth Basters show that they are a lower nation of mixed race. I can't remember the words which are horrible.' Ute read more by Dr Ehmann on Fischer's career and finally learnt the real truth about the kind old man to whom she had typed letters.

Because she did not wish to upset family members who were reluctant to discuss South West Africa's links with Nazism, Ute was at first reluctant to be interviewed on film about Rust and Fischer. She had already upset her family when she married a rabbi from Israel. Once we got to know each other better, however, Ute agreed to the interview. She would also come to play a significant role in the uncovering of my family's history in Berlin.

* * *

When Eugen Robinski died peacefully in his bed in 1931, he went to rest with the knowledge that he had left his mark on the Karoo town he had made his home. He had succeeded in his business ventures and also left behind a large and thriving family. His experiences in Africa were very different from those of his brother David in Berlin.

Nevertheless, anti-Semitism was rife in South Africa too, and reached all the way to the Karoo. Aubrey Herbst confessed to me that his family harboured a deep resentment of Jewish businessmen such as Robinski, who were blamed for the dramatic decline in local Afrikaners' fortunes in the 1920s and 1930s. By the 1920s, the Herbst family had lost almost all their land and had to live adjacent to Amandelboom, Williston's coloured township. Aubrey's father's dislike of Jewish merchants led him to join the pro-Nazi Greyshirts in the early 1930s.

As a boy of about nine, Harold Levy remembers being present when the rabble-rousing Afrikaner nationalist D.F. Malan gave a speech about Jews in Williston. Malan, then a member of Parliament in the neighbouring Calvinia district, had broken away from Hertzog's National Party in 1934 to form the Purified National Party. The party demanded not only the ending of Jewish immigration into the country, but also the enforcement of discriminatory laws against recent arrivals from Eastern Europe. They regarded Jews as 'unassimilable', claiming that they threatened Afrikaner interests because of their domination of commerce and the professions. In spite of these anti-Semitic sentiments, Malan still tried to book the local Williston hall, which was owned by the Jewish Abrahams brothers, Vaal and Swart, who refused his request, and Malan was forced to hold his meeting outdoors. Harold recalls making his way to the front of the large crowd and hearing Malan declare: '*Die Jood is soos 'n bosluis. Hy suig die bloed van die Afrikaner*' (The Jew is like a parasite. He sucks the blood of the Afrikaner). Harold says these words still send shivers down his spine. This was not Harold's only encounter with anti-Semitism in Williston, and he remembers that his Afrikaans teacher proudly wore a swastika brooch to school.

After Eugen Robinski died, his descendants began leaving Williston, moving to the cities of Port Elizabeth, Cape Town and Johannesburg, or relocating to England, Canada, the United States, Australia and Israel. Eugen had ensured that they all received good educations, and many went on to become successful in their chosen careers.

The movement of the Robinski clan was part of a much wider exodus, and by the 1960s there were hardly any Jews left in the Karoo. Gittel Oddes, who died in 1950, was the last person buried in Williston's tiny Jewish cemetery; the last Jew in Williston was Eugen's grandson Leonard Oddes, who sold his grandfather's hotel in the late 1970s and moved to Israel with his family. All that now remains of Williston's Jews is Robinsky Street, the dozen tombstones in the cemetery, and a repertoire of stories and jokes at the Williston Mall pub about the Jews and their money.

I met an elderly local who had passed on these stories to his son. They both rattled off a string of jokes and tales about Williston's Jews, some of which revealed how Jews had helped Afrikaners with loans in times of drought. All the accounts hid any reference to the Afrikaner resentment of the Jews who had once controlled Williston's economy.

Despite their complicated history in the Karoo, many Jews who grew up there are often deeply nostalgic about their experiences in towns like Williston. This is evident in *Memories of Williston: A Tribute to Leonard Oddes on his 70th Birthday*, which contains fond memories of an idyllic Williston where Jews lived comfortably among Afrikaners.

I had no attachment to Williston while growing up, and even though I was often in the company of three of Eugen's daughters – Evelyn, Lily and Laura – I did not know how they were related to my father, nor did I have any interest in my father's history. With my discovery of Eugen's footprint in this Karoo town, I came to view my family's past through different eyes. I realised the Robinskis had roots in the South African countryside – the ancestor who had laid our foundations in the country was a proverbial son of the soil, a tough and resilient *Boerejood*.

My family history had now become an obsession, and at the same time that I was learning about our history in the Karoo, the doors to my father's more immediate family were opening in a way that I could not have imagined.

EIGHT

Letters from Berlin

When Mark Kaplan and I began working on our documentary film on the Robinski family history in August 2012, one of our first interviews was with two of Eugen Robinski's granddaughters, Deirdre van Tonder and Colette Thorne. The sisters, who were then in their early eighties, had been raised in the small Northern Cape town of Calvinia, near Williston, as real *Boeremeisies* (Afrikaans girls). Their parents had very little to do with the local Jewish community, and it was only when they were adults that they learnt about Jewish customs and beliefs. During their childhood, Deirdre and Colette's mother, Anne, worked hard at submerging her Jewish identity and reinventing herself as an Afrikaner. She was active in local Afrikaner women's cultural organisations, and claimed that her maiden name was the common Afrikaans surname Loubscher, although it was actually Lipschitz. Deirdre and Colette's father David, a magistrate, was the first Robinski to change his name to Robins. He was a liberal man in a part of the country where racism was widespread, and was labelled a '*kafferboetie*' ('kaffir lover') by certain Afrikaners in the area for his views. David Robins' strong sense of social justice rubbed off on Colette, who married a South African communist.

On the day the interview took place at Deirdre's flat in Sea Point, I attended a family event of my own – evening prayers for the passing of Elsa Robins, the widow of my uncle Artur. It was at prayers that Aunt Elsa's children, my cousins David and Cecilia, told me about the letters. A couple of days earlier, while they were 'sitting Shiva' (the Jewish grieving ritual) at their mother's flat in Sea Point, they found a plastic bag full of loosely stacked letters in a cupboard in her bedroom. As the self-appointed archivist in the family, they thought at once of me.

Soon we were all sitting together around Cecilia's dining-room table, poring over the letters. There were about a hundred of them, and I again sensed a breach of the silence surrounding my father's family. It was a moment eerily reminiscent of my own discovery of David and Cecilie's photograph behind the portrait of Cecilie and her daughters. Was my family sending me a gift that would finally answer my questions about their past? I was hesitant at first to touch the letters lest they evaporate before my eyes.

A few of the letters were written or typed in English but the bulk of them were written in German Gothic script. Most seemed to have been sent to Herbert and Artur from Berlin between 1936, the year my father arrived in South Africa, and 1943, when his family were deported from Germany. Nearly all of them were written by my grandmother Cecilie and my aunt Edith, but there were also a few from other family members, from East Prussia, Sweden and Bolivia. We speculated that these were probably desperate relatives requesting help from Artur and Herbert to escape Europe. During the war years, letters were widely circulated among families all over the world. A family member would receive a letter, read it, and then send it on elsewhere, to another relative anxious for news. Letters became collective forms of communication at a time when worried relatives were doing all they could to remain in touch with one another.

Our unearthing of the Robinski family letters soon came up against the reality that, on our own, we were not going to be able to crack the linguistic code of German Gothic script. This was bitterly disappointing. Cecilia knew some German and tried her best to decipher what she could, but she wasn't able to fathom very much. Also known as Blackletter, this Gothic script was used throughout Western Europe from about 1150 until the seventeenth century, and continued to be used in Germany well into the twentieth century. Both Artur and Herbert had passed away in the early 1990s, and none of their offspring could read German properly, never mind Gothic script. I therefore needed to find someone to help me make sense of it – and soon. I was desperate to find out what my ancestors had to tell me from the depths of their buried past.

Every time I touched the brittle, translucent paper I was aware of the fact that I was coming into contact with the material remains of my father's parents and siblings. Their DNA was imprinted on these soft, yellow sheets. I had within my grasp their own words, the physical inscriptions of their thoughts, desires, hopes, fears and dreams. Edith's eyes appeared to implore me more than ever. She had been waiting for me to hear her story for close on eighty years.

I wondered why Artur had kept the letters hidden away in a dark cupboard for so long. Unlike my father, Artur was more willing to talk to his children about his past, and David and Cecilia learnt much more about

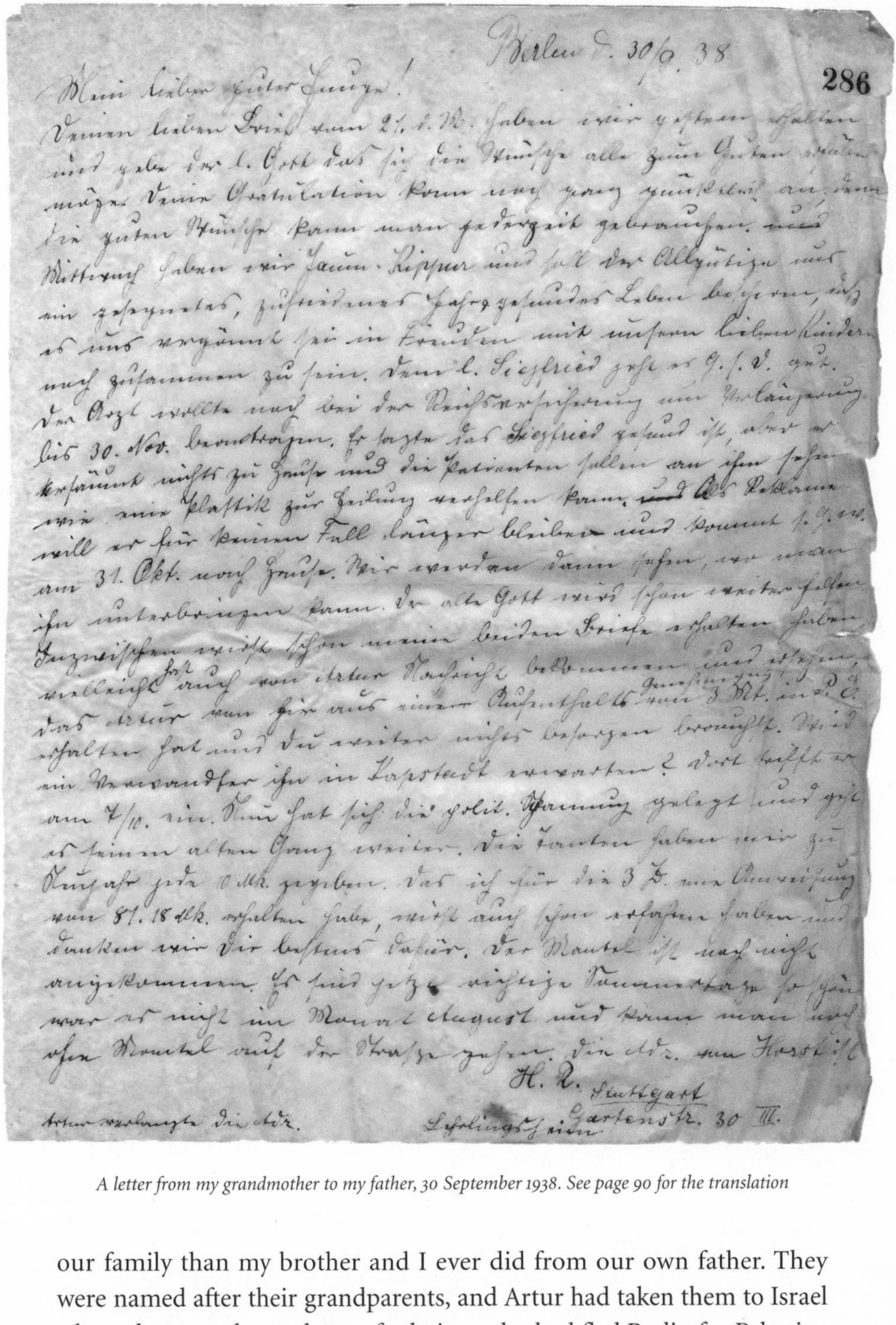

Berlin d. 30/9. 38

286

Mein lieber guter Junge!

H. R.

Stuttgart

Gartenstr. 30 III.

A letter from my grandmother to my father, 30 September 1938. *See page 90 for the translation*

our family than my brother and I ever did from our own father. They were named after their grandparents, and Artur had taken them to Israel where they met descendants of relatives who had fled Berlin for Palestine in the 1930s. Yet, for some reason, Artur had not told his children about the letters.

Why they were stored at Artur's flat, and why he had become their custodian, also puzzled me. Once Herbert and Artur knew the terrible truth of their family's fate, it probably became too painful to read the letters again. Yet they never destroyed or threw them out, but kept them safe and intact, even while transporting them from Ndola and Port Elizabeth to Cape Town. Perhaps they wanted the letters to survive for the next generation of Robinskis.

* * *

I found two German-speaking students in Cape Town to do the first translations, and sent them scanned copies of the letters to work with. One of these early translations was an undated letter from Edith to my father in South Africa. At last, I could hear the voice of the woman who had been an ever-present but unnamed face in a photograph throughout my childhood.

Dear Herbert
First of all thank you very much for your efforts. Hetty invited me in such a friendly and heartily manner that one could already be looking forward to meeting her.

There is a rumor going round that after all some more visitor visa shall be issued in December. I will start organising tomorrow, but I doubt that I will succeed as applying for a passport and other related formalities take much more time than I have got. Anyhow, I will try my very best.

Mrs Friedrich already left and most likely arrived by now.

The size of my class shrinks continuously because many children leave for Holland or other countries. Actually one can only be happy for them, although for us this marks the beginning of the end.

Maybe I need a confirmation from Hetty which states that you'll provide for me and I can stay with you, so that I do not need to work over there. I am not quite sure, but rather be safe than sorry.

Dear Herbert, many regards and best wishes
Sincerely,
Edith

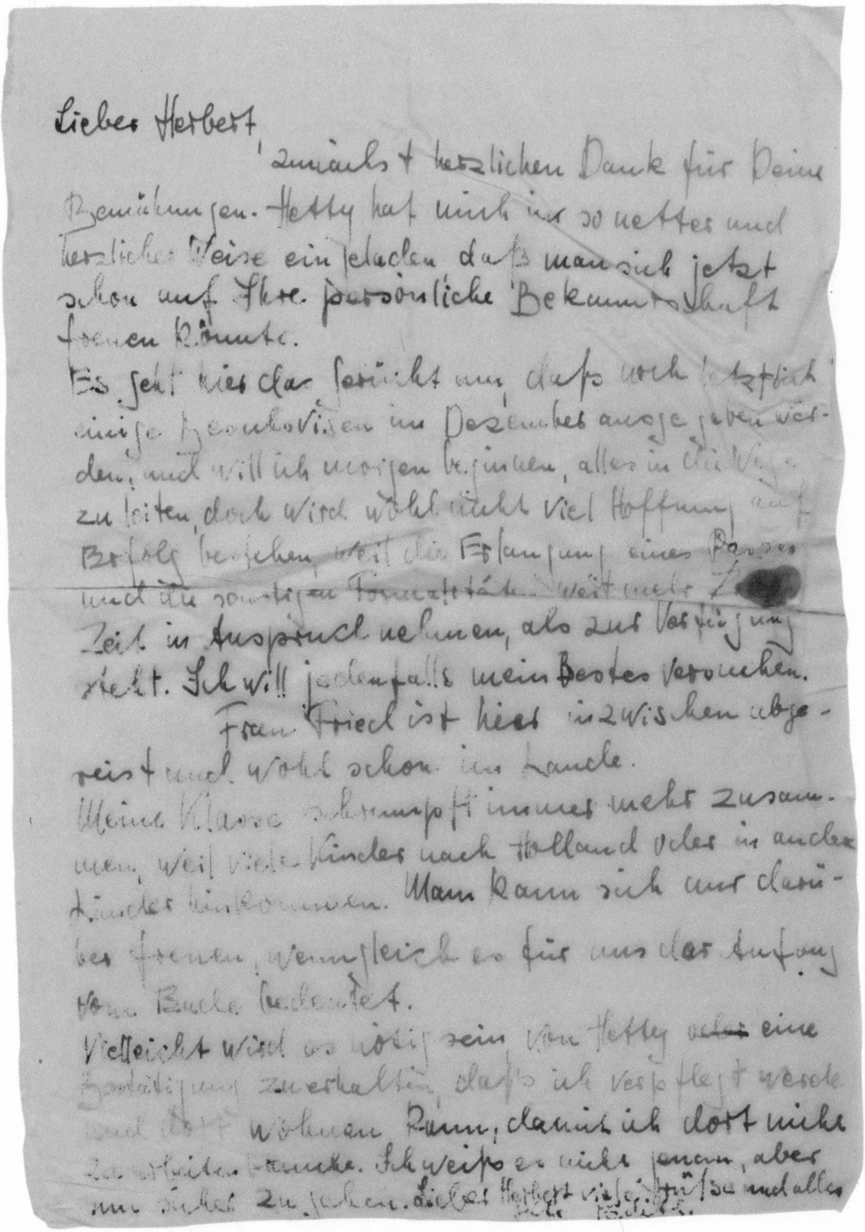

Lieber Herbert,
2mals herzlichen Dank für Deine Bemühungen. Hetty hat mich in so netter und herzlicher Weise eingeladen daß man sich jetzt schon auf Ihre persönliche Bekanntschaft freuen könnte.
Es geht hier das Gerücht um, daß noch letztlich einige Besuchsvisen im Dezember ausgegeben werden, und will ich morgen beginnen, alles in die Wege zu leiten, doch wird wohl nicht viel Hoffnung auf Erfolg bestehen, weil die Erlangung eines Passes und die sonstigen Formalitäten weit mehr Zeit in Anspruch nehmen, als zur Verfügung steht. Ich will jedenfalls mein Bestes versuchen.
Frau Fried ist hier inzwischen abgereist und wohl schon im Lande.
Meine Klasse schrumpft immer mehr zusammen, weil viele Kinder nach Holland oder in andere Länder hinkommen. Man kann sich nur darüber freuen, wenngleich es für uns den Anfang vom Ende bedeutet.
Vielleicht wird es nötig sein von Hetty ~~oder~~ eine Bestätigung zu erhalten, daß ich verpflegt werde und dort wohnen kann, damit ich dort nicht zu arbeiten brauche. Ich weiß es nicht genau, aber nur sicher zu gehen. Lieber Herbert viele Grüße und alles Gute

This letter expresses the urgency that Edith felt about getting out of Germany, as she speaks about visas and passports and other formalities necessary for emigration. 'Hetty' must be Hetty Levy, who was with my father in Port Elizabeth. It seems she offered Edith an invitation of some sort, and Edith looks forward to meeting her in South Africa. It is heartbreaking to read these words and to know that nothing came of this. Edith was a schoolteacher in Berlin, and her reference to her shrinking classes, and children leaving for Holland, reflects the fact that Jewish children were evacuated from Germany in the year before the war began. This letter must have been written in late 1938.

As the translations proceeded, we were faced with glaring gaps in some of the letters, as the students were struggling to decipher the Gothic script. Martin Düspohl, a friend and director of the Kreuzberg Museum in Berlin, offered to help with transcribing the letters into standard modern German, and a team of committed museum staff members immediately began this laborious task. I also realised that, because they were young, there were limits to my student translators' capacities to grasp subtle linguistic signs and emotional and psychological connotations in the letters. I needed a more mature translator and interpreter.

And so, through a series of strange and unforeseen circumstances, it was Ute Ben Yosef who became the translator of the Robinski letters. When I first met her at the Holocaust Centre café, I instinctively sensed that she was the right person to be entrusted with such a herculean task. A native German-speaker, she also has a doctorate in art history, was the chief librarian of the Jewish library at the Holocaust Centre, and is well versed in Jewish culture and history. Most importantly, she is a mature and sensitive woman who would be able to decipher the codes and submerged feelings inscribed in these letters. I was soon to discover that her assistance would go well beyond translation. She became for me the interpreter of the hidden stories and insinuations in the transcripts, of things that could not be openly stated. She also became a mediator to the emotional undercurrents pulsing through these carefully worded letters. She was my guide into the world of the dead.

The first translation Ute sent me, on 30 March 2013, was of a *Tafellied* (a celebratory song) created on the occasion of Siegfried's wedding to Edith Urbanski, which took place in Berlin in 1934. (This Edith is often referred to as Edith II in the letters, to distinguish her from Siegfried's sister.) Ute provided two versions of the *Tafellied* – one that she described as a poetic translation, and the other as a direct translation. The *Tafellied*, written by an anonymous composer, is sophisticated and playful, even in its English translation. At first I could not figure out who the other personalities in the *Tafellied* were, but eventually I began to piece together the family picture.

Tafellied

Your attention, people dear
Tidings we will bring you here
Do be seated first and hear
Wake your senses, prick your ear.

Here, there, everywhere
Marriage, that's what is done
A call there sounds to everyone
To marry above all else.

But Siegfried did not want to [marry]
Shrewd since boyhood
Now and then he'd find
For himself a girl as friend.

Freedom! This was his ideal
Here and there and sometimes yonder
To Schreter's to play 'skat' he'd wander
An alibi he always had.

It happened suddenly one day
To this confirmed bachelor
The way it came about
These verses here will say.

Whilst he with much dexterity
Dyed buttons, his eyes suddenly
Fell on Edith and he stared
And all the buttons turned to red.

The moment this occurred
All resolutions became blurred
Forgotten, as he lost his heart
Chose Edith straight'way from the start

Now have a look at this Chochem[1]
Turned husband on this very day
And Edith as his lovely wife
Fulfilled the yearning of her life.

And Edith too from her first glance
With Siegfried was forthwith entranced.
Said: 'Bet you thalers thousand
This boy I'll take to be my spouse'

In the *Tafellied*, Siegfried is portrayed as a happy-go-lucky, debonair and dapper young man. '*Skat*' is a card game, which he would play at the apartment of his friend Schreter. The *Tafellied* also reveals that, by 1934, Siegfried's occupation involved dyeing buttons. (From Berlin address books from the 1930s, an archivist at the Kreuzberg Museum discovered that by 1935 Siegfried had become a 'merchant' who owned a factory in Kreuzberg that manufactured buttons. It is likely that his business was one of hundreds that were confiscated by the Nazis after Kristallnacht in November 1938.)

This first translation turned out to be the most hopeful of all the others I would receive from Ute. By the time Siegfried married Edith, the long black night of fear and terror had already enveloped every aspect of German life. My father had experienced this fear himself in his arrest a year earlier in Erfurt. Ute probably chose to send me the translation of the *Tafellied* as a gentle introduction to this frightening world.

Ute translated a couple more letters with an equally playful and light-hearted tone. My father's correspondence with a young woman named Grete Fränkel provides surprising insights into the cosmopolitan and cultural character of a pre-war Europe – a world from which my father had only recently fled. On 18 July 1936, Grete writes to my father from Prague to thank him for his farewell letter. She describes her holiday travels in Prague and its thriving Jewish cultural atmosphere at a time when it was still possible for a young Jewish woman to travel freely and enjoy the city's tourist attractions. The tone of the letter is at times frivolous and flighty, and I initially found it strange that my father received letters like these during such a dark period of history. But of course, Grete's travels occurred before the Nazi occupation of Czechoslovakia.

It is unclear what the nature of Grete and Herbert's relationship was. They might have been lovers or friends, but how they envisaged continuing any relationship following my father's immigration to South Africa two months earlier is unclear.

Prague, 18 July 1936

Dear Robi (Mr Robi does not sound so good)
I was truly pleased with your[2] *farewell greetings which were sent to me from Prague, especially as I had not expected them at all. Therefore you should also receive a prompt reply.*

You are demanding a detailed travelogue, this is difficult. Where to start first? The trip became interesting from Dresden onwards, firstly because of very nice fellow travellers (Italians) and secondly because the scenery became very beautiful. The train travelled along the Elbe and one had a most beautiful view of the mountain range of sandstone. (I think this is the correct name for it, we call it 'Saxonian Switzerland'). At the station I was embraced by my uncle, beaming joyfully, although he first had to ask me whether I was indeed Miss Fränkel, as he had not seen me for many years …

Meanwhile many warm greetings
Your Grete F.

Five days later, on 23 July 1936, Grete responds to another letter from my father. Her writing is again peppered with playful banter, and at one point she comments, '*In the previous century one wrote letters about stars, moonlight, flowers etc.; the modern girl of 1936 writes about food.*' She jests about my father's previous letter to her, in which he attempted to decipher her personality from her handwriting. She goes on to describe some of the other places she has seen since visiting Prague.

Dear Robi, auspicious colleague of Raphel S.!
I have made an effort to enrich my knowledge and have viewed further places of interest. Thus I saw the old synagogue of Prague yesterday, which is over 1 000 years old and I also visited the old Jewish cemetery, at which the graves at the time were arranged in layers because of lack of space, and I also saw the tombstone of the old Rabbi Löw (of course you know the tale of the Golem) … The other day I swam in the Moldau. There are many swimming pools here [and] swimming competitions often take place at which many Jewish sportsmen participate, and win most of the time … On Sunday morning I will travel to Marienbad, I will then inform you of my new address.

Meanwhile I remain
With many warm wishes
Your Grete Fränkel

It is as if Hitler's rise to power three years earlier is the farthest thing from Grete's mind. Perhaps the naïveté of youth or a wilful, blissful ignorance prevented her from recognising the danger looming in Europe, or maybe she was simply unaware of the scale of Nazi terror infiltrating German society at the time. It is unclear whether she knew about Herbert's experiences in prison a few years earlier, or if he kept his planned escape so secret that his friends, like Grete, truly believed he was on holiday in Genova, or emigrating because of an economic opportunity in South Africa.

Ute followed Grete's letters with translations of the Robinski family correspondence to Herbert and Artur. We did not have a specific plan regarding the sequence in which I would receive the letters, but it was Ute who decided to start with two of the lighter, more celebratory ones. She seemed intent on shielding me from their distressing content; or perhaps she needed to enter this tragic story with more caution herself.

One of the early letters was written by my grandmother to my father in September 1938.

Berlin, 30.9.38

My dear good boy!

Yesterday we received your dear letters of the 21st of the month and may the good God grant that your wishes will all be positively fulfilled. Your letter of congratulations has arrived right on time; because one can use the good wishes at all times. On Wednesday we will have Yom Kippur and may the All-Merciful bestow on us a blessed, contented year and a healthy life, so that it may be granted us still to live together with our dear children in peace. Our dear Siegfried is well, thank God. The doctor still wanted to apply for an extension up to the 30th November from the state [medical] aid. He said that Siegfried is well, but that since he does not miss anything at home the [other] patients should see by way of his example, how a plaster cast can help towards healing. However, he does not under any circumstances want to remain there as an advertisement and will come home please God on the 31st October. We will then see where one can accommodate him. The ancient God will no doubt help. Meanwhile [you] will have received my two letters, perhaps [you] also have received news from Artur and have learned that he has obtained a residence permit of 3 months in P.E. from here and that you do not have to see to anything further. Will a relative meet him in Cape Town? He will arrive there on the 7/10. Now the political tension has abated and everything is going its previous course. The aunts have each given me 10 marks for New Year.

You will already have learned that I have received an allocation of 81,18 marks for the 3 pounds and we thank you most warmly for this.

The coat has not yet arrived. We now have real summer days, the whole of August it was not this lovely and one can also walk in the street without a coat.

Horst's address is:

H.R.
Stuttgart
Gartenstr. 30 III
Lehrlingsheim [home for apprentices]

Artur had asked for the address.

Since an offer was made to Artur from the London [Jewish] Friendship Society, to remain there in order to learn a trade, with a weekly allowance of 25 shilling, to be subsequently sent away, I have written to Norbert who is now with his parents waiting for a place in the Hachshara. He should request an invitation and then the same offer could be made to him in London. He is an intelligent boy and the Jews will definitely help him. He does have a passport. If Artur, with mazal, will be there he can write to Norbert about this. Today we received the news from Uncle Adolf, that he has received the allocation and he will thank you for it. The letter will arrive at your place after Yom Kippur and you will hopefully have fasted and broken the fast well. Were you at the aunt for Jontef? As from tomorrow many Jews here are losing their livelihoods, the doctors are not allowed to practise, with a few exceptions, hawking and street-market trade ceases and this continues all the time, slowly but surely.

Hopefully the Almighty will have mercy on us in the coming year and give us a little joy and contentment; so that it may be granted to the Jews to lead a worthy life as human beings.

Now we wish you together with Artur a very cheerful Sukkot and think of us too as we will think of you on that day. We send to you, our two boys, very warm greetings and kisses, your loving parents and sisters, and reciprocate the regards to Edith and the aunts. Nothing has changed as yet since Artur's departure. For Yom Tov I have bought a linoleum carpet 300 x 300 for 17 marks and the room looks quite clean. At last I have taken out the old dust trap. Regards to the dear relatives.

There is so much in this letter. It reveals that Siegfried was in hospital, presumably with a broken arm or leg, as he was wearing a plaster cast. Artur was about to leave for South Africa; it seems he was in London for a time. Someone named Norbert was trying to leave too, and was waiting for a place in the *Hachshara*, a German Zionist youth organisation that prepared youth for Aliya, or immigration to kibbutzim in Palestine. My grandmother mentions the political tension, but her letter is filled with domestic details. Her frequent appeals to God reveal a religiosity I had not expected. Because of my own upbringing, and based on what I had read about Jews in Germany, I assumed my father came from a typical secular German Jewish family.

Some members of my family were overwhelmed when reading the letters; Cecilia found those from our grandmother to her sons particularly sad and painful. Ute, too, found my grandmother's messages to her sons in Africa especially heart-wrenching in the way that they reveal her unwavering commitment to the protection of her family. In her encouragement of her sons and her hope that opportunities still exist to save her family, Cecilie Robinski tries her hardest to remain optimistic and cheerful despite the dreadful omens.

Ute's translations soon started arriving in my mailbox on a regular basis, and so began the journey into the lives of the Robinski family and their desperate attempts to get out of Germany.

NINE

Artur's Escape

When my father arrived in South Africa in 1936, he immediately set about getting his younger brother Artur out of Germany. It seems that Artur had already investigated the possibility of immigrating to the United States. On 18 August 1936, my grandmother's sister Minna and her husband Bernhard Rubenstein, who lived in Eydtkuhnen in East Prussia, wrote in response to a request from Artur for information about relatives in the US. The first part of the letter reveals their efforts to track down the addresses of these relatives. Minna then provides news about her children and their efforts to emigrate. They hope that if Artur is able to get to the US, their son Norbert will be able to do the same.

> *If you shall have arrived there safely, with God's help, then Norbert should also go there. We are pleased that you have good news from Herbert, thank God, and may the Almighty furthermore grant everything of the best. We hope that dear David [Robinski] is much better by now and that the Almighty may help him along. Heinz has already landed in Eretz [Palestine] on Monday and we received mail from him, when he was on the boat for 24 hours, and now we are waiting for further mail telling us how he has arrived. The departure from here was very difficult for the boy. May the Almighty hold a protecting hand over him.*
>
> *I think it also won't take long with regard to our dear Irma and it is terrible, how one tears away the children from us. Thank God that the border will be opened, perhaps one will be able to breathe more freely again. It is forbidden to take meat across, but 4 pounds of lard (Schmalz), 1 pound of butter, 6 eggs, fruit, vegetables and 1 piece of poultry are permitted weekly. Better than nothing. Even if one is just allowed to hustle over there, it is good. The main thing is that the business will come to life again. Margot is learning to sew gloves, there is nothing else on offer here and she is already making very beautiful collars and leather belts and you can as of now already place a big order. Here everything is as usual. Thank God we are well and this is the main*

thing. Wishing you everything of the best, warm greetings and kisses to you.

When I first read this letter, I was bewildered by the many names of relatives about whom I knew absolutely nothing. It took me some time to piece together that Minna was one of my grandmother's four sisters and that she had five children, Horst, Norbert, Heinz, Irma and Margot. As I read the letters, I would learn more about this wider family and how their lives intertwined with my more direct relatives.

* * *

Immigrating to the United States was almost impossible, thanks to the 1924 Immigration Restriction Act, which limited the number of Jews who could enter the country. In 1937, South Africa, too, closed its doors to German Jewish refugees with the passing of the Aliens Act.

The rapid economic successes and upward social mobility of immigrant Jews such as Eugen Robinski in the early twentieth century had stirred resentment among poor white Afrikaners in rural towns. Afrikaner nationalist politicians such as Malan and Verwoerd latched onto this growing antipathy and, along with Greyshirts such as Louis Weichardt, worked on demonising Jewish refugees as the embodiment of an antisocial, parasitic and unpatriotic Jewish capitalism.

Hendrik Verwoerd in 1945

In 1936, Professor Hendrik Verwoerd accompanied five colleagues from Stellenbosch University as part of a delegation to Barry Hertzog's United Party government to protest the entry of German Jewish refugees into South Africa. On 1 October 1937, Verwoerd, then editor of the influential National Party newspaper *Die Transvaler*, wrote an editorial titled '*Die Joodse Vraagstuk Besien vanuit die Nasionale Standpunt*' (The Jewish Question from the Perspective of the National Position) in which he defended the introduction of stricter regulations against Jewish immigration. While insisting that 'the [Afrikaner] Nationalist does not hate the Jews', he acknowledged that a conflict existed between the two groups because of a Jewish alliance with English and capitalist interests and Jews' hostility to the political and economic aspirations of Afrikaners. He justified the 1936 protests against the docking of the *Stuttgart* on the grounds that Jews presented unfair economic competition for poor white Afrikaners, and called for a tightening of restrictions on Jewish immigration as well as on trading licences.[1] Verwoerd's lobbying with government was ultimately successful, and in a parliamentary debate on 14 January 1937, the National Party called for stricter laws to prohibit Jewish immigration into the country, as well as to exclude Jews from South African citizenship and certain areas of the economy. Some of these measures would be implemented retroactively from 1 May 1930. The passing of the 1937 Aliens Act was Verwoerd's *coup de grâce*.

As Afrikaner nationalist leaders began flexing their muscles, South African Jews became increasingly fearful about their future in the country, the desperate situation of Jews in Germany heightening their anxieties. In a speech in 1937, Malan clarified his position on the Jewish Question: 'I have been reproached that I am now discriminating against the Jews as Jews. Now let me say frankly that it is so ... There are too many Jews here, too many for South Africa's good and too many for the good of the Jews themselves.'[2] In response to these rising anti-Semitic sentiments, the Jewish Board of Deputies wrote a letter to Malan on 15 December noting 'with deep regret and concern, the expressions of unfriendliness towards [Jews] which have been voiced by the leaders of the National Party, and in resolutions adopted at its conferences'.[3] They objected to efforts by the National Party to discriminate between Jews and other South Africans, asserting that South African Jews would 'protect and defend by every legitimate means their fair name, their honour and their full rights as citizens of the country'. The letter concludes with a call for a meeting with the National Party leadership to discuss the board's 'desire to maintain amicable relations'. Verwoerd's editorial on 'The Jewish Question' published two months earlier had, if anything, heightened the board's fears about the 'unfriendly' approach of the National Party towards the Jewish community.

The nature of this historical relationship between early Afrikaner nationalists, South African Jews and Nazi Germany remains contested terrain. Afrikaner historian Professor Hermann Giliomee denies that apartheid architects such as Verwoerd and the influential anthropologist Werner Eiselen were in any way inspired by German racial science and Nazi ideology. Giliomee contends that early Afrikaner nationalists and apartheid ideologues were primarily influenced by US segregationist Jim Crow laws and conservative theological interpretations of the Dutch Reformed Church. He also rejects the idea that Volkekunde, the style of anthropology taught at Afrikaans-speaking universities such as Stellenbosch, was in any way influenced by German racial science. South African historian Andrew Bank disputes this line of thinking, maintaining that the founding father of Volkekunde at Stellenbosch University, Werner Eiselen, was strongly influenced by German imperial and missionary racial ideas. In fact, during his doctoral studies at Hamburg and Berlin universities in the 1920s, Eiselen became a disciple of Carl Meinhof, a scholar of African language and religion whose work was steeped in German eugenics and who joined the Nazi Party in 1933.[4]

A 1959 essay by political correspondent Stanley Uys provides revealing insights into Verwoerd's wartime past and his anti-Semitic and pro-German views, for which he was already well known by the time the war broke out, and which developed somewhat differently from Eiselen's. In 1943 Verwoerd took the Johannesburg *Star* to court for publishing an article titled 'Speaking Up for Hitler', which alleged that Verwoerd's newspaper, *Die Transvaler*, was a German propaganda instrument that falsified news stories about the war. Verwoerd lost the case and was accused of making his newspaper 'a tool of the Nazis in South Africa', thereby causing damage to the 'war effort of the Union'. During court proceedings, the defence showed Verwoerd an article from *Die Transvaler* that urged the British to make peace with Germany, which the article claimed was close to winning the war. To the allegation that such a piece of news would provoke alarm and despondency among the population, Verwoerd retorted, 'It is not my business to comfort the English.'

Verwoerd certainly did not see it as his business to comfort Jews either.

* * *

Herbert would have watched this rising hostility towards Jews in South Africa with anxiety, having just escaped such conflict in Germany. He would have also been more determined to get his family out of Europe before the Nazi threat grew big enough to prevent their escape.

He must have known that the 1937 Aliens Act would make it almost impossible for his brother to acquire a residence permit for South Africa, but he somehow managed to get Artur a job as a storeman in Bulawayo in Southern Rhodesia (now Zimbabwe). On the basis of this job offer, Artur could apply to immigrate. Artur must have been ecstatic when he received the offer from Rhodesian Agencies Ltd in 1938 – a position that offered him refuge and a chance for a new life.

17th May 1938

Artur Robinski, Esq.
Wallnertheaterstr. 45
Berlin 027

Dear Mr. Robinski,
We refer to the conversation we had with Mr. H.L. Robinski of Port Elizabeth and we confirm as follows:

Upon your arrival in Bulawayo you are to join our firm in the capacity of a storeman. You will have to take charge of the entire store and despatch and to keep monthly records. We are prepared to pay you a salary of six pounds per month board and lodging found. It is understood that, after being acquainted with the conditions prevailing in this country, you will join our sales staff as a commercial traveller. Your remuneration will be fixed on the lines usually observed.

Please oblige and advise us immediately at which date you presume to be able to commence your duties.

It seems the family hoped that Artur would somehow manage to stay with his brother in South Africa once he landed there, even if this was unlikely. When he set sail from Hamburg, his future was uncertain and he had no way of knowing whether he would ever be able to return to Germany or see his friends and family again.

Artur travelled to South Africa via London, where his mother sent him a letter:

Berlin 18.9.38

My dear boy! We have received your cherished postcard and we are pleased that you have landed happily in London. We are still expecting a more detailed letter in which you describe how you have survived your trip and what the farewell from the aunts was like ... [Sending] the suitcase will probably cost 20 mark for freight and so 50 mark will remain for you as boarding money. Hopefully this will be adequate for you; because you will depart from England on the 22.9. and will be in P.E. on the 10.10. Thus a trip of 18 days. I had the money sent telegraphically and there were still charges of 3 mark. The main thing is everything is completed and may it all be for your luck and blessing. As the New Year festival will begin today for 8 days and you will not receive news from us prior to that, the next letter will follow [you] to Cape Town, so I want to send you today our warmest congratulations.

May the All-Merciful grant you everything of the best in the New Year, which brings with it a new phase in your life. May the All-Merciful grant you the best health and may He bless you with happiness and contentment. May He hear the prayers of your parents and be by your side on your life's paths so far away, that you may find the happiness, which your heart yearns for, in your new home. You can say a prayer on the ship; because I am sure that many Jews will be on that boat and there will be no lack of minyans.[5] *I have forgotten to give you a machzor*[6] *for your journey. Buy one in London in the Jewish Quarter. Pray for a good, healthy and happy new year with heartfelt greetings and kisses from your loving parents and siblings. Once again, happy journey and a heartfelt farewell. Your portion is always left over after the meals. For me this still is like a dream. Your departure was too sudden, although we had been prepared for it and I am very glad to know that you will be sheltered there. Write to us often and also send our regards to your friend [masculine]. What happened with regard to the bride and the 1000 pounds? This is the last letter to Europe. The next one will be sent to Africa.*

Cecilie is evidently very protective of her youngest son, as revealed in the control she takes of his finances and travel arrangements. Her injunction to Artur to pray on the ship, and her appeals to the 'All-Merciful', again reveal an unexpected religiosity.

Artur arrived in Cape Town in October 1938, and soon went on to his brother's home in Port Elizabeth. In a letter to his former colleagues in Berlin, dated 30 October 1938, Artur describes his initial impressions of the city and the adjustments he has had to make to some of its strange customs.

1 Westbourne Road
Port Elizabeth
30-10-1938

Dear Sirs
After I failed to comply with my writing obligations for such a long time, I have set aside this day to send you a little report, straight from the African wilderness.

It is now three weeks since I arrived in this country and I have assimilated very quickly, to the extent that I regard myself as an African. I use the English 'hello' for greetings and I do not any more feel the urge to shake hands. I have virtually forgotten this weird German custom, and now my hands simply belong to my pockets and if I had more hands, then I would require more pockets! I am no longer surprised when a young black girl serves me my dinner, as there are only black housekeepers here. I also no longer find it strange when the ladies go to cinema on Saturday night, dressed in long evening dresses and silver shoes, and the gentlemen appear in their smoking [suits]. Everything is so natural for an African. I should not forget to tell you that I am feeling the cold like the others, even when the sun is shining. It is still winter here, you know, and whilst I am writing this, my legs are frozen. I am most delighted by this fact, for the heat was one of my biggest worries.

Artur's main concern upon arrival was whether he would be allowed to enter South Africa and remain there, especially since he had brought little money with him:

Another little worry of mine was whether, and in what way, I would be permitted to enter the country, and I want to tell you about this now. After 18 days of uninterrupted travel by boat, we sighted Cape Town, where the general customs clearance for immigration for the entire Union takes place. The uncertainty whether everything would be successful did not permit me to indulge in a holiday mood and I forced myself to feel as detached as possible under the circumstances. Upon my arrival in Cape Town I had received a letter from my brother, telling me that he had had a word with the immigration officials and that I was not to worry, and I was happy about this and headed straight to the court, armed with £1, in order to procure the much-needed permit. But nothing came of that. The official had indeed been aware of my existence, but after I could only reply with 'Sorry' to his many questions about my financial situation, I could not get the permit. He told me that I would be obliged to pay £50 upon my arrival in P.E., and I would then be able to obtain a permit for the duration of two months. And only after my brother here paid the amount, was I allowed to disembark from the ship. Here you can get anything with money and had my brother been in Cape Town, everything would have been easier and probably also cheaper.

Artur later told his daughter Cecilia that my father had tried, unsuccessfully, to bribe one of the officials to grant him a South African residence permit. Instead, Artur was given a temporary residence permit for two months. Despite these concerns, and the worries he must have had about his family back home, Artur finds some space in his letter to convey his excitement about his newfound freedom and to describe all of the new things he has encountered on his travels.

He describes his two days in Cape Town, which he calls '*the second most beautiful city after Rio*', but adds:

I saw little of it because of the rain, which washed away the differences between Berlin and Cape Town. The pavements are in both cases equally slippery and so I spent my time doing the usual – eating and drinking, tea and cinema, which here is large and elegantly furbished. After a further 24 hours of coastal journey by sea, I arrived here [in P.E.], to commence a new chapter of my adventurous journey …

Artur is charmed by Port Elizabeth:

We were anchored at sea before docking in Port Elizabeth because the ship was unable to enter the harbour, as there was no room. And when I saw before me the city, which would perhaps become my new home, stretched out, with tall houses, amidst lush green surroundings, like a little New York – everything that I had been suppressing for months broke forth in me. This intensely happy feeling of freedom [and] the joy of the reunion [with my brother], and the satisfaction following my anxious desire to begin a new life …

Later on he writes:

Here in P.E. they have hotels eight storeys in height! About this city, I can only sing my praises. Life here is really great, because, firstly, the climate is very good and a strong breeze always blows. The surrounding is ideal for parties and the sea is, so to speak, situated directly on your doorstep. One can drive to the beach in a bathing suit and, if one finds parking, one can jump directly from the car into the water. There are beautiful, well-tended parks in African style, with small ponds, which during the holiday season are suffused with a magical light, the most modern street lights, that light up the beach at night. There is a modern harbour and big shops with hyper-modern designs, with escalators etc. It has the latest London buses, and cars as numerous as sand on the beach … All of this could make one forget that one is on the opposite side of the world, in the midst of the African wilderness. There are also many industries, shoe factories, chocolate and car factories. Ford and Chevrolet have their own factories here, and the car market, mostly American, is enormous. Among these one will often see the small DKWs which over here cost over £200. Among the local immigrants there are only a few who do not drive big American cars, whose price is about £300. Of course, nobody pays cash and the whole economy is based on credit. However, on the whole, earnings are good; one does not conduct business simply for its own sake.

Artur is also a fine observer of South African life. He describes in detail, and with a certain degree of parody, the 1938 centenary celebrations of the Voortrekkers' Great Trek.

I will remain here for a further 14 days to continue with my English studies, which I have already started. This is most important and I have drawn up a timetable, for which I have reserved four hours daily for studying. Whilst we have wonderful weather outside, I sit inside and listen occasionally to radio stories, prayers – which form a large component of the programmes and news reports. These radio programmes are of great

> *value to me, for they allow me gradually to acquire the sound and rhythm of the language. The English here is not too good because Afrikaans is mostly spoken by the Boers, i.e. the formerly Dutch people. In the coming weeks, a huge celebration will take place, to commemorate the great journey which the Boers undertook with their ox wagons in 1838 in search of new land and to establish farms. So ox wagons will be driven along the same roads as part of the centenary celebrations. Because these people, called Voortrekkers, once had long beards, in commemoration the Dutch [Afrikaners] will also grow beards, which looks ludicrous. The English people seem quite tolerant of this…*

Artur clearly finds these commemorative rituals rather eccentric and quaint. But he also perceives the similarities between such exuberant displays of Afrikaner nationalism and other forms of flag-waving back home in Germany – a similarity that increased his fears that the Nazi threat was not confined to Europe. '*After the political experiences lately in this regard only bad things are to be expected. Why not here? The soil for this is fertile*,' he wrote to his Berlin colleagues in 1938. Artur arrived in South Africa a few months after a general election, in which the United Party of Barry Hertzog and Jan Smuts had retained power. D.F. Malan's Purified National Party, which had broken away from Hertzog's party after its union with the more liberal Smuts, became the official opposition in Parliament. Meanwhile, leading National Party figures such as Malan and Eric Louw continued to target Jews as being pro-English liberals, harbingers of 'international Jewish communism', and economic parasites who were sucking the blood out of poor white Afrikaners.

The same year witnessed the emergence of a new paramilitary fascist movement, the Ossewabrandwag (Oxwagon Sentinel). Founded by the former United Party minister of defence Oswald Pirow, the Ossewabrandwag identified Jewish money and Jews' supposed allegiances with the British, Freemasons, imperialists and capitalists as some of the biggest threats facing Afrikaners at the time.[7] By 1941, the Ossewabrandwag would claim a membership of 300 000, which included its paramilitary elite unit, the Stormjaers. Oswald Pirow founded the pro-Nazi Nuwe Orde (New Order), and, two weeks after Kristallnacht in Berlin in November 1938, visited Hitler at his Berghof in Berchtesgaden.[8] Given all these dangers looming on the horizon, Artur's relief is palpable when he tells his colleagues he feels fortunate to be leaving for Southern Rhodesia.

Ossewabrandwag leader Dr Hans van Rensburg (centre), flanked by torch-bearing members during a rally, 1941

By the mid-1930s, the groundwork had been laid for the ascendancy of right-wing Afrikaner nationalism, according to South African historian Saul Dubow. The powerful Afrikaner secret society, the Broederbond, had already transformed itself into a Christian national organisation with widespread influence in political, religious, business and educational institutions throughout the country – and it viewed Jews as a special kind of problem because of their alliance with English capital.[9] The growing poor white population in the 1930s strengthened the Broederbond argument that such an unholy alliance made it impossible for Afrikaners to compete with the uncanny commercial acumen of Jews. This ideological stance, with its echoes of Nazi political rhetoric, was reinforced by influential Afrikaner intellectuals such as Nico Diederichs, Piet Meyer, Geoffrey Cronjé and Hendrik Verwoerd, who had all returned from studies in Germany and Holland in the 1930s.

With this confluence of political and intellectual currents firing the militancy of the Voortrekker centenary celebrations, it is therefore unsurprising that Artur writes of these events with such despondency and foreboding during his stay in Port Elizabeth. These striking convergences between Nazism and Afrikaner nationalism were a reminder to Artur that he had not entirely escaped the dangers he had faced in Europe. Moreover, almost everyone he loved and cared for was still trapped there.

Everything that was before lies far behind and I do not know whether others feel the same way as I do. But today I am unable to understand how people can still live in G. [Germany]. And when someone asks me here, how the Jews actually live in G? then I do not know what to reply. I feel great sympathy for all those who still have to live there, submitted to all the pressures, afraid, after [reading] each sentence in a newspaper and listening to each speech and figure of speech, to hear whether this will bring new punishments. I am asked of the state of mind of the people who have to endure such a nerve-wracking atmosphere and I do not know what to say to that. It just is to no avail.

* * *

Although Artur had been offered a job as a storeman by Rhodesian Agencies Ltd, something appears to have gone wrong, because he writes in another letter that not only was he unable to remain in South Africa, but he had to apply for a new job in Southern Rhodesia.

As I have already written before, I only got a temporary residence permit for two months and a Capetonian lawyer [Joe Levy, Hetty's husband], who is a relative of mine, is trying to get an extension, and we could also count on surely getting it. But a couple of days ago he wrote that there is no longer any prospect of getting one. Now we tried from day one to get a contract for Rhodesia and we put the most possible and the most impossible things in motion but we could achieve nothing positive. The situation was very risky and I must admit that my relatives, who until the day of my arrival had no idea of my existence, outdid themselves in getting me the necessary contract, and I was deeply moved by their extremely warm welcome which I did not count on at all, since after all they were strangers to me with whom I had never been in contact. And my application ended up being successful – two days ago I received not only a contract from Rhodesia but a proper job offer. It's in a factory that manufactures pants and sports jackets, as well as shirts and the company will provide all necessary guarantees. However, I will have to bring along £200/250 Vorzeigegeld[10] which for the most part will be held in safekeeping by the immigration officers. But I hope that this affair will also go smoothly and that I won't even need to use the above-mentioned residence permit here until it expires, but that I will be able to go to Rhodesia as quickly as possible, before new difficulties arise.

Cecilie writes to the brothers on 14 November 1938 to express her relief that Artur has managed to enter Southern Rhodesia legally:

> *My dear boys! We have received your dear letter of the 2.11 on the 12th and it took 10 days which is quite long and we were very pleased that you [plural] are well thank God and that Artur has managed to get to Rhodesia legally. May God grant that he will find the yearned-for happiness there and we want to hope for the best for his further well-being. When will he move into his home? And this should only be with much mazal and broches.*

But then something must have gone wrong with the job and Artur had to move on. In an undated letter to Artur, my grandmother comes across as dismayed and perplexed as to why he is now planning to move again:

> *Why do you want to travel further? Is there not hope for livelihood over there? Are you a bit anxious? After all you have much time to reflect about things in your present state of inactivity. We thank you very much for both the little pictures. As small as your ponim appears on the boat, I have still recognized you immediately. You can send us another little photo from R.d [Rhodesia] occasionally, so that we can be convinced that you are well.*

Edith, in an undated letter to Herbert, also expresses her disappointment and regret that her brother is still not settled. '*It is a great pity that A. has not yet found his feet. Now he will probably have to move on again, the poor boy.*' Artur had to leave Southern Rhodesia, but he managed to get into Northern Rhodesia. In a letter to my father on 25 December 1938, my grandmother writes:

> *The fact that Artur did not manage to remain in S.R. is really very unpleasant and now he has transferred his residence to the 3rd place, and may that now be to his happiness and blessing. From there it will probably be possible to get Siegfried there faster. Please write to us whether he has found employment and how he likes it there … I have already had a feeling that things were not going well with Artur; I had missed his punctual mail. May it all be for the best and may the All-Merciful grant that he will find happiness there; because he has deserved it.*

Artur's daughter Cecilia believes that Artur's position in Southern Rhodesia was linked to an application for Edith for a teaching post in Bulawayo, but that this had been unsuccessful, which adversely impacted on Artur's request for a residence permit. According to Cecilia, the local reverend's wife, who also happened to be a Hebrew teacher, was offered the job for which Edith had applied.

In a letter from Siegfried to Herbert dated 25 January 1939, the family still seem optimistic that Artur will find a job in Northern Rhodesia and will then be able to assist the rest of the family:

> *We also received mail from our dear Artur. He wrote that he stands a chance to get work on the [copper] mines. Hopefully he already got the job as this will increase his ability to assist us with all our immigration applications.*

Two months later, on 31 March, Cecilie seems satisfied that Artur is at last settling down in his new country:

> *This week we have received 2 letters from d[ear] Artur and we are very pleased that at last he has found a job. Even though the salary is very small; but it will increase. I am sure that the boy will make an effort to satisfy the boss. Is NDola situated close to Nkanar? Is it a clothing shop?*

Cecilia recalls that Artur brought with him to Northern Rhodesia an elegant white suit made by a Berlin tailor before he left. She also remembers her father telling her that at precisely 5 p.m. every day he would take his malaria pills. His new life in a small African town could not have been more different than his life in Berlin.

In 1939, Artur became engaged to a woman named Edith Glatter, who lived in Salisbury in Southern Rhodesia. In a letter to Herbert, my grandmother expresses excitement and relief about the engagement. She was worried about Artur being on his own in Ndola, and the prospect of her youngest son settling down with a German Jewish woman would have reassured her about her sons' well-being in Africa.

> *Berlin, 28.7.39*
>
> *My dear Herbi! … Yesterday we received the news from dear Artur that he has got engaged and that he is a happy bridegroom, we congratulate*

him heartily on this move and wish that he will find his yearned-for happiness by the side of his chosen one. So he has outdone you; but luck will also blossom for you …

Cecilie writes to Artur three days later to congratulate him:

Berlin, 31.7.38 [sic]

My dear boy! The happy news about your engagement surprised us all, [although] you already have given us some hints. We congratulate you with all our hearts and may the good God grant you His support. Hopefully you have made the right choice and may the knot be tied in a happy hour, so that your dear bride will soon be a loving, loyal wife to you, and to us a good daughter and that you will at last find the yearned-for happiness that you abundantly deserve. The blessing of your parents will accompany you on all your footsteps and may the All-Bountiful help you further towards the good. When do you think the wedding will take place? It will probably not be granted to us to celebrate this great day together with you. The distance unfortunately is too vast. But as far as it is, we do not want to give up hope. I expect to learn more from you soon. Do you have the intention and the possibility to move to S.R.? We would be very pleased and we are waiting to receive a few lines from our future daughter-in-law. I have not yet received her photo from Herbi. I do not doubt your good taste.

But the wedding never happened. In a letter sent from Salisbury on 29 September 1939, Edith Glatter informs Artur that she has since become engaged to another man, and that they 'have to forget any future plans'. This letter must have been devastating, both for Artur and for his mother.

Artur eventually recovered from the heartbreak Edith Glatter caused him and married Elsa Benatar, a woman whose Sephardic family had lived in Alexandria in Egypt before moving southwards to the Congo. Artur and Elsa settled in Ndola and had two children, my cousins David and Cecilia. In 1972, the family left Zambia and moved to Cape Town. Artur was a gregarious and witty man with wild strands of grey hair, a large nose and sparkling eyes. His sense of humour was often quite dark and offbeat. When he discovered that I didn't eat red meat, he observed, with a deadpan expression, that Hitler had also been a vegetarian. To this day, I am not sure what he meant by this remark. Perhaps he was implying that one cannot depend on vegetarians to be kind to humans. I later learnt that Hitler took to vegetarianism because of a particularly bad problem with body odour.

Artur in Ndola with his two children David and Cecilia

As a student at the University of Cape Town I would regularly visit Artur and Elsa's flat in Sea Point for Shabbat dinner on Friday nights. They lived on the ninth floor and I would soak up the panoramic views from the balcony of the beachfront promenade and the Atlantic Ocean. I would sometimes stare pensively at Mandela's Robben Island prison. This was the early 1980s, the country was in turmoil, and I was living in Observatory, a mostly student and white working-class suburb on the other side of Table Mountain. My dilapidated bohemian house had no sea views.

Elsa was born in 1927 in Suez, Egypt, where her father was a shopkeeper, and moved to Alexandria when she was five. When she was eighteen the family moved once again, this time to Sakania, a small mining town in Katanga Province in the far south of what is now the Democratic Republic of Congo, near the border with Zambia. As a Sephardic Jew who grew up in the cosmopolitan port town of Alexandria, Elsa had a multicultural upbringing that impressed me as an anthropologist. She could speak Ladino, French, Italian, English and Spanish, and told fascinating stories about Egypt and the Congo. Her father and most of the other Jewish shopkeepers in small Congolese towns were also fluent in the local African languages. Elsa was a lively and generous woman who paced about the flat with a determined gait. She also had a spirited and droll sense of humour. Elsa and my mother Ruth did not get on from the moment they set eyes on each other. Artur, who could never refrain from teasing the very sensitive Ruth, generally aggravated any tension between his wife and sister-in-law, and relations between my mother and Artur's family remained strained as a result. David and Cecilia later revealed to me that they always felt like Ruth treated them shabbily whenever they visited us in Port Elizabeth. They believed she looked down on them as her husband's relatives from the Northern Rhodesian hinterland.

My mother had been determined from a young age to escape the working-class Port Elizabeth neighbourhood of South End – a predominantly coloured area until the apartheid-era forced removals of the 1960s – and she loved nothing better than to mingle with well-to-do folk. After marrying my father, she soon established a place for herself in Jewish high society in PE. Herbert had already opened his men's retail clothing shop, Novelty Fashions, when he married Ruth in 1955. Although he experienced some difficulties with this business, my father's fortunes eventually recovered enough for him to purchase Flair Fashions, an upmarket retail store for women's clothing. My parents were never wealthy, but they nonetheless found a way to include themselves in upper middle-class Jewish society.

Ruth always felt that our Ndola relatives could never fit in with her charmed inner circle of affluent PE Jews. Her disdain kindled a lifelong family feud – one that lasted almost fifty years, and which only intensified when Artur moved his family to Cape Town in the 1970s. Regardless of my mother's feelings towards Artur and his family, I always enjoyed my Friday-night visits to their beachfront flat, completely unaware of the hidden letters in Aunt Elsa's bedroom.

* * *

While cleaning out her late mother's flat in April 2014, my cousin Cecilia found a photograph of Artur with his sister Edith. This was probably taken in Berlin in the mid-1930s – perhaps shortly before his departure. Artur looks handsome and dapper in his suit and tie. The two siblings seem close and affectionate towards each other. This is the only photograph of Artur in Berlin and the only one of Edith with her brother. It is also the only photograph I have of Edith in which she seems happy and at ease.

TEN

The Noose Tightens

On the back of the photograph of my grandparents is an inscription in my grandmother's handwriting: *Berlin 10.11.38*, which I assume refers to the date 10 February 1938. By this time, the situation had become especially precarious for the Robinski family, as German Jews had already been subjected to a host of racial laws. Cecilie appears to have aged since she was photographed with Edith and Hildegard the previous year, and both she and my grandfather David look almost shell-shocked, and defeated. The final loopholes allowing Jewish immigration into South Africa had been closed, and they were probably beginning to give up hope that they would succeed in leaving Germany. A few months later they would learn that Artur's application to stay in South Africa had been turned down, and that he was unable to remain in Southern Rhodesia either. Edith and Siegfried, however, were still trying against all odds to get into South Africa, Rhodesia, or any other country that would give them refuge.

* * *

It was widely believed by many German Jews that Hitler's ascent to power in 1933 was a passing phenomenon. Many assumed that ordinary Germans and the political and military establishment would not be able to tolerate this uncouth rabble-rouser corporal for very long. They were proven horribly wrong when Hitler and his Nazis began to establish control over all state institutions and nearly every aspect of daily life in Germany. Strangely enough, my father was probably fortunate that his imprisonment in Erfurt in 1933 forced him to confront the reality of the Nazi regime, and through this, was compelled into planning his escape. But his parents Cecilie and David, siblings Siegfried, Edith and Hildegard, as well as Artur until he managed to emigrate in 1938, had to live through each stage of this relentless intensification of Nazi terror.

Following a barrage of anti-Semitic laws and the repression of any form of political dissent, 1936 witnessed something of a lull in Jewish oppression. The Olympic Games were being held in Berlin in August and

Hitler did not want to draw too much negative international attention to his regime. The attack on Jews' rights and citizenship resumed between the autumn of 1936 and the spring of 1937, when the Aryanisation of Jewish firms occurred in February. By this time, the Nazis had announced their key objective of completely eliminating Jews from German economic life in the next four years.[1]

Despite the imposition of an extremely inhospitable living environment on Germany's Jews, by January 1938 only 135 000 of the country's 525 000 Jews had emigrated. Over the next year, life for Jews would worsen dramatically. In April 1938, only 40 000 businesses remained in Jewish hands out of 100 000 in 1933, and about half of all Jewish workers were unemployed. From July onwards, all Jews, including infants, had to carry identity cards. In August 1938, all Jewish doctors were expelled from their profession and Jews could no longer own motor cars.[2]

Such crippling restrictions would have undercut any attempt by Jews to hold onto a sense of citizenship and civility. Yet, in spite of being subjected to this kind of degradation on an almost daily basis, as well as witnessing its effect on her family, Cecilie Robinski never complains about these measures in her letters to her sons in Africa – in fact, they are mentioned almost casually.

One reason for Cecilie's silence was no doubt due to legitimate fears that her letters would be intercepted by Nazi censors; but it also reflects her fortitude and reluctance to burden her sons any more than she needed to. While she betrays her fears very rarely, when she does, she continues to be hopeful that there will be some delivery for her and her family from their plight. Her letter to my father on 30 September 1938 is one of the few instances in which she reveals her true feelings about the daily onslaughts on Germany's Jews, when she reports, '*As from tomorrow many Jews here are losing their livelihoods, the doctors are not allowed to practise, with a few exceptions, hawking and street-market trade ceases and this continues all the time, slowly but surely*.' The words following this report are heartbreaking in their expression of the most basic of human desires: '*Hopefully the Almighty will have mercy on us in the coming year and give us a little joy and contentment; so that it may be granted to the Jews to lead a worthy life as human beings*.'

In October, Jews of Polish origin were expelled from Germany – a situation the Robinski family were able to avoid, notwithstanding their Polish roots. Then, on 7 November 1938, a young Polish Jew assassinated a

German official, Ernst vom Rath, at the Paris embassy, as vengeance for his parents' expulsion from Germany a month earlier. The Nazi leadership used this event to incite the notorious Kristallnacht pogroms, with propaganda Minister Goebbels' speech on 9 November in Munich setting the tone for the response in his commemoration of the fifteenth anniversary of the Nazi putsch. Nazi officials and Sturmabteilung leaders in Munich circulated instructions to local party structures for retaliatory measures, and Goebbels' Propaganda Ministry and the Gestapo dispatched telegrams to district and subordinate authorities. One such order to the 'North Sea' SA office spelt out exactly what had to be done.

> All Jewish stores are to be immediately destroyed by SA men in uniform ... Jewish synagogues are to be immediately put on fire, Jewish symbols should be confiscated. The fire department may not intervene ... The Führer wishes the police not to intervene. All Jews are to be disarmed. Shoot on sight at any sign of resistance. Signs are to be hung over the destroyed Jewish shops, synagogues etc. with the following text: Revenge for the murder of vom Rath. Death to international Jewry. No compromise with people who are Jews.[3]

That night, Jewish homes, public institutions, businesses and places of worship were damaged or destroyed by Nazi foot soldiers and members of the SA and SS. Shortly thereafter, young Jewish men were arrested and sent to camps such as Dachau and Sachsenhausen, where living conditions left many of them very ill. Historian Mark Roseman describes how trains transporting Jews to Dachau on 16 November were overcrowded and did not have lights or sanitary facilities, while the inmates were forced to wake up at five in the morning to stand to attention for hours on end. At the camps themselves, the men had to endure arduous labour, hunger and other horrors, and for thousands of Jewish men, this was the most terrifying ordeal they had ever experienced.[4]

In a letter to Herbert on 14 November 1938, a few days after Kristallnacht, Cecilie, who has to be extremely cautious in her wording, writes: '*Thank God that Artur has managed to get to Rhodesia legally ... I am so happy that he is away from here, because you will have read in the newspapers about all that happened. We will have to follow soon.*' She tells my father that '*since Friday the Jewish community has been dissolved, and for the time being no [synagogue] service will take place*', adding, as if in passing, that '*Hermann*

Holz has been absent since Friday and Aunt Hildchen is quite heartbroken'. Hermann Holz was married to my grandmother's sister Hilda; the Nazi terror had struck very close to home.

Two weeks later, on 28 November, Cecilie writes to my father to stress the urgency of the Robinski family leaving Germany.

Berlin 28.11.38

My dear boy! We have received your dear lines of the 16.11 on the 26.11 and I can inform you that we are all, thank God, well, and I have not experienced anything bad. It would be very desirable if we would also succeed in emigrating as soon as possible and you [plural] must try to submit an application on our behalf. Since dear father is above the age of 60, an application for him can probably not be made together with that of his wife. For young people it is probably easier to get into Rhodesia, and Artur must try to do his utmost for Siegfried. I have written a letter to Artur 3 days ago … Horst is in Dachau, if only the boy could manage to emigrate. The only question is: where. Little Jochim of the Urbanskis is going to Holland as many children can be accommodated there. Father's card club in the café has been dissolved and the skat players will now take turns in continuing their entertainment in the family home. Hilde is occupied with the school feeding scheme and is very happy there. She is earning 3 mark per week, and is very proud of that. Siegfried thank God looks very well, like a count, but has no employment. Perhaps Artur can organise a job for him as a dyer, colour remover for dresses and buttons. 14 days ago I sent you a single letter with Edith's photo. Have you received it? We spent my birthday in our intimate family circle, and only Mrs Urbanski was present. We spoke a lot about you and Artur …

The rest of the letter is torn.

Cecilie's simple pronouncement that '*Horst is in Dachau*' hints at the incarceration of Jews in camps after Kristallnacht. Horst was the son of Cecilie's sister Minna and her husband Bernhard Rubenstein. (They were the relatives living in Eydtkuhnen, East Prussia, who wrote the letter about family members in the United States, and who hoped that their son Norbert could move to London around the time that Artur left Germany.) It is not evident whether Cecilie and the rest of her family realised what it meant to be sent to these camps at the time, but her letter does reveal a heightened sense of anxiety in its emphasis on the urgency of the Robinskis leaving Germany and her references to other people who are trying to emigrate. At the same time, she seems at pains to assure her sons that their family still participates in some of their regular routines, such as David's card games. These card games become a refrain in the letters. Nonetheless, Herbert and Artur would probably have feared the worst when they read these letters.

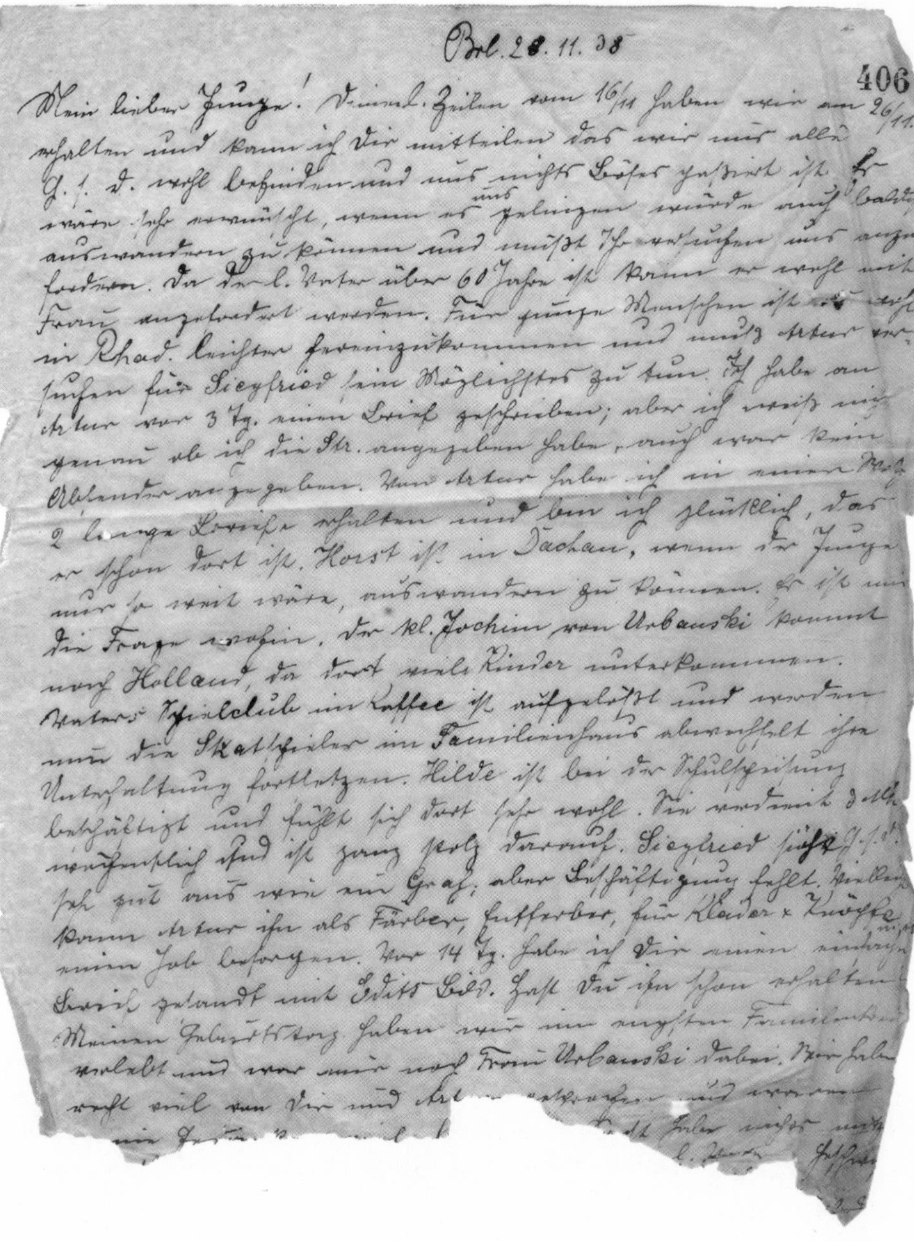
Brl. 28. 11. 38

406

There is more to the comment about Hildegard. In a later letter Cecilie writes: '*She feels very proud, when she presents me with her weekly salary of 3 marks.*' I read these statements as confirmation of my suspicion that Hildegard had a mental disability. My cousin Cecilia, who is a clinical psychologist, recalls her father telling her that his sister was 'slow'. Even though Hildegard labours under extremely poor conditions for very low pay, her mother believes this work is good for her and makes her feel useful. It could even have functioned as a form of occupational therapy. Frustratingly, I have no window into Hildegard's inner world. There is not a single letter from her, and all I can do is surmise who she was from the letters her mother wrote to Artur and my father.

Cecilie's comment that '*Siegfried thank God looks very well*' refers to the fact that he is recovering from some sort of accident. Two months earlier, on 24 September, Cecilie wrote to Artur: '*Our dear Siegfried will remain in Soden until the end of October, the state [medical] insurance has authorised another month and the doctor said that he will then be discharged as a completely healthy person, which after all is the most important thing.*' In a letter to Herbert a week later, Cecilie mentioned that Siegfried was wearing a plaster cast.

On 1 December, Cecilie writes to Artur to reassure him that Edith is doing all she can to apply for a teaching position, including asking for a reference letter from a certain Dr Bamberger. As in the letter to Herbert, she refers to a photograph of Edith that she has sent. (My cousin Cecilia found a portrait of Edith in her late parents' Sea Point flat in April 2014; this might be the photograph referred to in the letters.)

Berlin, 1.12.38

My dear boy! As I have written a letter to Herbi on Tuesday I want to write to you today. First of all, many thanks for your heartfelt congratulations on my birthday and may the Almighty grant that all your wishes be fulfilled for the good. I wish you good health and a life without worries so that we will always hear glad tidings from you [plural] … I am relatively well. The only problem is that Edith is so impatient and she complains all the time that she will not get out. She has requested Dr Bamberger to write a very good [testimonial] report for her and she still intends to learn to make lady's finery in addition, [but] whether she will manage to do that is questionable. Have you already received her photograph? I have sent it by normal mail, which is 10 pfennig cheaper

than airmail. Siegfried now has hardly any chance to learn anything, as the Jewish institutions have been dissolved. He wants to learn to dye clothes and to remove stains with an acquaintance of his. Would he have the possibility to earn something there with that? It would be a blessing if the boy could get out. I probably have already told you that Horst is in Dachau, Norbert in Stallupönen [a town in East Prussia], Hermann in Sachsenhausen, Katz is also gone.

Dear father's health is good thank God … Each Wednesday a skat evening takes place at our house [and] Siegfried also participates. For the time being I shall continue to live here, and the old lady also still lives here. This month we have not received anything from Schn. [the tenant Schnitzler]. Father will go there on Monday. Siegfried was there last week, together with a client and the cashier told him that they are now totally

> *impoverished. S. is very ill and in bed and E. is very nervous so that his mouth twitches whenever he speaks. Aunt Hildchen intends to go to Bolivia, as well as Fritz Cohn. She has already paid a 500 mark deposit. Egon [Holz] likes it very much in P. [Palestine] except that he receives no money there. Otherwise everything is as usual. Please write to us in detail how you are faring over there. Does the expenditure not exceed the income? With heartfelt greetings and kisses from us all, your loving parents and siblings. Siegfried, Edith and Aunt send their regards.*

Cecilie is clearly frustrated with her daughter, even as she acknowledges her efforts to get out of Germany. Perhaps she felt that she could report on Edith's anxieties but was unable to express such thoughts herself. She then turns to older brother Siegfried's equally precarious predicament. We see that Siegfried has been unable to acquire a new trade to improve his chances of emigrating because the Jewish institutions responsible for technical training have 'dissolved'. Cecilie seems to become increasingly resigned to the reality that Siegfried's chances of emigrating are diminishing daily. Edith has a much better chance, she feels, because of her teaching qualifications, but she needs to overcome her defeatist attitude.

By the time this letter was written, three weeks after Kristallnacht, my grandmother would surely have had no illusions about Hitler's Germany. In a single sentence, she conveys the terrifying reality of that time: '*Horst is in Dachau, Norbert in Stallupönen, Herman in Sachsenhausen, Katz is also gone.*' As always, she tries to reassure her sons in Africa ('Otherwise everything is as usual'); she is determined to be stoic, silent and vigilant. She cannot, or rather she chooses not to, express the pain and fear that she and her relatives must be going through. Like my father, all of this had to be buried beneath the quotidian, practical concerns of family life and basic survival.

Ute told me that when she visited Sachsenhausen many years after the war, she learnt that flimsily clothed Jewish men were made to stand to attention in the open for hours in freezing winter temperatures. The men who survived the experience returned to their homes broken, sick and defeated.

What exactly does Cecilie mean when she writes '*S. is very ill and in bed and E. is so nervous that his mouth twitches whenever he speaks*'? Who are S. and E. and what caused their afflictions? Could S. be Siegfried and E. Egon? There is so much that remains unknown. If only my father and Artur were still alive.

* * *

When Ute sent me her translations of the letters, she would often apologise for their agonising content and worried about the effect it would have on me. In an email in April 2013, she wrote, 'I have translated two more letters, wanted to hold them back because I wanted you to enjoy Shabbat. But o.k., I will send them to you now.' A few days later, she asked if we could meet to discuss two letters she had translated the previous evening.

Over lunch at the Holocaust Centre café, Ute suggested that I join the Legacy Forum, a Cape Town–based organisation for second-generation survivors of the Holocaust. According to some psychoanalysts, the children of survivors tend to carry inside themselves a black box of unconscious emotions and traumatic memories inherited from their parents. Ute believed the Legacy Forum could help me cope with my own distress over my family's ordeal during the Holocaust. Soon thereafter, she ended another email with the words: 'Wishing you, your wife and family Shabbat Shalom and much strength when reading these letters.' Two months later, I received an email from Ute responding to an early draft chapter of this book:

> Dear Steven
>
> I have completed the revision, scribbling into the margins … What does come across is the incredible pain that you are carrying with you … Every culture has specific archetypal myths. I am thinking of the Medusa of the Greeks. Whoever came face to face with her turned to stone. In the Jewish myth: the Story of Lot: in the face of horror one turns into a pillar of salt. Be careful, Steven. Your father kept these things from you because he wanted to shield you from them. And he wanted you to be happy, to live a normal life. I am relieved that you are joining the Legacy group on Thursday. Sharing this terrible burden with others may give you some relief …

I never did attend the meeting of the Legacy Forum that night, or any other night thereafter. I received news earlier that day that one of the members had committed suicide; his father, a survivor, had killed himself some years earlier. It did not seem like a good idea to me to join the group under such circumstances. I felt uneasy as well about being given the label of second-generation Holocaust survivor. Maybe I really did belong to this category and carried with me traumas and grief inherited from my father. Perhaps, like him, I was displaying these feelings unconsciously, and would not be able to keep them hidden for much longer. As I read and reread the letters from my grandmother and Aunt Edith, I opened myself up to their tragic content. The letters pulled me back into a world of ghosts and shadows, and the past continued to leak uncontrollably into my present.

After my aunt Elsa's consecration at the Jewish cemetery, a year after her death, I drove my wife and two boys along Beach Road in Sea Point to lunch at Cecilia's home. In the car, Lauren and I had an explosive argument while discussing the consecration, the spectral world of Berlin once again creeping into my everyday life. Lauren, who is not Jewish, mentioned that she found Jewish rituals of death far more meaningful than the Christian ones with which she grew up. The conversation then shifted to why she had not converted to Judaism, even though she supported our son Joshua having a bar mitzvah – a choice Lauren explained was partly due to her deep discomfort with South African Jews' unquestioning loyalty to Israel, regardless of its policies and military actions. I responded that the state of Israel was merely a blip on the horizon of a much longer history of Judaism, and that it would never have come into existence had it not been for the genocide. For me, the most valuable aspect of Judaism was its cultural and intellectual legacies and not its religious, nationalistic and Zionist aspects. By then, however, I had completely lost my composure and was spitting mad.

I had put a lot of effort into holding on to an idea of Judaism that was not tainted by Israel's occupation of Palestinian lands. While I shared Lauren's criticism of Israel's actions in this regard, I rapidly lost any capacity for rational debate when she offered her views on this particular occasion. She then unwittingly plunged the knife deeper into the wound when she told me she'd heard of orthodox Jews who claimed that the Shoah was somehow part of God's plan for the creation of the state of Israel. I was furious at this pronouncement, and yelled that this was a twisted, lunatic and extreme viewpoint.

Later I tried to reflect on my outburst with less anger. Like Lauren, I too am offended by those who invoke the Shoah to justify Israel's military actions. I too criticise Zionists who use and abuse this catastrophe for ideological purposes that deflect attention from the suffering of Palestinians in occupied territories. So what was I doing lashing out at my wife for views that I shared? I had been completely incapable of logical thinking or debate during the argument, and there was something raw and forceful in the way I was expressing myself. The boundaries between the past and my present seemed to be collapsing.

The letters from my family, while an incredible gift, had also opened me up and made me vulnerable to a world of ghosts and shadows that I had sought for so long to avoid. I realised with greater clarity how significant my appointment of Ute as translator of the letters was at this particular point in my life. Ute seems to have known how important this role was, too, because she took to it with an incredible amount of understanding and empathy – without me ever having to ask. She read and translated these letters knowing full well the fate that awaited the letter writers. Leading me gently by the hand, she helped me to peer over her shoulder into this dark pit. As I caught glimpses of the abyss, I prayed that I would not turn to stone.

ELEVEN

The Boomerang

The year my father was imprisoned, in 1933, Hitler appointed his favourite racial scientist, Dr Eugen Fischer, as rector of the Friedrich Wilhelm University (now Humboldt University). Fischer was already the director of the Kaiser Wilhelm Institute of Anthropology, Human Heredity and Eugenics (KWI-A) in Berlin, and he was one of the signatories of the 'Loyalty Oath of German Professors to Adolf Hitler and the National Socialist State'. By the late 1930s, with Hitler's unequivocal support, Fischer became one of the most influential scientists in the Nazis' implementation of eugenics programmes, which included the forced sterilisation and euthanising of mentally and physically disabled people. The discrimination against and murder of the Reich's Jews, which included my family, was underpinned by the science of anthropology, and by eugenics in particular.

The sciences of anthropology and eugenics colluded with biologically inflected state programmes that claimed to improve the health and welfare of national populations but, in the process, sent those deemed unworthy of belonging to a race or population to their deaths. In the words of political philosopher Giorgio Agamben, 'For the first time in history, the possibilities of the social sciences are made known, and at once it becomes possible both to protect life and to authorize a holocaust.'[1] This is the tragic story of the complicity of Western Enlightenment thinking in the genocidal violence of the last century. A significant strand of this story, somewhat surprisingly, begins, not in the heart of metropolitan Europe, but in a remote section of the colonial periphery of southern Africa.

During my 2012 visit to Williston in search of Eugen Robinski's legacy to the town, I stumbled on the footprint of the other Eugen. Like so many of my discoveries on this journey into the past, this encounter had an uncanny quality to it. It was on this visit that I learnt about how the mixed-race Basters, despite living under the protection of the Rhenish missionaries at Amandelboom, were dispossessed of their land in the 1860s by trekboer pastoralists and white commercial wool farmers. Losing access to their grazing lands, many had to move northwards, eventually settling in Rehoboth in South West Africa, in 1870.

In 1884, South West Africa became a colony of the German Empire, and the Rehoboth Basters were treated thereafter as an intermediary class of colonial subjects, sandwiched between the indigenous population and white German-speaking colonisers. In 1904, following an escalation of conflict between the indigenous population and German colonial authorities, the Herero rebellion erupted and was brutally suppressed, resulting in the deaths of an estimated 24 000 to 100 000 Herero between 1904 and 1907, and 10 000 Nama. In a letter written in 1904, the German General Lothar von Trotha outlined his strategy for dealing with this rebellion:

> I believe that the [Herero] nation as such should be annihilated, or, if this is not possible by tactical measures, [they] have to be expelled from the country ... This will be possible if the water-holes from Grootfontein to Gobabis are occupied. The constant movement of our troops will enable us to find the small groups of the nation who have moved backwards and destroy them gradually.[2]

General von Trotha eventually defeated the Herero at the Battle of Waterberg in August of that year, driving them into the Omaheke Desert, where most of them died of thirst and hunger. The survivors of this massacre, the majority of whom were women and children, were herded to detention centres such as the notorious Shark Island concentration camp off Lüderitz, where they worked as slave labourers for the German military and settlers. Prisoners were categorised into groups designating their suitability for work, and they were issued death certificates even before they died, indicating their 'death by exhaustion following privation'.[3] Many interned Herero died of disease, overwork or malnutrition, with estimates of the mortality rate varying between 45 and 74 per cent.[4] It took over a century, until July 2015, for the German government to acknowledge that General von Trotha's actions were 'part of a race war' that culminated in the first genocide of the twentieth century – a trial run for a genocide that would occur two decades later in Europe. German colonial rule continued in South West Africa until 1915, when it was invaded by South African forces during the First World War. When the war ended in 1918, South Africa took over administration of the territory, a situation that continued until Namibia achieved independence in 1990.

In 1904, four years before Eugen Fischer arrived in Rehoboth to study the Basters, Theodor Mollison, who would later become Josef Mengele's doctoral-thesis supervisor, studied Herero people in prisoner-of-war camps.[5] Fischer also apparently visited the camps to conduct race studies on Herero children and children of Herero women and German men.[6] However, his study does not mention that it took place in the aftermath of an anti-colonial rebellion and genocide. Hannah Arendt and contemporary historians have provided chilling accounts of how the Herero and Nama genocide set the stage for what would happen in Nazi Europe only a few decades later.[7] Fischer's scientific ideas, developed in Rehoboth in the early twentieth century, would likewise boomerang back to Europe.

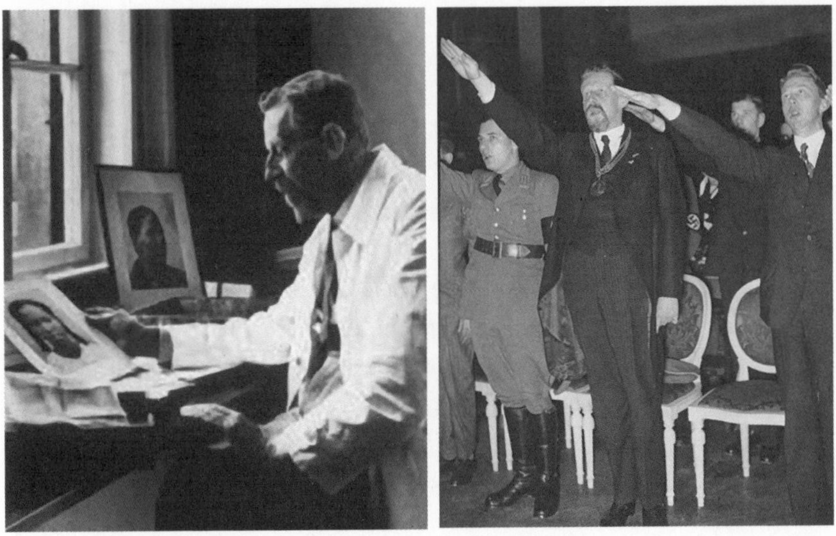

Left: Dr Eugen Fischer looking at photographs of Rehoboth Basters from his 1908 study.
Right: Fischer as rector of the Friedrich Wilhelm University after being appointed by Hitler in 1933

Fischer's study of 310 Basters, who were the offspring of white fathers and Khoikhoi mothers, was part of a scientific enquiry into the role of heredity in human evolution, with a focus on the effects of racial mixing.[8] The study was of great significance at the time, when German scientists and colonial officials in South West Africa were debating the cultural and biological consequences of miscegenation. Historian George Steinmetz writes that, in the early 1900s, some scientists argued that 'mixed-race' populations could become a genetically stable 'new type', while others maintained that they would 'remain "in flux", expressing a mishmash of traits from both parent races, splitting into two opposing types, or reverting to one of the two ancestral genotypes'.[9] German colonial officials were perturbed by what they regarded as this racial and cultural instability of mixed-race peoples such as the Rehoboth Basters, making them the perfect population for Fischer's study. They were also curious about whether the 'admixture of white blood' rendered the Basters more reliable and amenable to colonial rule, or if their 'in-between status' (*Zwitterstellung*) made them more dangerous, unpredictable and troublesome. The rediscovery of Mendelian genetics in 1900 further fuelled Fischer's interest in 'race-mixing' in the colonies and in Germany.[10]

During his four months in Rehoboth, Fischer measured the size, facial structure, nose, lips, ears, hair, eyelids and eye colour of the Basters to determine, among other things, whether the interbreeding of peoples of different races would result in a 'new type' of mixed-race *Mischlinge* (mulattos). He concluded that Khoikhoi and European features appeared in a myriad of possible combinations, and, because of this, the Rehoboth Basters could not constitute a stable mixed race. Fischer consequently abandoned his initial eugenics research programme and classified the Basters as a *Mitteldi ng* (literally a 'middle thing'), or an intermediate class between the Khoikhoi and the Boer, as well as a 'wedge' between the Herero and Ovambo on the one side and the Nama on the other.[11] While assets to the colonial administration, they were nonetheless relegated to the biologically determined category of natives who would forever be racially inferior to whites.

The Rehoboth Basters had entrenched their intermediary position in the colonial social hierarchy in 1885, when their leaders signed a 'Treaty of Protection and Friendship' with the German colonial government. Through this, they were able to secure protection and a privileged status within the regime, as well as self-governing capability in Rehoboth. In return for these privileges, they fought alongside German soldiers to suppress uprisings by the indigenous Herero and the Nama, between whom some two or three thousand Basters had been living as a wedge for three decades of German colonial rule. In Fischer's view, General von Trotha had 'honoured the Basters' by allowing them to fight on the front lines during the Herero campaign.[12] Notwithstanding their privileged status, Basters were still targets of colonial panic about intermarriage, as expressed in the growing concern that German men, and soldiers in particular, would marry Christian, Europeanised and Dutch-speaking Baster women. This would swell the numbers of *Mischlinge* who qualified for German citizenship and who could then move into European settler society. The culmination of this sexual panic was the 1906 decree banning mixed marriage in the colony.

By the time Fischer arrived in Rehoboth in 1908, the colony had already assimilated popular eugenics ideas that racially mixed peoples were politically unreliable, potentially dangerous, and subject to cultural degeneration and biological decay. Although the Rehoboth Basters continued to be loyal and useful allies to German officials, the possibility of a Baster rebellion remained a worry. In 1913, Fischer's ethnography, *The Bastards of Rehoboth and the Problem of Miscegenation in Man*, was published to widespread acclaim. Its appendix provides practical recommendations for German colonial policy, including the use of Basters as low-level officials, foremen and native police to reinforce German colonial rule. Fischer also recommends that the ban on mixed marriages and racial miscegenation in the German colonies be upheld, which would later influence Nazi laws to promote 'the protection of German blood and honour' through the Nazi Marriage Act of 1935 and what became the Nuremberg Laws. These laws forced my father to hide his relationships with his gentile girlfriends in Erfurt.

Fischer's study in Rehoboth was also deployed by National Socialists to support the idea that the recessive genes of racially mixed populations led to physiological, psychological and intellectual degeneration. By the late 1930s, Fischer was one of Germany's most influential scientists, with his institute in Berlin laying the foundations for Nazi eugenics that would find their ultimate expression in the Final Solution.

Fischer's contribution to Nazi racial science was not straightforward, however. On 1 February 1933, a mere two days after Hitler formed his cabinet, Fischer delivered a public lecture in Berlin called 'Miscegenation and Intellectual Achievement', in which he presented ideas at odds with those of Nazi ideology. Written before Hitler became chancellor, Fischer's lecture did not line up neatly with the National Socialist brand of racial-hygiene thinking, shown particularly in its conclusion, which was drawn from *The Bastards of Rehoboth*:

> The crossing of intellectually very capable races with intellectually less capable ones, e.g., Europeans with Negroes, yields a product that is between these races intellectually ... Occasionally, an individual half-breed of this kind can also be strikingly intellectually capable (Pushkin, [Booker T.] Washington), as is to be expected from the laws

> of heredity. The assumption that half-breeds are always worse than both parents intellectually – or even morally – is incorrect.[13]

Fischer's claim that some Jewish genetic material contained 'Nordic parts' made it difficult to categorically define the 'Jewish races' as inferior. Hans-Walter Schmuhl notes that Fischer's categorisation of Jews as a racial mixture, with Nordic and Oriental elements, resonated instead with his earlier Rehoboth findings concerning the 'exuberant growth of the bastards'. But such a notion of 'hybrid vigour' opened him up to attack from National Socialist ideologues.

In his lecture, Fischer also noted that Central Europe, despite being a miscegenation 'hot spot', possessed 'the entire development of great art and culture from the Gothic era over the Renaissance and Baroque periods'. His discussion of the Jewish question led him to deduce that the outcome of interbreeding between Nordic races and Jews depended on Nordic people either crossing with the offspring of old, cultured Jewish families or those from more recently immigrated, and less cultivated, Eastern Jewish families. Some German academics had been contemplating the exemption of the Jewish bourgeoisie from racial legislation created solely for Jews, which they endorsed for 'uncultivated' Eastern Jews. Fischer claimed that cultivated Western Jews and 'philistine' Eastern Jews could be understood as separate biological races. For Nazi ideologues, however, such views conflicted with their anti-bourgeois passions, which would not make any exceptions for an acculturated Jewish bourgeoisie.[14]

Criticised for his February 1933 lecture, Fischer's response was that of a man of unbridled ambition and nationalist fervour. From then on, in something of a Faustian bargain, he made sure that his public views conformed to official lines of Nazi racial thinking, and adjusted his scientific formulations accordingly.[15] He refrained from stressing the 'hybrid vigour' of mixed races and from openly questioning Nazi policies on stringent racial segregation of the Jewish minority.[16] He also no longer referred in public to his earlier endorsement of the scientific findings of German Jewish anthropologist Franz Boas, which emphasised the dynamic influence of environment on the development of 'races'. Fischer's enthusiastic promotion of Nazi eugenics policies, aimed at enhancing the genetic health of the German nation, began in earnest. These policies included euthanasia and sterilisation programmes to isolate 'elements alien to the nation'.[17]

In Germany, this racially alien element was the Jew.

In a public address on 29 July 1933, Fischer, now rector of the Friedrich Wilhelm University in Berlin, offered his position on the Jewish question. Titled 'The Concept of the Volkish State, Considered Biologically', the lecture laid out the following viewpoint:

> That there are physical and intellectual differences no one can objectively deny. I am not pronouncing a value judgement when I declare this. I even go so far as to say that a nation mixed and crossed equally of Aryan and Jewish components could theoretically create a very credible culture, but it would never be the same as one that grew on purely German national soil; it would not be a German culture, but an entirely different, half-Oriental one.[18]

Fischer's revised position on Jews as a foreign body in the German Volk allowed him to promote his institute as Germany's foremost architect of racial-classification policies, including the notorious 'genetic and race science certificates of descent'. Fischer was also appointed a judge for Berlin's Appellate Genetic Health Court, thereby helping to implement the Sterilisation Law of 1933 to combat hereditary medical conditions.[19]

Fischer's story provides sobering lessons for science, and for my own discipline of anthropology. He was an ambitious man who believed that scientific expertise ought to determine state policies, but he had struggled to influence policy during the Weimar Republic period, because of the accountability structures of liberal democracy. To influence policy one had to lobby and pressure parliamentarians, which was a slow and laborious process. The Nazis' rise to power presented him with unprecedented opportunities to short-circuit all of this. In no time he had a direct line to the most powerful state officials. As director of the Kaiser Wilhelm Institute in Berlin, Fischer and his colleagues offered to provide the Nazis with scientific expertise to guide their eugenics policies. In return, Fischer attained unprecedented access to state resources for research. Medical scientists and doctors became virtual gods during the Third Reich. Their expertise was seen to hold the key to the modern eugenicist state so desired by the Nazis.

One outcome of this pact was the sterilisation of the so-called Rhineland bastards, who were the children of German women and African men serving as French colonial soldiers in the occupied Rhineland region after World War I. The Nazi authorities regarded these children as racially

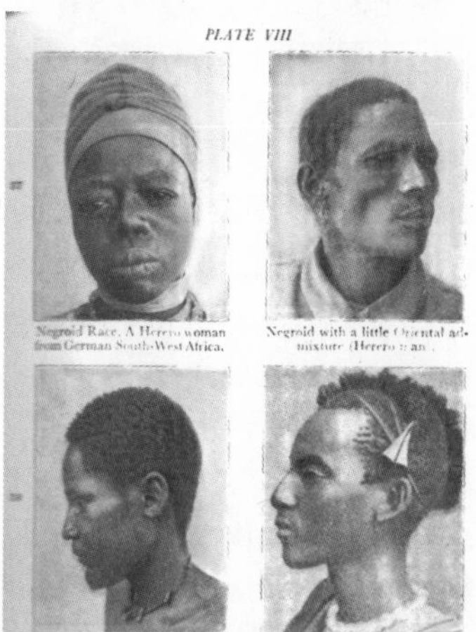

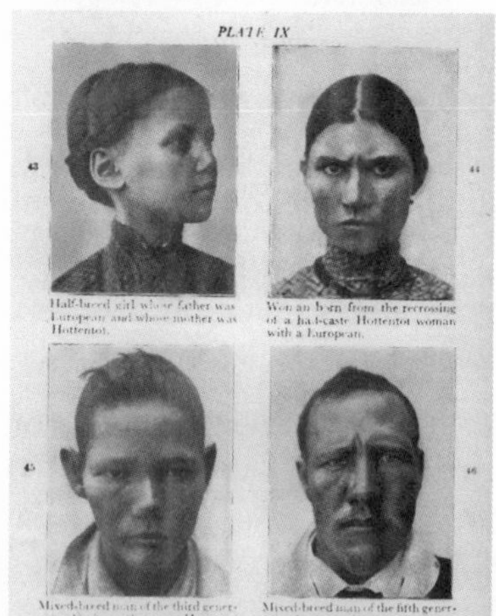

'Racial Types' in Baur, Fischer and Lenz's Human Heredity, *first published in Germany in 1921*

inferior and in a programme supported by Fischer's institute beginning in 1937 subjected them to forced sterilisation.

In 2013, I found a copy of *Human Heredity* by Erwin Baur, Eugen Fischer and Fritz Lenz in the Stellenbosch University library.[20] Hitler had read the book in 1923 while in prison in Munich, when it was already the standard text on German eugenics. Once it was translated into English in 1931, it became a bible for a burgeoning international eugenics movement. Fischer wrote Section Two of the book, 'Racial Differences in Mankind', which includes anthropometric photographs of 'racial types' arranged in the following sequence: Nordic, Alpine (Maritime Alps), Oriental, Mongoloid, Negroid; the section ends with photographs of 'Cross-Breeds between Europeans and Hottentots in German South West Africa'.[21] The faces of the Basters photographed by Fischer seem to reflect their resentment and indignation at the cold objectification of his science – a science that classified them as *Mitteldinge*. I felt contaminated simply touching the book, and was relieved to return it to the library. It had been borrowed eight times – four times in the 1950s, then again in 1963, 1980 and 2000. I wondered what the other borrowers had been looking for in this tainted bible of eugenics.

There are striking similarities in the ways officials and scientists such as Fischer classified European Jews and the Rehoboth Basters. The Basters' unstable, in-between status led German colonial officials to vacillate between viewing them as loyal subjects and potentially dangerous troublemakers. Jews in Europe occupied a similar position and were often seen as constituting a political threat to the nation, either as communists, or rootless cosmopolitans and unpatriotic capitalists. Their dual loyalties meant that they could never be trusted. Like the Basters, Jews had also tried to subvert doubts about their patriotism by fighting the wars of their political masters. My grandfather David Robinski fought for the Germans in the First World War only to become disillusioned with the Kaiser and his military exploits. The payback for his loyalty to Germany was the removal of his citizenship and his execution in the forests of Riga.

Through Fischer's work, a barbaric and lethal science incubated in the colonial laboratories of southern Africa had boomeranged back into the heartland of 'civilised Europe'.

TWELVE

Edith's World

Born in Culmsee in 1915, Edith Robinski was barely eighteen years old when Hitler came to power; she was twenty-two when she qualified as a teacher, and twenty-four when the war broke out. As a young woman, she would have witnessed all her dreams fade before her eyes.

When I began this journey into the past, I knew very little about Edith. The only information I had of her life was based on that photograph taken in 1937, a couple of lines on her fate in the *Berliner Gedenkbuch* and the file from the Landesarchiv. Then came the discovery of the letters from Berlin. Suddenly, a window had opened onto Edith's personal world. I learnt that the photograph of Edith, her mother and her sister was taken the same year she received her qualification to become a teacher at Jewish elementary schools. A certificate found in my aunt Elsa's flat states that she had trained for three years in Berlin and was admitted, on 12 March 1937, to write an examination essay on 'Fairy tale songs in the lowest four forms of elementary schools'. On 23 September she took an oral examination, which she passed, and could thereafter work as a teacher. The certificate, translated from the original German into English, must have been included, along with various testimonials, as part of her application to immigrate to South Africa. On 3 January 1939, the Jewish Congregation of Berlin Department of Care for Juveniles in 2–4 Rosenstrasse provided Edith with the following testimonial:

3rd January 1939

Sworn Translation from German

EDITH ROBINSKI

born on January 26th, 1915,

a German national,

residing at 45, Wallnertheaterstr., has been known to us for many years. She is a lady teacher who underwent her training and professional education at the Training Academy for Teachers at this place, and who is endowed with genuinely valuable features of character. Miss. ROBINSKI in her relations to the children proved to be highly reliable and efficient. She also displayed [these attributes] at the holiday camps of our congregation.

We are able to recommend her in every regard for a similar kind of work, requesting you hereby to let her enjoy your assistance in her efforts to the greatest possible extent.

Department caring for Juveniles and maintained by the Jewish Congregation

sgd. Engländer

As a qualified teacher of music and religious instruction, Edith and her family probably assumed she stood a chance of immigrating, either to South Africa or Rhodesia. In an undated letter to Herbert she explains how hard she is working to achieve this. This was one of the first letters I received from the students who did the initial translations. Ute's is slightly different:

Berlin

Dear Herbert

First of all, I appreciated your effort. Hetty has invited me in such a loving and caring manner that I am really looking forward to meeting her personally.

There is a rumour going round that some more visitor visas shall be issued in December. Tomorrow I will start making arrangements to obtain a visa, but I doubt that I will succeed as applying for a passport and other related formalities will take much more time than I have got. Anyhow, I will try my very best … The size of my class shrinks continuously because many children leave for Holland or other countries. Actually one can only be happy for them, although for us this marks the beginning of the end …

Regards, Edith

Edith writes a similar letter to Artur on 30 November 1938, updating him on her progress. She also alludes to the unravelling of Jewish communal life in Berlin and the impact this has had on her as a young woman witnessing such events.

Bln, 30.11.38

Dear Artur
Many thanks for your prompt mail. Due to my forgetfulness I requested a [teacher's reference] certificate which does not mention anything about drawing. I will have it changed and get it translated and submit it together with the other documents. If you could get me any job – no matter what it is – I'd be very grateful. The community is dissolving and one does not know how long the school will continue to function. Besides that, many children leave for England and Holland and so on.

Herbert's letter included a very warm invitation from Hetty. But only one that is officially sanctioned by the local authorities will be of use for me; and my visit needs authorisation from P.E. Please be so kind to let Herbert know this and also send my best wishes and many thanks to Hetty.

Otherwise we are fine. It would be very good if Siegfried could also leave. I doubt that my attempts will bear fruit, but I spare no efforts. Today I will try to obtain a 'letter of no objection'.[1] *Hopefully it works.*

Apart from that I do not have any special news. All of us are in good health, except Norbert, Uncle Hermann, and Horst who are still sick. Auntie Hilda will most probably leave for Bolivia.

We wish you all the best, and have fun at your work,
Best regards,
Edith

The parents of Hildchen, Siegfried and Edith also send their warm regards.

PS. If an employment contract is not possible, then an authorised invitation to visit Rhodesia might work, if P.E. is not possible any more.

Edith's correspondence with Herbert and Artur reveal how her moods regularly swing between hope and despair that she will be able to leave Germany. The events of Kristallnacht, only three weeks earlier, would have plunged her into an even deeper anguish. Her report that '*Norbert, Uncle Hermann and Horst … are still sick*' is confusing, seeing that Cecilie writes to Artur the next day that '*Horst is in Dachau, Norbert in Stallupönen, Hermann in Sachsenhausen*'. It is possible that Edith was writing in code, using the word 'sick' to imply that these men were incarcerated. The sentence '*The community is dissolving and one does not know how long the school will continue to function*' is a carefully worded statement

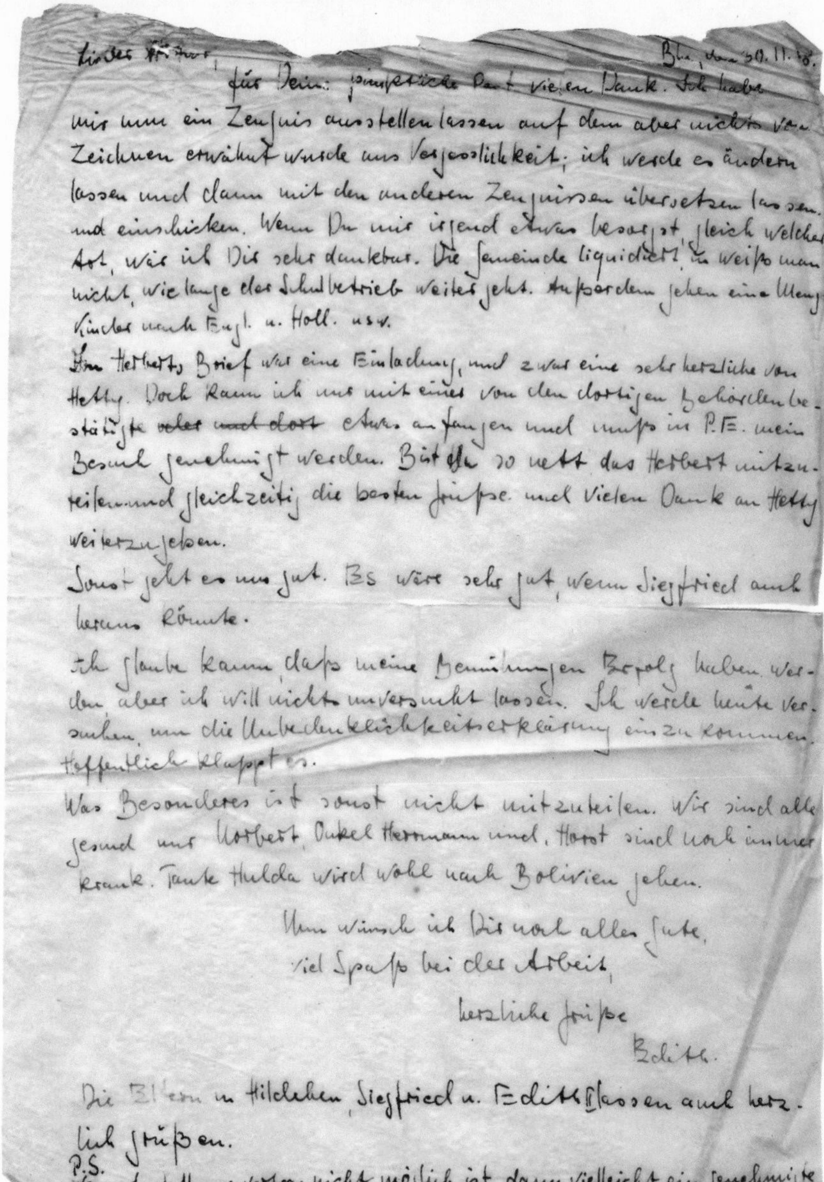

Liebe [illegible], Bln, den 30.11.38.

für Deine [illegible] Karte vielen Dank. Ich habe mir nun ein Zeugnis ausstellen lassen auf dem aber nichts von Zeichnen erwähnt wurde aus Vergesslichkeit; ich werde es ändern lassen und dann mit den anderen Zeugnissen übersetzen lassen und einschicken. Wenn Du mir irgend etwas besorgst, gleich welcher Art, wär ich Dir sehr dankbar. Die Gemeinde liquidiert, u. weiss man nicht, wie lange der Schulbetrieb weiter geht. Ausserdem gehen eine Menge Kinder nach Engl. u. Holl. usw.

In Herberts Brief war eine Einladung, und zwar eine sehr herzliche von Hetty. Doch kann ich nur mit einer von den dortigen Behörden bestätigte ~~oder und dort~~ etwas anfangen und muss in P.E. mein Besuch genehmigt werden. Bist Du so nett das Herbert mitzuteilen und gleichzeitig die besten Grüsse und vielen Dank an Hetty weiterzugeben.

Sonst geht es uns gut. Es wäre sehr gut, wenn Siegfried auch heraus könnte.

Ich glaube kaum, dass meine Bemühungen Erfolg haben werden aber ich will nichts unversucht lassen. Ich werde heute versuchen, um die Unbedenklichkeitserklärung ein zu kommen. Hoffentlich klappt es.

Was Besonderes ist sonst nicht mitzuteilen. Wir sind alle gesund nur Norbert, Onkel Herrmann und Horst sind noch immer krank. Tante Hulda wird wohl nach Bolivien gehen.

Nun wünsch ich Dir noch alles Gute,
viel Spass bei der Arbeit,
herzliche Grüsse
Edith.

Die Eltern u. Hildchen, Siegfried u. Edith [illegible] lassen auch herzlich grüßen.

P.S.
Wenn Anstellungsvertrag nicht möglich ist dann vielleicht ein genehmigte Einladung nach S.A. Wenn nach P.E. nicht mehr möglich.

and can only allude to the effect Kristallnacht has had on the Jewish community. Edith's teaching career was also in a precarious condition as the numbers of Kindertransports increased.

The Kindertransport ('children's transport') was a rescue operation before the war that transported almost 10 000 children from Germany and Nazi-occupied countries to safety in England, Holland and other countries.[2] For Edith, shrinking numbers in the classrooms signalled the diminishing of hope for her own fate.

Edith was no doubt relieved that some of her students had found refuge outside Germany, but she would have been under no illusion of what this meant for her: that she would soon be without a job. Such an occurrence would exacerbate her family's already dire financial predicament. Her teaching probably also gave her a sense of meaning and purpose during these uncertain times; once this was taken from her, there would be nothing left.

Edith is young, in her twenties, but not young enough to benefit from the Kindertransport rescue operations herself. The dreams of her youth are gradually being destroyed, and she is desperate to do any work, anywhere in the world, for the chance of having some kind of future.

In contrast to Edith, the deeply religious Cecilie was unrelenting in her faith that her family would find some salvation from their predicament, even in these darkest of hours. On Christmas Day 1938, she writes a letter to Herbert thanking him for his efforts to get the family out of Berlin and asking for his assistance in encouraging Edith, who seems to have lost faith in her own ability to save herself, to continue trying.

Berlin 25.12.38

My dear, good Herbi! Your cherished letter of the 16th of this month has just arrived and I want to reply to you immediately, as it is Christmas today and I have a bit more time to chat to you. My previous letters always were so curt due to time constraints, therefore I want to chat to you today more lengthily, which I love to do so much because then I get the feeling that you are together with me in person. You are exerting yourself so much on our behalf and you are attending to each one of our fates, which is really touching, particularly as Edith and Siegfried are a bit negligent with regard to their emigration. I am always thinking how much effort you made on behalf of Artur at the time, incessantly and in each of your letters, and how you took everything into consideration, until he succeeded at the last hour, thank God. Artur will probably have told you about Edith and how she sometimes suffers from feelings of inferiority and this also is her mood today. She just states that she knows nothing, neither Hebrew nor playing the piano and she does not want to work as a teacher; despite the fact that she is a good teacher. Write to her in the near future that she should accept a position as a teacher there, even if this is done under pretence, and that she has the biggest chance to get married there, that you have someone suitable for her. It is not impossible that she will make a good match there. She has developed to her advantage. Beautiful figure and also likeable; but she does not want to know anything regarding this.

Tomorrow Siegfried will come here and he must also prepare for his departure. He is able to prove that he has previously owned a business and that he is familiar with the work. As I have already written to you, we lack for nothing thank God, were it not for the worries about the children.

Financially I am getting along for the time being. Should I need something at a later stage, I will come forward. The fact that Artur did not manage to remain in S.R. is really very unpleasant and now he has transferred his residence to the 3rd place, and may it now be to his happiness and blessing. From there it will probably be possible to get Siegfried there faster. Please write to us whether he has found employment and how he likes it there. Here the people are sitting and wait longingly to get somewhere and they would be happy if they could [even] go into the wilds. Unfortunately Horst and Norbert have still not returned, Aunt Minna is quite despondent.

In a later, undated letter to my father, Cecilie, rather uncharacteristically, communicates her feelings about what is happening. She is worried about Artur, who is on his own in Northern Rhodesia, and laments the dispersal of the Robinski family: '*Now the poor boy is so far away from everything and among entirely strange people. It is a hard lot for us Jews, all scattered far apart and also with an uncertain future. But we must have courage and hope for a good future.*' Cecilie quickly changes the topic and discusses Edith's behaviour, which has improved somewhat: '*Your reprimand has helped, she is behaving more decently now.*' Edith, who seems to have been expressing her fears and anxiety about her situation more openly, much to her mother's disapproval, has decided, after receiving a letter from her brother, either to fight these feelings or to mask them. Perhaps Cecilie's constant fussing that her daughter work harder on her emigration has left her frustrated and angry, and contributed to the entire family suffering through this tension.

In an undated letter to my father, Edith reveals how anxious the situation in Germany is making her. This 'nervousness' pervades all her correspondence, even when she does not overtly refer to it.

Dear Heppchen,
Enclosed please find the translated [teacher reference] reports. I think they are in order like that. If necessary I will also send legally attested ones. You will have to inform me about that. Otherwise there is nothing special except that the atmosphere makes one a bit nervous. On the other hand one is, with regard to time pressure alone, so occupied by the school, that one neglects the most important issue, namely to get out. As probably in a few months' time it will not be possible to achieve this. Artur should please kindly send me the address of Hans Segal [in London]. If he then would be in a position to organise a position for a domestic worker or a job with children, there would be a prospect to get out. It is a great pity that A. has not yet found his feet. Now he will probably have to move on again, the poor boy. Well, hopefully soon something favourable will come up for him. Next time I want to write more. Still everything of the best. Be well … Again everything of the best. With regard to the position in Cape Town I wish myself and you much success. Warm regards, Edith

In another letter, Edith reassures my father that she is still working hard on her emigration, although she would have known by then how difficult it would be to get into South Africa. The letter is undated, but she seems to refer to my father's birthday, which was on 29 March, so she probably wrote it in March 1939. It appears that by then the position in Cape Town that she hoped for in the letter above had been taken by someone else, adding to her gloomy outlook.

Dear Heppchen,
Now you have once again put an entire year behind you and I hope this is not the only thing which you have put behind you. I specially wish you a continual good health and much happiness in all your undertakings. May the Goddess who is watching over the lottery show her gracious side! That would definitely not be a bad thing. Have a very pleasant day and also think a bit about us.

I have sent the transcripts of my reports by airmail to Artur and would be very pleased if I could get there [i.e. Northern Rhodesia]. By the way, a colleague of mine who attended a seminar together with me has obtained a position as religious instructor and cantor in Cape Town. His name is Sabor, Rudi – as a result of this I presume that I do not have very many prospects, but perhaps it would still be possible. Do you have any news from Joe [Levy]? I am saving some money for the voyage, because, really, sometime somewhere something has to work out. Many teachers and also other girls have gone to England to work as housekeepers. This possibility still exists. Only it is better to first obtain a written invitation, as there is little prospect to get away by way of the [Jewish] Committees. Now I want to wait and see whether Artur perhaps achieves something through Segal and meanwhile will try to suppress the 'nervousness' which you mention in your letter.

Dear Heppchen, notwithstanding, everything of the best. Give my regards to Hetty and thank her once again on my behalf.

My heartfelt congratulations and everything of the best
From Edith

The turn of phrase '*May the Goddess who is watching over the lottery show her gracious side!*' is striking. If life is a lottery, Edith does not have fortune on her side. Nevertheless, she tries hard to convince Herbert and her mother that she is doing her best to remain positive. She tells Herbert that teachers and young girls are leaving for England to work as housekeepers, and she hopes to find similar work in London. She is doubtful that she will succeed, but says to him: '*Meanwhile, I will try to suppress the "nervousness" which you mention in your letter.*'

* * *

I have walked through the area in Mitte where Edith lived with her parents and Hildegard at Wallner-Theaterstrasse 45. This was one of the parts of Berlin almost entirely destroyed during the war, the buildings replaced with modern high-rise *Plattenbauten*. I have strolled through the streets Edith walked, sat in cafés near her old home. I have spent time contemplating her world amid the ruins of the Heidereutergasse synagogue near Rosenstrasse where she must have attended services. The more I walked in her shadow, the more aware I became of the barriers preventing me from learning about her life. Notwithstanding these gaps in my knowledge, I have learnt much from the letters. I found out that Edith and her family frequently visited the South African consulate at Tiergarten, either to drop off documents or check the progress of their visa applications. Despite many diligent efforts, which included sending required documentation to Pretoria, their applications were repeatedly rejected. In another letter Edith confesses her fears that nothing will come of these efforts. The first part of the letter is missing; only the last page survives. Edith appears to be telling my father about a woman who was successful in her application.

She herself gave me the advice to go along the same route as she did in order to get out, but everything is much more difficult, as I don't have a passport. Her father is a nice person, he eagerly wants to help me. Only he says that I first have to have a written invitation from you [plural, i.e. Herbert and Artur] in order to submit [an application] for the possible procurement of the passport.

The possibility of immigration to which the South African consul has referred was probably based on English cordiality. I believe that it has no factual basis.

I have had a photo taken, but it is so cranky and appalling that I first have to have another one made before I can send it off. I have had the photos from the camera developed; only one of Mutti [Mother] was reasonably exact, with regard to the others the prints were not worth it. I will hand in the box this week.

Now I want to close as we are soon going to Edith II. Next week Mutti will travel to Eydtkuhnen [where Minna and Bernhard Rubenstein live], she actually wanted to go there this morning, but Aunt Hilda had troubles with her gall bladder.

Hoping that you [plural] continue to be well, and everything in your lives will remain satisfactory.

With warm regards and kisses, also from the parents and Hilde, Siegfried and Edith II.

Your Edith.

In another letter to Herbert, Edith, in one simple sentence, captures the fear and despondency that stems from the realisation that her labours will probably come to nought: '*It is difficult today to get accommodated anywhere.*' By now, Edith understood that it was only those Jews with financial resources or special skills and qualifications who could leave the country; the rest were trapped.

On one of my visits to Berlin I was wandering through the exhibits at Centrum Judaicum when I came across a group of elderly women who had been evacuated from Berlin to England in the late 1930s as part of the Kindertransports. When I approached their guide, he told me that he had also been a teacher in Berlin at that time. Realising it was a long shot, I asked him whether he knew of a teacher called Edith Robinski. He seemed mystified at first, observing that there were probably many women with that name in Berlin, but he began to page through a booklet, *Judische Schulen in Berlin* (*Jewish Schools in Berlin*), stopping at a photograph of a group of teachers from the Volksschule Choriner Strasse. The caption beneath it reads: *Early summer 1939. Teachers at the Volksschule Choriner Strasse.*

I picked Edith out immediately, seated on the far right. The guide is in the back row, the third teacher from the right. The members of the tour group, who had gathered around us to look at the photo, told me how one of them, who now lived in England, had been a favourite pupil of Edith's, and that Edith was always especially kind and patient with her. The lady hadn't been feeling well that day and had remained behind at the hotel, so the group suggested I meet with her there. But before I could take the proposition any further, the tour guide ended the conversation, insisting that I had enough information. The group started to protest, but I had already backed away, leaving them as soon as I could. I am not sure why I gave in, but it is a decision I regret to this day. The guide's reluctance to have me talk to Edith's former student is confusing, and I wonder if he knew something about her that he was hesitant for me to learn.

THIRTEEN

Cecilie's Burden

Most of the letters to my father and uncle were written by their mother. Her correspondence tells the story of the family's ceaseless attempts to emigrate while Nazi racial laws continued to undermine their livelihoods, rights and dignity, but it also contains details of everyday activities such as birthday parties, religious festivals, card games, shopping trips and visits from family members.

Cecilie's unflagging faith and indefatigable optimism, as well as her ceaseless attention to practical family matters, find expression in a letter to my father on 8 December 1938.

Berl. 8.12.38

My dear boy! During this week I have received 2 letters from you and you should not worry about us. With us thank God nothing has changed and we have personally experienced nothing unpleasant. Your dear father and Siegfried are at home and are well and every Wednesday a skat afternoon game takes place, together with Father's regular guests from the café which has meanwhile been sold. I then give coffee and cake and the two foreign gentlemen linger until 6 o'clock. One merchant, one member of the public health department and Siegfried. It then becomes very cosy as the old doctor is quite funny and amusing. As you see, you do not need to worry about us.

For the time being I also do not need money because I still have savings. Edith is at the school, still working and gives 100 mark each month. Sch. [Schnitzler] has also paid up until now. I don't know what it will look like next month. I have let 2 rooms and they bring in 45 mark. Now some winter aid will come in too and we should always have so much to eat as we have now …

One of these days Edith will collect her [teacher's reference] report and send it to Artur; perhaps there is a possibility that she comes to Rhodesia. It would be desirable if something would materialise for

Siegfried. He is learning to dye material and remove spots. Perhaps one can do something with this in Rhodesia. Uncle Hermann came home yesterday…

My dear Herbi, [our] best thanks for your good wishes and we can all use them well. Especially health and happiness, that it will still be granted to us, to find ourselves together in joy and after all these worries, to experience very happy and joyful times. I am full of trust and hope to the Almighty that everything will find a good end. Hildchen [Hildegard] still works daily from 8 to 6 o'clock at the school feeding scheme, tomorrow she will again bring 3 mark. So she already has a saving of 15 mark. How is your business developing? You have many costs, let alone the instalments for the car.

The Aid Society is making efforts for Horst's [immigration to Palestine] because he has after all worked for the Hachshara. Norbert is expecting a permit from London. I hope the poor boy will soon succeed to get out. Furthermore I wish you best health and good parnose.

Heartfelt greetings and kisses from us all from your loving parents and brothers and sisters. Siegfried, Edith as well as the aunts send their regards.

Cecilie again paints a picture of a cosy, convivial atmosphere in her home, using David's Wednesday *skat* evenings as confirmation to her sons of their well-being. The card games feature routinely in her letters, probably as a means of deflecting attention from the impending danger. The *skat* sessions were initially held at David's Lichtenberg Strasse Café in Kreuzberg, which I once visited, but after Kristallnacht, the games took place in the players' homes. Along with communal organisations, Jewish homes became the only spaces where Jews could feel some semblance of security. Cecilie refrains from mentioning the names of the players in her letter, simply referring to them as '*two foreign gentlemen*' – a merchant and an employee of the public health department. She might be protecting these men from the censors checking the letters, as non-Jews were not allowed to fraternise with Jews. Despite the constant fear in which she and her family have to live, Cecilie still writes the familiar refrain to her son – '*you should not worry about us*' – and repeats it insistently: '*As you see, you do not need to worry about us.*'

After explaining that their financial situation is all right, Cecilie writes: '*Winter aid will come in.*' Although this is meant to reassure her sons, it also signals the family's reliance on welfare, which one in four Jews in Berlin would depend on by 1940.[1]

Cecilie reports in her letter that Hermann Holz has returned from Sachsenhausen, and that Horst and Norbert Rubenstein have likewise been released. If she knew more about their experiences, she does not tell Herbert. The rest is left to the imagination.

In light of what I know, it is painful to read her wish '*that it will still be granted to us, to find ourselves together in joy and after all these worries, to experience very happy and joyful times*'. Buoyed by her religious faith, she clings to hope: '*I am full of trust and hope to the Almighty that everything will find a good end.*'

The letter ends with three sentences from David and two short lines from Siegfried.

> *My [dear] Herbert*
> *Since dear Mutti has already imparted everything to you, so I do not have anything more to do but to wish you the best of health and to send you heartfelt greetings and kisses. Please give our regards to the dear relatives . . . All the best your father.*
>
> *My dear boy! I too want to send you a sign of life, and dear Edith and I are well as far as health is concerned. In case you or our dear Artur have the address of Lieselotte from Amsterdam, please write directly from there regarding an invitation to me, because I do not at all know the people and it is also better if you would write to them, possibly also to Segal. Now dear boy, warm regards from Siegfried and Edith.*

This is one of the very few times my grandfather writes to his sons. Perhaps he was unwilling to talk about the horrors that he saw around him, but not prepared to write as if everything was all right. My grandmother was the one who tenaciously sustained the lines of communication between the family members.

There is something quite formulaic about Cecilie's letters. A sentence saturated with foreboding and fear is usually followed by one interlaced with the levity of card games, family events, religious festivities and daily domestic life. Further ominous revelations then follow such light-hearted news. Cecilie's tendency to juxtapose pleasant or ordinary matters with menacing developments could be partly attributed to the conventions of letter writing in those days, when messages to relatives living far away conformed to a standardised style and structure and were generally not informal, even between mothers and children. Letters would consist of opening greetings, enquiries after individuals' well-being, family news, wishes for health and prosperity and, finally, closing greetings. It is likely that Cecilie was schooled in this traditional style of letter writing.

Nowhere in Cecilie's letters does she discuss larger political issues, such as the rise of Nazism or the possibility of war, although she does hint at how these developments are affecting the lives of Jews. Mainly, her letters are filled with details on the minutiae of domestic life. After she read Cecilie's letters, Jean Comaroff, a South African–raised Jewish anthropologist based at Harvard, suggested that what was happening in the outside world probably gave Cecilie 'a sense of her world getting narrower and narrower'. To cope with these traumatic occurrences, she carried out what 'anthropologists write about as the rituals of everyday existence that keep things going. The card games, the küchen (cake) and coffee become important.' Jean explains that 'as people see the larger edifice of the world coming down around them, they realise that the true things that matter are the very small rituals of dignity, of life, of getting from today to tomorrow. Even just surviving through the day. And that those things, those small graces are what life is about, what dignity resided in. I imagine for her that when they could not have the cake and coffee and card games any more, then civilisation would really have imploded.'

While reporting on everyday events may have been Cecilie's attempt to hold onto an idea of normality in such abnormal times, I also wonder how much my grandmother actually knew about what was happening beyond her home. There were many forces bearing down on her and her family at this time: fear of the censors, the hostile conditions of the streets, and the racial laws of the late 1930s, which included the eradication of Berlin's Jewish organisations and the prohibition of Jews from sports clubs, baths, swimming pools, beaches, cinemas, operas, concert halls and theatres. For many Jews, the home became the only relatively safe space left, as Cecilie indicates in her retreat to home life for sanctuary, and she may well have been in denial about what was going on in the outside world. As the weeks went by, and Jewish social life outside the home continued to disintegrate, Cecilie could no longer ignore many of these occurrences, and the reports on birthdays, religious festivities, family arguments and *skat* evenings are increasingly interrupted by accounts of the hardships facing her relatives.

On 24 December 1938, my grandmother is more frank about the urgency of emigration for Siegfried and Edith, but, again, her letter is punctuated with an array of domestic matters.

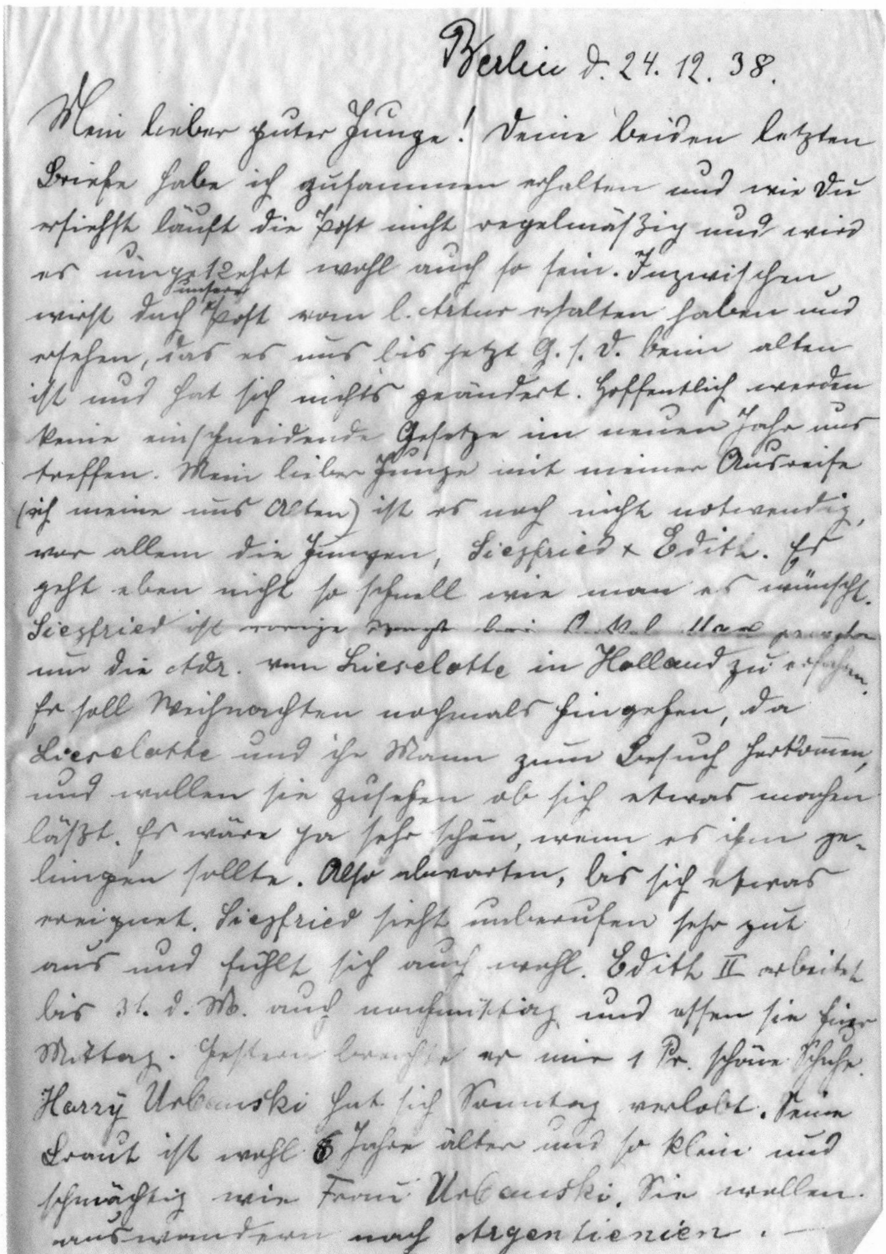

Berlin d. 24. 12. 38.

Mein lieber guter Junge! Deine beiden letzten Briefe habe ich zusammen erhalten und wie Du ersiehst läuft die Post nicht regelmäßig und wird es umgekehrt wohl auch so sein. Inzwischen wirst Du unsere Post vom l. Vater erhalten haben und ersehen, daß es nur bis jetzt G. s. D. beim alten ist und hat sich nichts geändert. Hoffentlich werden keine einschneidende Gesetze im neuen Jahre uns treffen. Mein lieber Junge mit meiner Ausreise (ich meine uns Alten) ist es noch nicht notwendig, vor allem die Jungen, Siegfried + Edith. Es geht aber nicht so schnell wie man es wünscht. Siegfried ist vorige Woche bei [illegible] gewesen um die Adr. von Lieselotte in Holland zu erfahren. Er soll Weihnachten nochmals hingehen, da Lieselotte und ihr Mann zum Besuch herkommen, und wollen sie zusehen ob sich etwas machen läßt. Es wäre ja sehr schön, wenn es ihm gelingen sollte. Also abwarten, bis sich etwas ereignet. Siegfried sieht unberufen sehr gut aus und fühlt sich auch wohl. Edith II arbeitet bis 31. d. M. auch nachmittags und essen sie hier Mittag. Gestern brachte er mir 1 Pr. schöne Schuhe. Harry Urbanski hat sich Sonntag verlobt. Seine Braut ist wohl 6 Jahre älter und so klein und schmächtig wie Frau Urbanski. Sie wollen auswandern nach Argentinien. —

24.12.1938

My dearest son
I received your last two letters simultaneously and, as you can see, the post does not arrive regularly. You will have received news from our dearest Artur in the meantime, so you are informed of his well-being and also that – thank God – nothing changed on our side. We hope that no new laws will be implemented that could lead to further obstacles. My dearest child, emigration is necessary, especially for the young ones Siegfried and Edith. Sadly, things do not go as fast as one would like. Siegfried visited Uncle Max [David Robinski's brother who lived in Elbing, Poland] last week, to ask for the address of Lieselotte in Holland. He is supposed to go there once again over Christmas, because Lieselotte and her husband are free over the festive season and will try to do what is necessary to see Siegfried. Siegfried looks very good and he also feels very good. Edith II is working until the 31st of this month and also in the afternoons – they eat here. Yesterday he brought me nice shoes. Harry Urbanski [the brother of Siegfried's wife, Edith II] got engaged on Sunday. His fiancée is supposedly 6 years older and small and petite as Mrs Urbanski. They wish to immigrate to Argentina.

Yesterday was skat day again and Siegfried plays too. From 2 until 7 the gentlemen are lost in their conversations. I expect news from Artur tomorrow, as 14 days have passed.

Today, my dearest son, I cannot write much to you because it is Friday and Siegfried and Edith are playing chess. I wish you a happy new year and best wishes from everyone here.

In a letter dated 2 January 1939, Cecilie provides my father with further updates on the Robinskis' home life.

Berlin, 2.1.39

My dear boy! Today we received your dear letter of the 12th December and we are very pleased that you are well thank God and that everything will fall into place with regard to your business. Yesterday we received news from Artur, and as I do not know whether he will receive the letter at his present address, I am writing to your address and you can send it on to him. I hope that he has meanwhile found a job and that the climate there agrees with him. He asked so many questions and I want to reply to them as fully as possible. I have forwarded his letters. He does not have to send them to London first and from there to me. With me for the present everything is thank God as usual. We do have the apartment and we have let the 2 rooms. The old woman still lives in the small room and 1 young man.

Today Edith was at Schmutzler's and wanted to buy material for a costume. She bought very good material for 6 mark per metre and a beautiful dress which had cost over 1 mark, for 70 pfennig. She also received the 53 mark from us, and Edith said that Artur has written a new letter, which he did not need to do. Mr Schwarte was here and wants to collect the piano in the next few days. The aunts have not yet sold the houses. They do not yet have approval. Helmut [Cohen] has not yet advanced with regard to his departure. You have probably heard that both aunts have booked seats for Bolivia. Ali Belitzer is still here and is waiting for [the] exit [permit]. The Wolffs are also waiting for visas.

Today we have skat day. Siegfried also participates and you will probably conclude from my letter that my thoughts are jumbled; I am distracted, Edith is now making strenuous efforts with regard to emigration and is trying to attend to all the necessary things. She is now learning [to make] lady's finery and will send in her reports tomorrow. Siegfried will also try everything in order to be successful.

Heartfelt greetings and kisses to you as well as to dear Artur from us all your loving parents and siblings. Soon I will write more, in detail and more relaxed; but the letter should still go off today.

Ute believes the disjointedness of this letter mirrors Cecilie's fragmented state of mind at the time of writing, a symptom of the precarious and chaotic times in which she is living. Short staccato statements report on the activities and predicaments of family members, and she jumps from one bit of family news to the next in an almost garbled manner. Fear and uncertainty are growing, and the Robinskis' financial situation is worsening – the piano has had to be sold, either to support the household or to raise funds for emigration taxes. Cecilie's sisters, Frieda and Hilda, are also trying to sell their houses in order to emigrate to Bolivia. Her apology for her 'jumbled' writing and for being 'distracted' – one of the few times she apologises for this aspect of her letter writing – perhaps unwittingly exposes the cracks that are forming in her armour.

While studying the letters, Ute and I identified other patterns that signal Cecilie's growing anxiety – the innocuous news about family, followed by one-line intimations of possible threats. Her fitful switching from topic to topic is typically separated by a comma, where Ute felt a full stop was necessary. Ute insists this is not because Cecilie struggled with basic rules of punctuation and grammar, but rather because, as the pressures of daily life intensified, her use of language and syntax started to break down. Not even the stoic, uncomplaining and ever-hopeful Cecilie Robinski could suppress the unconscious linguistic signs of psychic turmoil and anxiety.

When Ute first began the translation process, she noticed that my grandmother would often use virtually the same words to describe a fact or event she had already written about to Herbert or Artur, sometimes only a few days earlier. She did this more frequently in the late 1930s, as her fears for herself and her family increased.

Cecilie also sometimes 'turned around the sentences, almost in a Yiddish manner', an inversion of German sentence structure that was often accompanied by 'poor grammar'. As a result, she would 'get weaker in her expressions' and use simple language. Ute again attributes these changes to stress and anxiety, and sometimes, not wishing to reveal my grandmother's vulnerability to me, she would edit out some of the more glaring signs of linguistic breakdown. 'I often translate it the way she wants to say it,' she told me, 'but not the way she says it, because I actually can't, because it would look as though she is naïve, and this would convey a wrong impression.' Cecilie would quickly recover from these disruptions in her linguistic composure: 'She picks herself up again and writes quite normally. I can then see that her writing is very good.'

Cecilie might also sometimes have used indistinct language because she was deliberately hiding something – disguising a statement to elude the censors, or concealing her fears from her sons. But most of the linguistic disruptions appear to be unconscious.

Ute explained to me how she had to learn to identify and interpret these linguistic signs and silences, usually because my grandmother would strive to come across as if she was coping with everything being flung at her:

> What I read in these letters is a situation of great fear and a sort of reluctance to say what they want to say. And, one knows from the history about the things that must have been happening, like Kristallnacht. But they can write nothing about this – except your grandmother writes, 'You probably have heard what happened already. Luckily nothing happened to us' … They are always positive, they never complain, they

> just say, 'Please find a way for us to get out of here.' And I felt that this must have been a terrible strain on your father, a terrible strain. Because when these letters [were written] the Aliens Act was enforced in South Africa, and he must have known better than they did, that he can't get them out here.

In contrast, Edith never resorts to light repartee or the discussion of mundane domestic matters to displace fears and anxieties. In her direct, modern-German writing style, she provides frightening snapshots of the nightmare she and the rest of Germany's Jews are living. Edith's refusal to suppress the truth of what is happening is what, in all likelihood, triggered her quarrels with her mother, who, as Ute emphasises, 'comes across as very noble, because there's never a complaint. She's always trying to be positive.' But in a letter written on 20 January 1939, Cecilie does complain to Herbert about how Edith's focus on her teaching is preventing her from concentrating on more important or pertinent matters.

> *Berl. 20.1.39*
>
> *My dear Herbi! Today I must write to you, particularly because I have already received 2 letters from you of the 1/1 and 6/1 from C.T. ... Edith's reports will hopefully go off these days, she is a wearisome auntie. Nu! All is well that ends well, which is also a consolation. She is, as before, fully occupied in the school, from 8 to 2 and then still from 4 until 7 o'clock, and little time remains for her to translate the [testimonial] reports, with her nervousness and all.*
>
> *Siegfried also was here yesterday and he can only attend to the issue of emigration next week. Yesterday he sold his bedroom for 350 mark, and he receives beds and a cupboard from the community. For the time being they sleep on 2 chaise-longues, because she [Edith II] received the 2nd one from the lawyer as a keepsake, as well as the Mercedes typewriter, and on this she does small private work at home. Her work finishes on Saturday. S. [Siegfried] has let one room for 25 m[ar]k ... the apartment costs him 17 mark per month and he has submitted an application for support. Today Father collected the medical certificates for himself as the Jewish day (Judentag) will take place at the Wohle [Jewish Welfare Centre] on Thursday; the officials were very courteous and obliging. Now our father's name is David Israel R., my name they have not as yet registered as Sarah.*

Cecilie here reveals the dire financial situation of Siegfried and his wife, who has lost her job as a typist at a paralegal firm because of racial ordinances preventing Jews from working in the legal profession. They have had to sell their bedroom furniture and now sleep on chaises longues, one of which was given to them by Edith's employer. Siegfried is expecting to receive furniture from the Jewish welfare organisation ('*the community*') and has applied for welfare support.

Cecilie's comment about middle names refers to the decree passed on 17 August 1938 requiring all Jews to adopt the middle names of 'Israel' or 'Sarah'. She must have recognised this racial ordinance as yet another bad omen, but cannot afford to dwell on such matters. Her letter, after referencing the plight of a few family members, returns to the usual subjects: emigration, the familiar comfort of her husband's *skat* game, and her constant reassurance to her son that she is all right.

> *Has A. [Artur] sent my letter on to you? In it I had told him that Uncle [Hermann] Holz has celebrated his silver wedding anniversary, that Uncle Bernhard [Rubenstein] was here with Norbert last week for a few days and that Norbert will get to Sweden at the end of January, Horst to London. I have sent your letters to Uncle Isidore [Robinski] in Königsberg so he knows about the matter of presentation of moneys. Meanwhile Trinidad is blocked. His son-in-law works on the building site and he earns quite well. Harry Manusch Urbanski also worked on the building site but Siegfried told me that he has collapsed there today, so the work is too heavy for him. Everyone wants to leave and it is more and more difficult with regard to this. Slowly but surely some remedy has to be found in this matter. Does your friend Katz have a business in C.T.?*
>
> *With me thank God everything is still as it was, if it remains like this, I am satisfied. Father has had his skat day today again from 2 to 7 o'clock in Lichtenberg [the café] and Monday at our place. It is quite cosy then as the gentleman of the public health department (title: Sanitätsrat) Dr Bomke is full of jokes and there is a lot of laughter. Yes, laughter. I then give coffee and cake. For the time being you do not have to worry about us. Main thing, that we are all well. Now over there it is real summer and here it is beginning to get warmer; but at the beginning of January the days were quite cold.*
>
> *Otherwise, my dear boy, I do not have anything of interest to impart to you. We wish you the best of health and a very good business. Many*

tender greetings and kisses from your loving parents and grandparents and the entire mishpoche. During the coming days Manfred Holz is going to P. [Palestine], Egon likes it more there every day. Helmut [Cohen] has not progressed with his emigration. Meta [Cohen] will meanwhile work as a nurse in the hospital. Helmut will not be able to survive that long without income, as he also pays for his parents in the aged home and as his brother lives with him. Again wishing you everything of the best.

Regards to the mishpoche over there.

As everyone continues to expose their fear and desperation to escape – to London, Sweden, Trinidad, Palestine, South Africa, Australia, Shanghai, Chile, Uruguay and Bolivia, to anywhere – Cecilie, as always, has to be the rock around which this frantic activity revolves. She must have felt unimaginable pressure to save her children.

Five days later, Siegfried, the oldest sibling, types a letter outlining the same developments mentioned in Cecilie's letter: that he has sold his furniture and that his wife Edith has had to leave her job in a law firm. If anything, his tone is even more optimistic than his mother's.

Berlin, 25 January 1939

My dear boy
Today I will answer your letter of the 13th. We all were delighted to hear about your well-being and all of us will keep our fingers crossed that everything works out with your position [job]. Here everything is still the same and we will now – at full steam – put our shoulders to the wheel regarding our emigration. I already started by selling our bedroom furniture – in fact for 350 mark – so that we now have to sleep on chaise-longues. I also asked my clients for references regarding my work as a button dyer and manufacturer. In case the immigration freeze will – hopefully – soon relax, I will submit those documents to the consulate. Suggesting Shanghai certainly is not a bad idea, but I fear that the climate may not be optimal for me and I would like to first consider the other places. Dear Edith [Siegfried's wife] also had to resign but she really enjoys the temporary retired life. As a farewell gift she received a Mercedes typewriter from her boss. So don't be surprised when I type with this machine – or rather try to type. We also will make an effort to get some typing work.

We also received mail from our dear Artur. He wrote that he stands a chance to get work on the [copper] mines. Hopefully he already got the job as this will increase his ability to assist us with all our immigration applications. In terms of health I am very well and with a weight of 150 pounds I feel quite mobile. Yesterday I did not manage to finish this letter as I went to Edith's birthday party. We had a very big party. Besides the five of us, more guests were present and of course we also thought of you. Today it is Harry's birthday and celebrating seems to never stop these days. He is also still here and together with his bride he wants to go to Argentina where his father-in-law – who also has not left yet – will request his immigration. I will finish for today.

Best wishes to you and dear Artur.

Sincerely,

Siegfried

Dear Edith, the parents and siblings also send their regards.

I have no photographs of Siegfried. Based on correspondence to my father and from what others have written about him, such as his mother in her letters, and in the *Tafellied* written in 1934, he was a charming and debonair young man. One line in the *Tafellied* reads, '*And Edith too from her first glance, with Siegfried was forthwith entranced*'.

Siegfried's writing is humorous and light-hearted. He makes a joke of his wife's dismissal from her job, saying she '*enjoys the temporary retired life*'. He insists that he is '*very well*', and suggests their world is filled with fun and joy: '*celebrating seems to never stop these days*'. He is optimistic that he will get out of Germany, even though there is a 'freeze' on immigration. In fact, he is choosy about where to go, believing Shanghai's climate would not suit him, and preferring to go somewhere else. His letter seems out of touch with reality – but I make this judgement, perhaps unfairly, with the benefit of hindsight.

Like his mother, Siegfried's letters reveal that he was determined to be strong and optimistic; he probably could not bear to let his siblings and wife spot any signs of doubt and dread in his demeanour. He may have felt he had no choice but to continue playing the part of the heroic, strong and courageous Siegfried of ancient German and Old Norse lore – the one who fought the dragon and triumphed.

But Siegfried is neither practical nor in possession of the requisite skills

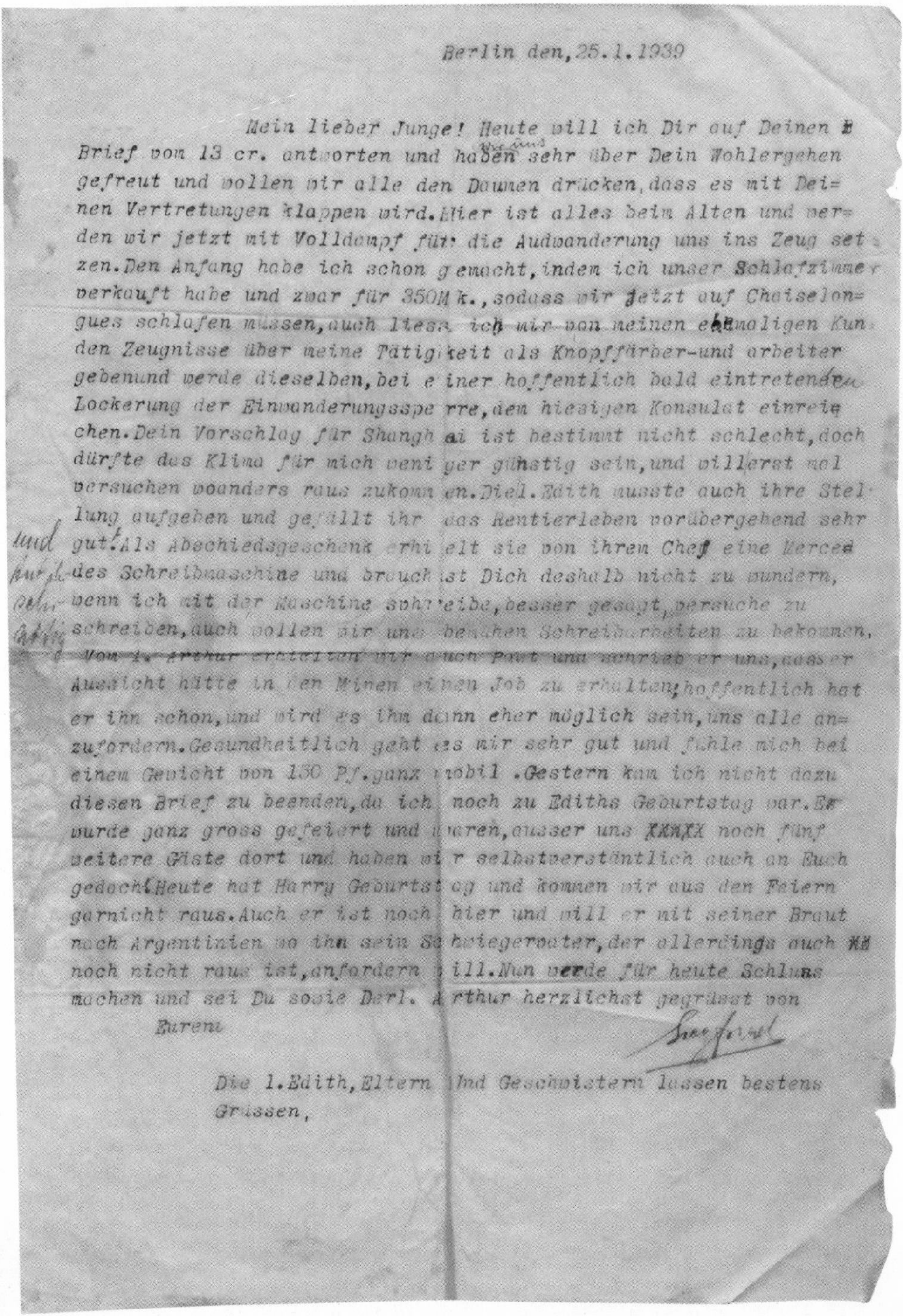

Berlin den, 25.1.1939

Mein lieber Junge! Heute will ich Dir auf Deinen Brief vom 13 cr. antworten und haben uns sehr über Dein Wohlergehen gefreut und wollen wir alle den Daumen drücken, dass es mit Deinen Vertretungen klappen wird. Hier ist alles beim Alten und werden wir jetzt mit Volldampf für die Audwanderung uns ins Zeug setzen. Den Anfang habe ich schon gemacht, indem ich unser Schlafzimmer verkauft habe und zwar für 350Mk., sodass wir jetzt auf Chaiselongues schlafen müssen, auch liess ich mir von meinen ehemaligen Kunden Zeugnisse über meine Tätigkeit als Knopffärber-und arbeiter gebenund werde dieselben, bei einer hoffentlich bald eintretenden Lockerung der Einwanderungssperre, dem hiesigen Konsulat einreichen. Dein Vorschlag für Shanghai ist bestimmt nicht schlecht, doch dürfte das Klima für mich weniger günstig sein, und willerst mal versuchen woanders raus zukommen. Die l. Edith musste auch ihre Stellung aufgeben und gefällt ihr das Rentierleben vorübergehend sehr gut. Als Abschiedsgeschenk erhielt sie von ihrem Chef eine Mercedes Schreibmaschine und brauchst Dich deshalb nicht zu wundern, wenn ich mit der Maschine schreibe, besser gesagt, versuche zu schreiben, auch wollen wir uns bemühen Schreibarbeiten zu bekommen. Vom l. Arthur erhielten wir auch Post und schrieb er uns, dass er Aussicht hätte in den Minen einen Job zu erhalten; hoffentlich hat er ihn schon, und wird es ihm dann eher möglich sein, uns alle anzufordern. Gesundheitlich geht es mir sehr gut und fühle mich bei einem Gewicht von 150 Pf. ganz mobil. Gestern kam ich nicht dazu diesen Brief zu beenden, da ich noch zu Ediths Geburtstag war. Er wurde ganz gross gefeiert und waren, ausser uns XXXXX noch fünf weitere Gäste dort und haben wir selbstverständlich auch an Euch gedacht. Heute hat Harry Geburtstag und kommen wir aus den Feiern garnicht raus. Auch er ist noch hier und will er mit seiner Braut nach Argentinien wo ihn sein Schwiegervater, der allerdings auch noch nicht raus ist, anfordern will. Nun werde für heute Schluss machen und sei Du sowie Darl. Arthur herzlichst gegrüsst von Eurem

Siegfried

Die l. Edith, Eltern und Geschwistern lassen bestens Grüssen.

to immigrate, and it is doubtful that his proficiency at dyeing buttons was in high demand in other countries. He tries to reassure my father that everything is on track – he has sold his belongings, requested references from his employers, and is waiting for immigration rules to relax – but this optimistic spirit must have taken a battering when he realised his chances of getting out were fading fast.

Artur once told me that Siegfried was a communist and a friend of Martin Buber, although my father said that Siegfried 'never was a communist; he was a little bit rightish, a little bit leftish'. This, and what I have gleaned from the letters, is all I know about Siegfried. In 2014, while travelling through Namibia, I dreamt a Chagall-like scene in which Siegfried and Herbert, both seemingly tipsy, were dancing on the roof of a moving train. Siegfried resembled my father as a young man, and also looked remarkably like my brother Michael and cousin David Robins. In my dream he was nattily dressed, tall, well built and handsome. While I watched them dance, I became aware that they were supposed to be looking after my two young boys. I was relieved to see that the boys were fine, and then I slipped out of the dream.

In a letter to Artur on 27 January 1939, Cecilie is optimistic that Edith will get out, but is acutely aware that Siegfried and the rest are not making any progress with their own plans.

Berlin, 27.1.39

Yesterday we celebrated Edith's birthday and we thought much about you and Herbi. Both of you brothers are so far away, and soon she will perhaps also be there. She has invited 2 friends [female] and 1 gentleman acquaintance. We spent a cosy time together until 10 o'clock. As gifts she received many sweets, as well as handkerchiefs and from me lingerie. With God's help she will send off her [teacher reference] reports this week. There is no great hurry with her departure as she will get away all right, even though a few weeks later. After all, [Edith] is a tenacious auntie. With the departure of the aunts, as well as the other relatives, no progress has been achieved, everyone has to wait…

I am surprised at my grandmother's confidence that Edith would be successful, given the difficulties that so many relatives were facing. Maybe she felt that Edith's teaching qualifications would be enough to save her.

On 31 March 1939, my grandmother writes a letter to my father full of short accounts of the small, quotidian aspects of daily life – birthday parties, Pesach (Passover) festivities and, as always, her husband's weekly *skat* games.

Berlin, 31.III.39

My dear Herbi, again 14 days have passed since I sent you post and I have meanwhile given news about myself to d[ear] Artur. Now it is your turn again and I want to chat with you a little. Last Sunday Aunt Frieda celebrated her birthday with coffee, cake, tarts, bread rolls, fish, and so on and it was very cosy. Helmut, Meta and child, Albert, Hanny and child, Mrs Kissmann and daughter and I were present. Hopefully you have celebrated your day of honour festively. I have celebrated it at home with coffee and cake, my speciality, and have thought a lot about you. Does one also give birthday presents over there? Now we are a few days before the Pesach holiday and I have a lot of work. Edith came today to spend 19 days of holidays. She began by sleeping. Right after lunch I packed her to bed and she sleeps like a Rohrspatz [a bird]. For this time of the year it is still quite cold and I must heat the oven a lot. D[ear] Father today has again his famous skat day and he will come home shortly before shabbes [Sabbath]. Yesterday Edith II had her birthday. We were not at her place because some time ago Father had a small argument with her. Siegfried often comes here and is always pleased when he can read your post.

I wonder what underlay the argument between David Robinski and Siegfried's wife. Cecilie's letters also hint at simmering conflict between herself and Edith. Despite these tensions, my grandmother somehow managed to maintain the social fabric of the Robinski family.

Cecilie goes on to talk about other people's emigration prospects. She also mentions a new law, introduced on 1 February 1939, which required Jews to hand over all gold, silver and gem jewellery.

Norbert will probably be in demand in London as a decorator. He has imparted this to me from Sweden. With regard to the departure of Uncle [Hermann] Holz there is nothing definite as yet. He must report daily to the police until he has emigrated. When he receives the permit from the sale of the house he will no longer be permitted to stay. He does not know where to go, he also does not have the presentation money

[Vorzeigegeld]. He did not have anything to give to poor relatives, now he has to help himself. Today a letter arrived from Uncle Wolff and he misses news from all the relatives from Africa. After all, you cannot make efforts for everyone. Let him ask there again, then they will surely reply.

Today is the last day on which the Jews have to deliver, apart from two sets of cutlery and small pieces of silver, everything of gold, silver and gems. Uncle Hermann and Aunt Frieda are most agitated. This year there is a scarcity of mazzas [Passover matzos] and one has to go about them sparingly, so as not to have to eat chometz [leavened bread and fermented grains such as wheat, oats, barley and rye that are forbidden on Passover]. Do you not have any news from Joe [Levy], on behalf of Edith? Hildchen works all day and looks very pale. She is missing the daily walks which she had before. Today she is also coming for a holiday of 14 days and will surely recover during this time. She feels very proud, when she presents me with her weekly salary of 3 marks. Apart from this everything is the same here. We wish you the best health and much success in your business.

A very good Yom Tov (Jontef) and many warm greetings and kisses from us all your loving parents and siblings. Siegfried is struggling for Bolivia. Whether he will succeed is questionable.

Cecilie criticises members of the wider family who did not share their wealth when they had it, such as her brother-in-law Hermann Holz, and says they must now help themselves. She also seems slightly disparaging of relatives who were well-off before, such as her sister Frieda, and who have now been brought down to the same level as her own family. Even when it comes to the immediate family, there is a hierarchy of who to help. There seems to be an unstated assumption that my father and Artur should prioritise Edith, then Siegfried, and finally, the parents and Hildegard. A tragic form of triage is starting to unfold within the family. The reference to Hildegard, who suffered from a mental disability, is particularly poignant.

On 14 April 1939, Cecilie again assures my father that both she and my grandfather are doing their utmost to emigrate. She remains steadfast in her conviction that Edith is the one who has the best prospect of getting out, but now she is far less optimistic when it comes to the rest of the family. They can only wait and see what unfolds.

My dear Herbi! We have received your dear letter of the 4.4. on the 12th and were very happy that you are well. The days of the festival were very pleasant, I missed our two boys at the Seder [Passover] table and my thoughts were with you a lot. We received post from dear Artur on the same day and he has told us that he was invited to the Seder evenings, and we of course were very pleased to learn by this that Jews are living there too [i.e. in Northern Rhodesia]. If the business there will improve, he will be satisfied, which is a great satisfaction for us. He did not write any more details about the place and the business situation there, the main thing is that the climate agrees with him and that he earns his upkeep.

Cecilie then reports on two of their relatives, Dr Helmut Cohen and his wife Meta.

Professor Strauch at the hospital has made efforts on behalf of Helmut and he has got his [medical] practice back. He will practise in the hospital and will move in there tomorrow. Whether Meta will carry on practising the nursing profession there I do not yet know. Helmut has to pay for his parents in the old age home, and he would not have been able to accomplish this in the long run had he not gotten back the practice.

As it turned out, Helmut and Meta Cohen somehow managed to continue working at the Jewish Children's Hospital throughout the war, and they were the only relatives of my father's left in Germany when the war ended. Historian Dr Annegret Ehmann told me that the Cohens could only have survived if one of them was not Jewish, as 'mixed-race' couples (*Mischlinge*) were given some degree of protection from deportation. Being married to a woman of 'Aryan blood' must have protected Dr Cohen. Cecilie continues:

Edith II has obtained a position in the kitchen of the Jewish hospital; but I hardly believe that she will succeed there. The salary is also minimal, 45 mark with free meals [this could also mean board and lodging]. Siegfried still wants to learn to manufacture buttons.

Norbert is in Sweden and has obtained a permit [visa?] to London. He still lacks the travel fees; but Horst will probably provide for him. He has prospects to find work there as an interior decorator. Helmut's sister has found household work in London.

Now my dear boy, you are really moving heaven and earth to set things in motion in order to help us. Your dear father has written today to Mr [Max] Israel and we will visit him on Sunday. We just want to orientate ourselves a little and we will also send along hair-covers. They are thinking of travelling [to South Africa] in the middle of May.

Edith was very pleased about the affidavit and this is now proof that she will after all get out, as she said. Now we have to await further developments and see what help is forthcoming. Perhaps also Hachshara abroad or Rhodesia.

Here early spring has set in all of a sudden with at least 25 degrees especially since it was quite cold with rain during the festival days. 2 days ago I have stopped feeling cold and have taken out light clothing. How is your shop getting on? Do you sell en detail? We wish you much success in this. Otherwise here everything is as it was. Siegfried will probably come for supper, he will also write you a letter shortly. Things are not so easy with regard to his emigration, everything is really quite hard, also with regard to all the others.

Today on Friday I still have to see to a lot of things and want to close my letter. Father has skat day again today, [although] it would be better for him now to be in the fresh air; but the game really does have its attractions. To you the best of health and wishing you good business success, we greet and kiss you with all our hearts, your loving parents and grandparents.

Edith has gone away to do some shopping, as the school is beginning again next week, otherwise she would have added a few lines herself. In any case she asked me to thank you very much for all your trouble and to send you heartfelt greetings and kisses. Hilde will also soon come home from her work today again with her weekly salary of 3 mark, very little but in her heart she is proud of it. Please give regards to our dear relatives …

A week after her letter to Herbert, Cecilie wrote to Artur on his birthday. She expresses relief that he is safe in Northern Rhodesia, but it is also clear that she greatly misses her youngest son.

Berlin 20.4.39

My dear good boy! As your birthday is drawing close, I want to send you our most heartfelt congratulations already today, together with the most fervent wishes for your further well-being. The All-Merciful should above all grant you the best and ongoing good health, and may you find a happy home in the faraway continent, where you will experience the fullest contentment and the fulfilment of the dreams of your yearning. For us it is not a pleasant feeling to know that you will be so alone on that day, but my thoughts will be with you. We will sit at the birthday table with coffee and cake, your photo in the middle and celebrate your special day and you will be with us in spirit. How time flies, you have been away for ¾ years by now, perhaps God means well with us and will unite us again in peace. Still, a tear has fallen on the paper, but it is a tear of joy and I am happy …

My family was desperate to leave Germany, where laws rooted in Nazi racial science had made life increasingly dangerous for Jews. But it was also science that kept the doors of other countries firmly closed.

FOURTEEN

The Scientific Pathways to Destruction

Eugen Fischer's brand of eugenics was not a uniquely German invention. By the 1920s it had become an international scientific movement. In Britain and the United States, the eugenics movement largely derived its ideas from the English scientist Sir Francis Galton, who was the younger cousin of Charles Darwin. Galton studied the English upper classes and determined that their dominant social position was based on their inheritance of superior physical and mental characteristics. His ideas were also influenced by his experiences in southern Africa in 1850, when, for most of his visit, he travelled on the back of an ox through the hot, dry and dusty interior of what is now Namibia – interestingly, the same territory where Fischer forged his ideas half a century later. Galton returned to London in 1852 and published his 300-page memoir, *Narrative of an Explorer in Tropical South Africa*, a year later. Not for the last time, scientific ideas incubated in the laboratories of the violent colonial frontier found their way back to Europe.

South African historian Keith Breckenridge notes that Galton's first-hand encounters with 'native life', colonial rule and settler racism in South Africa in the 1850s, together with his observations of the urban poor in Britain, helped to inform his new science of eugenics.[1] Upon his return from southern Africa, he developed a science of empirical statistics that was used to investigate what he believed to be the growing decline of 'the better sorts'. This programme met with little enthusiasm or political interest at first, but following major British military setbacks against the Boers in the South African War, it began to gain momentum. Along with Charles Booth's findings about the deleterious effects of poverty in London, Galton's programme incited panic in Britain about the country's potential physical and moral decline. It was in this context that Galton became the pioneer of a popular eugenics movement that lasted until the First World War.

Like the eugenicists who would follow his example, Galton was concerned that the supposedly physically and mentally inferior poor and working classes were having more children than intellectual and professional classes – a trend that would ultimately undermine Britain's national stock. These ideas circulated widely in Europe and North America in the early decades of the twentieth century, when the urban poor and lower classes were viewed as both a biological and political threat. By then, Galton's followers baldly began calling for drastic measures to diminish this danger, which included selective breeding, euthanasia and sterilisation.

Galton used composite photographs to create character types of Jews. He claimed that the physiology of 'the Jewish face' that he captured on photographic film mirrored the essence of the Jew's pathological soul. This 'scientific finding' was then used to reinforce his concern that, left to their own devices, the Jews and the 'Orientals' could destroy his ideal English type. Later, the anthropologist Hans F.K. Günther, whose anthropology of Jews was a standard work during the Third Reich, drew on Galton's photographs to make the same point.

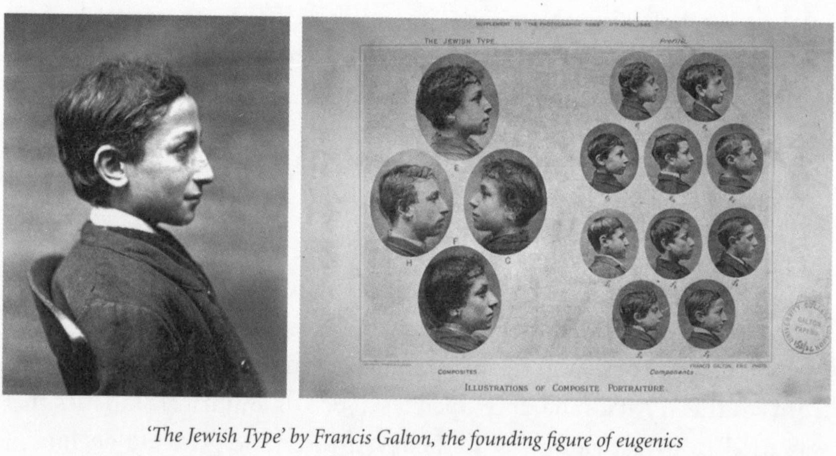

'The Jewish Type' by Francis Galton, the founding figure of eugenics

In his later life, Galton seemed to distance himself from any claims that Jews were a biologically and intellectually inferior race that constituted a threat to 'the better sorts'. Indeed, in an interview with *The Jewish Chronicle* on 29 July 1910, the eighty-nine-year-old Galton suggested that the hygienic regulations of the Mosaic Code could have indirectly contributed to the fitness of the Jewish race. In response to a question about his visit many years earlier to the Jews' Free School in London where he took a number of composite photographs of Jewish children, he said, 'They are, I think, the best specimens of composites, I have ever produced ... They were children of poor parents, dirty little fellows individually, but wonderfully beautiful.'[2]

Galton's ideas were continued by his protégé and biographer Karl Pearson. Pearson was a Renaissance man who was passionate about law, science, mathematics, philosophy, poetry and German literature, and he was a founder of modern statistics. Above all, he was determined to prove that science, and statistics in particular, should be the basis for all government policies and programmes for human improvement. What is intriguing about Pearson and so many other eugenicists is that they believed their work was driven by a virtuous quest for scientific truth, not racial prejudice.

Left: Portrait of the British eugenics scientist Karl Pearson, by Elliott & Fry, 1890.
Right: Pearson seated on the left with the eighty-seven-year-old Francis Galton

Pearson was certainly a man of his times. In the early decades of the twentieth century eugenics was embraced by scientists and politicians across the political spectrum – progressives, liberals, socialists and fascists. They all shared the belief that this was the appropriate scientific solution to improving the wealth, health and welfare of nations. As a committed nationalist and socialist devoted to the growth and welfare of Britain, Pearson had little patience for sentimentality, and believed there was nothing wrong in evicting indigenous people from their land if this was done in the name of Britain's improvement. 'No thoughtful socialist,' he claimed, 'would hesitate to cultivate Uganda at the expense of its present occupiers if Lancashire were starving. Only he would have done this directly and consciously, and not by way of missionaries and exploiting companies.'[3] In the aftermath of English military failures during the South African War, Pearson – shocked at how thoroughly Boer guerrilla fighters, with their tactical and military prowess and superior physiques, had outmanoeuvred British soldiers – called for scientifically based eugenics programmes to advance the British nation. Eugenics was the panacea that would not only remove the inferior mental and physical qualities of the poor and working classes, but redeem the British nation as a whole. Pearson also claimed that there was abundant quantitative evidence to prove the superiority of the professional classes over the idle aristocrats and the lazy and incompetent lower classes.[4]

In his musings on the rise and decline of nations and races, Pearson did not hesitate to accept the inevitability of the elimination of inferior elements: 'Mankind as a whole, like the individual, make advances through pain and suffering only. *The path of progress is strewn with the wreck of nations [which are] the stepping stones on which mankind has risen to the higher intellectual and deeper emotional life of today.*'[5]

* * *

In the United States, leaders of the eugenics movement demanded restrictive immigration policies which would prevent genetically inferior individuals from southern and Eastern Europe from contaminating the superior Nordic, Germanic and Anglo-Saxon genes of Western Europeans, found in upper-class Northerners in the US.

It all began with a 1912 study by eugenicist H.H. Goddard, who was invited by the US Public Health Service to use his intelligence tests for identifying 'morons' among immigrants arriving on Ellis Island. Goddard in fact invented the term 'moron' when he was director of research at the Vineland Institute for Feebleminded Girls and Boys in New Jersey. Drawing on his Ellis Island findings, he claimed to have scientific evidence that Jews, Russians, Hungarians and Italians were disproportionately predisposed to 'feeblemindedness'. The study provided the scientific justification for immigration officials to send back those deemed feebleminded, and was followed, in 1917, by the US army's decision to test 1.75 million World War I recruits with a set of examinations designed by Goddard.

Significantly, environmental and cultural factors had no bearing on Goddard's IQ tests, even though most of his Ellis Island subjects were illiterate, spoke very little English, and had just disembarked from a gruelling sea journey.[6] The tests instead measured familiarity with the dominant national culture of the United States rather than any objective indicator of intelligence. Nevertheless, Goddard's Ellis Island studies led to a dramatic increase in deportations for mental deficiency, which were not enough for him to entirely prevent the immigration into the US of individuals from countries 'swarming with morons'. He got what he wanted a decade later, however, when immigration was regulated by national quotas.

By the 1920s, eugenics was established as a respectable science by Ivy League universities, prestigious funding agencies and the US Congress.[7] Influential organisations such as the American Immigration Restriction League, along with their affiliates such as the American Breeders Association, successfully lobbied Congress into introducing the 1924 Immigration Restriction Act, which aimed to prevent 'inferior races' from entering the United States. Eugenicists such as Goddard, Charles Davenport and Madison Grant were key players in this eugenics movement. Moreover, eugenics programmes to prevent 'feebleminded' foreigners from diluting the Nordic national stock spread from the United States to Germany, where they found fertile ground.

The common thread running through all this eugenics research was its fundamental hostility to the idea that what appeared to be innate hereditary traits were in fact profoundly shaped by environmental factors. In the early decades of the twentieth century, the German Jewish anthropologist Franz Boas, one of the founding figures of cultural anthropology in the US, insisted upon this importance of environment in physical, psychological and intellectual make-up – a theory he developed while teaching at Columbia University, and which I would assimilate during my own studies at the university in the mid-1980s. In one of his most important studies, he demonstrated that the cephalic index (a scientific measurement of human skulls) of second-generation Jews in the United States underwent significant changes that could be attributed to improved conditions in occupation, nutrition and climate. But while Boas finally won the scientific debate in the US, his argument would prove incapable of quelling the rise of fascist ideology in Europe in the 1930s, or of persuading the US to open its doors to Jews who were trapped in Germany.

In *The Mismeasure of Man*, Stephen Jay Gould ridiculed the unscientific character of 'these absurd [intelligence] tests, which measured linguistic and cultural familiarity with American ways [and] ranked recent immigrants from southern and eastern Europe well below the English, Germans, and Scandinavians who had arrived long before'. Since most Jewish immigrants came from Eastern Europe, quotas based on country of origin ended up preventing Jews from entering the United States; and when quotas were established for the Immigration Restriction Act of 1924, they reduced the influx of Slavs, Italians and Jews to a mere trickle. In his history of scientific racism in America, *The Legacy of Malthus*, Allan Chase claims that the quotas prevented an estimated six million Southern, Central and Eastern Europeans from entering the US from 1924 to 1939. As Stephen Jay Gould concludes in *The Mismeasure of Man*: 'We know what happened to many who wanted to leave but had no place to go. *The pathways to destruction are often indirect, but ideas can be agents as surely as guns and bombs*.'[8]

By the mid-1930s, my father's family, who originated from Eastern Europe, stood no chance of immigrating to the US. My aunt Hildegard, who was mentally challenged, would have been blocked for two reasons. The Robinskis' chances of escaping to South Africa were equally bleak. Britain, too, where Edith hoped to find household work, had its own justification for restricting Jewish immigration.

* * *

In 1925, a year after Congress passed the US Immigration Restriction Act, Karl Pearson co-authored a paper titled 'The Problem of Alien Immigration into Great Britain, Illustrated by an Examination of Russian and Polish Jewish Children'.[9] Pearson's study investigated whether Eastern European Jews exhibited inferior physiological, psychological and intellectual traits and capacities that disqualified them from immigrating to Britain. Its purpose was 'to establish a standard of admission, which would insure that only immigrants of good physique and high mentality gained entrance'. Eastern European Jews failed Pearson's standard.[10]

In Pearson's enthusiasm and justification for national eugenics programmes, one cannot help but see the similarities to National Socialist racial policies, even though Pearson, who died in 1934, was not particularly interested in Nazi eugenics. He sought to solve the Jewish question in Britain through less brutal means – the 'civilised English way'.

Although he attempted to use eugenics to influence immigration policies, Pearson's eugenics did not have nearly as much influence over British immigration policy as was the case of the eugenics movement in the United States. Yet, by the mid-1930s, Britain too began to shut its doors to European Jews.

In the 1880s, Britain, much like the United States and South Africa, had witnessed a massive influx of Eastern European Jews.[11] This flood of Jewish immigrants into all three countries resulted in a backlash and calls for stricter immigration control, which in Britain culminated in the Aliens Act of 1905. As in South Africa in the early 1900s, the debate surrounding the Aliens Act stirred up considerable xenophobic and anti-Jewish sentiment, leading anglicised Jews to try even harder to fit into British society by reforming their religious services, emphasising their Englishness, and pressuring Eastern European Jews to anglicise.[12] With the Nazis' rise to power in 1933, the Anglo-Jewish leadership feared an escalation of anti-Semitism at home, which already had a long history in Britain, and this led to their guarded response to immigration matters. Their fear was also exacerbated by violent anti-Jewish persecution experienced by British Jews travelling abroad, which intensified their efforts to present themselves as loyal British subjects who posed no threat to Queen and Empire.[13]

The Board of Deputies of British Jews was therefore reluctant to petition Whitehall to open the doors to the British mandate of Palestine, and even actively tried to restrict the number of exiles to the country. The fear of drawing attention to Jewish sectional interests in Britain also led the board to refuse its support for a boycott of German goods in 1933.[14] Such actions would impact on my father's family in Berlin who were exploring every possible means to escape. But for restrictive British immigration policies, Palestine would have been their destination of choice.

* * *

German racial science was influenced by eugenics in the United States, and during the 1920s and early 1930s, the Rockefeller and Harriman foundations and the Carnegie Institute backed German eugenics to the hilt. Influential US eugenicists such as Davenport collaborated in Fischer's research programmes. These ties of mutual support were buttressed by the major American and international institutions, including the Eugenics Research Association, the Galton Society, the International Federation of Eugenics Organizations, the Third International Congress of Eugenics and the *Eugenical News*, which was published at the Carnegie Institute offices in Cold Spring Harbour. Even after Hitler came to power in 1933, the *Eugenical News* celebrated eugenics developments in Nazi Germany.[15] The Germans, in turn, had been inspired by the sterilisation programmes in twenty-seven states in the US. Meanwhile, the premier US eugenics researchers at Cold Spring Harbour rushed to get a complete copy of the 1933 Nazi sterilisation law from the German consul. It was translated and published in *Eugenical News* with glowing accompanying commentary:

> Germany is the first of the world's major nations to enact a modern eugenical sterilization law for the nation as a unit ... The law recently promulgated by the Nazi Government marks several substantial advances. Doubtless the legislative and court history of the experimental sterilization laws in 27 states of the American union provided the experience, which Germany used in writing her new national sterilization statute. To one versed in the history of eugenical sterilization in America, the text of the German statute reads almost like the 'American model sterilization law' ... In the meantime it is announced that the Reich will secure data on prospective sterilization cases, that it will, in fact, in accordance with 'the American model sterilization law,' work out a census of its socially inadequate human stocks.[16]

Even though the influence of eugenicists on policy in the US was by then on the decline, they were breathless in anticipation of the possibilities presented by the Nazis' new mass sterilisation programme.

Goddard, Pearson and their colleagues had unwittingly created ideas that germinated at Eugen Fischer's Institute for Anthropology, Human Heredity and Eugenics in Berlin, channelling eugenics down the dark tunnel that ultimately led to the gates of Auschwitz, a destination that they could not have anticipated. They had also played their part in laying the scientific foundations for immigration restrictions that kept Jews trapped in Germany.

FIFTEEN

The Tragedy of Triage

I don't have my father's letters to his family in Berlin, but their correspondence reflects what he must have communicated about his attempts to rescue them. On 25 December 1938, Cecilie writes to him: '*I am always thinking how much effort you made on behalf of Artur at the time, incessantly and in each of your letters*'; and on 14 April 1939: '*you are really moving heaven and earth to set things in motion in order to help us*'. Edith, too, writes, '*I appreciated your effort*'; and on 2 June, Siegfried says, '*we are so thankful that you are supporting us with the process of immigration*'.

Herbert seems to have found Edith a job in Southern Rhodesia, but that fell through. He also consulted a law firm in Port Elizabeth in May 1939 to assist him with his family's immigration application. With war on the horizon, however, their chances were looking increasingly slim.

20th May, 1939

H. Robins, Esq.,
1, Westbourne Road,
Port Elizabeth

Dear Sir
With reference to the discussion we had with you regarding your desire to assist your parents to immigrate to this country, we do feel that your chances of success in this direction would be magnified if your sister [Edith] could leave Germany before them, so that she would be in a position to obtain employment and to give an undertaking to assist you in the support of your parents, thereby ensuring that even though anything should happen to you, she would support them and thus prevent them from becoming a burden on the Union Government.

Yours faithfully,
Herbert Burman & Loon

Even four months before the war, Herbert was still working hard to get his family out. His efforts ultimately came to nothing, but at the time he must have clung onto the hope that he could at least rescue some of them. It would nevertheless have been a crushing responsibility to choose who to save first, or who to save at all.

In times of war, doctors and medical orderlies often have to make decisions about who to save and who to let die. The imperative of getting injured and ill soldiers back to the front line makes it necessary to prioritise which lives should receive treatment. Such practices have continued into our own times, even in conditions outside warfare. During the 1990s, practices of triage shaped access to HIV treatment in West Africa, when antiretroviral therapy was not available in the countries' public health systems.[1] For many of these medical professionals, having to judge which individual life should take precedence over another must have been an excruciating and traumatising experience. My father was tasked with the same burden in the years preceding the war; but in his case, the life-and-death decisions he had to make were about people he loved.

Herbert was the first to leave Germany – his experience as a salesman and buyer for a large department store in Erfurt meant he could save enough money to leave, establish himself relatively quickly in the new country, and then work to help the rest of his family escape. His obligation to his family after his escape resonates with many people today, particularly those who have escaped wars, genocides, political violence, poverty and other human and natural disasters in their own countries. The relatives who are left behind may view this person as holding the key to their salvation, and may overestimate the power, influence and agency of the ones they believe can rescue them. They also sometimes try to convince themselves that the 'civilised world' will come to their rescue. But, as subsequent genocides in Cambodia, Indonesia and Rwanda demonstrate, this often does not happen.

But if every member of the family cannot be saved, which ones should then be chosen? In such a scenario, a tragic type of selection process would have to be exercised, whereby a decision is made to save the youngest or the most educated, or the family member with the best business acumen and skills, the one who is likely to become a successful immigrant.

Artur was the next to leave Germany, in 1938. By now the Aliens Act had blocked entry to South Africa, and Artur's planned move to Southern Rhodesia had foundered for some reason, but he was able to settle into

Northern Rhodesia where, at that stage, immigration legislation was still less stringent. Both my father and Artur then turned their attention to getting Edith out. It was assumed she would succeed because she was a young, qualified teacher, and great effort was made to facilitate her emigration from Berlin. Siegfried, the eldest, dyed and manufactured buttons, an occupation that was not in great demand abroad, and by the late 1930s, my grandmother no longer held out much hope for him. Hildegard and my grandparents were the least likely to succeed.

On 12 May 1939, Edith thanks my father for organising a marriage affidavit. It seems that the family thought Edith might be able to escape by an arranged marriage with a Jewish man from Rhodesia. It is clear she sees this as a last option, but she is pleased that she is now in a stronger position to get a permit to enter that country. She again reassures my father that she is actively preparing herself for her new life, either in South Africa or Rhodesia. She is learning typing and shorthand in English.

Berlin 12.5.39

Dear Heppchen, first of all heartfelt thanks for organising the marriage affidavit. In the worst case one can always fall back on it and it really is a relief to me. So I have taken cognisance of the fact that I am now engaged. This after all is already something. Isn't it? Artur wrote that he hopes and trusts to receive the permit for Rhodesia. This would be simply wonderful, although I still doubt whether the authorities there will respond to it. In any case I am now beginning to learn German shorthand transferred to English. The same applies to typewriting, only with the school work so little time remains. I am already longing very much for my two big brothers and … often hold you in my thoughts. You write that I will perhaps not like A., I don't believe this and nobody is making such high demands. Main thing is, one can work and breathe fresh air. [Then all] is well.

I assume that 'A.' refers to the man she was to marry, but I can't be certain.

Edith's note comes at the end of a letter from Cecilie, in which she updates him on their documents for immigration. She reveals that they considered sending Hildegard to Palestine as part of a *Hachshara* Zionist youth preparation programme, but that this was impossible because of her disability.

Berlin, 12.5.1939

My dear Herbi!

We have received your dear letter of the 28/4, again coinciding right on time with Artur's post, and we were very pleased to learn about your personal well-being. So, you have the intention of expanding your business. We wish you much luck and blessing for your new project, which you richly deserve because of your good deeds. Thank God that dear Artur also likes it there and that the climate agrees with him. Meanwhile you will surely have received our dates of birth and the marriage date just has to be added, on 4.10.1904 in Strasburg. In case you need originals, I am sending you a photocopy. It is all well and good but I cannot accommodate Hilde at the Hachshara. Yesterday I went with her to the Palestine Office and so many people are already booked, and they have to be accommodated first, so it will take at least 4 months until new applications can be absorbed. Also, there is a lot of sifting, so that only people of high intelligence are admitted, who have been members of a Zionist movement for a considerable length of time. So, for Hilde, it is hopeless. I have already thought a lot about this. In case Edith should get to Rhodesia, then the only alternative would be to change the marriage document for Hilde. To leave her here with strange people would be terrible for me, as she is also not so independent. There must also be a solution for people like her. In case it will not get to a war, there would after all still be a possibility to get out.

This is the dreadful logic of triage: '*for Hilde, it is hopeless*' because she is in some way mentally challenged ('*not so independent*'). It is these cruel, seemingly unavoidable 'lifeboat ethics' that lead her mother to lament: '*There must also be a solution for people like her.*' Cecilie was certain that Hildegard should not be left on her own in Germany, and that she would not cope if sent abroad by herself, even if the latter was an option. As she discovered at the Palestine Office in Berlin, only committed Zionists with organisational affiliations and highly educated Jews – intellectuals, writers, artists, scientists, musicians and businesspeople – stood any chance of receiving emigration assistance. Cecilie would have known that Hildegard stood no chance at all in this selection process. She even suggests that, should Edith get out by other means, her marriage affidavit could then be transferred to Hildegard's name. But, for reasons we don't know, nothing came of the marriage plans in any case.

Cecilie informs my father of all the immigration efforts of relatives, but doesn't leave out her husband's upcoming birthday celebrations.

> *With regard to Siegfried there is still nothing definite. Edith II has found employment in the [Jewish Friendship] Society and will start work on Monday. Siegfried, thank God, is looking very well and also feels well. Today he will probably come here. Perhaps Aunt Frieda will immigrate to Bolivia. Her niece who went there for Christmas will apply on her behalf, as the husband is earning well as a shoemaker. What do you think with regard to Uncle Hermann, can something be achieved there? For the time being he is learning to clean clothes. I have already learned to sew collars and could open a business with this, which could be very lucrative. Edith can also sew leather gloves, which is very profitable as well, should there be a demand. This week dear father met Mrs Israel in the street … They are running about with regard to [emigration] taxes and this greatly delays the departure. Is Miss Bloch still in the Union [of South Africa]? Willy Pich is in Shanghai; but he is not well. He will try to stay above water by sewing shirts. His bride, a widow with an eight-year-old boy, followed him last week. On Tuesday dear father will celebrate his birthday and he has invited his skat friends, and this will hopefully be very cosy. Also a diversion …*

The next paragraph of the letter expresses Cecilie's intense desire for her sons to be happy and successful in their new homes far away in Africa. Now that Artur looks set to marry, she jests about consulting a matchmaker for Herbert. But lurking beneath this playful repartee about finding a wife for my father, I read signs of imminent catastrophe:

> *With the next chance I will go and consult a [marriage] broker. Perhaps she has a suitable partner for you. It must be something very special for our Herbi. I have told you or Artur that Jews are to live in Jewish houses; but it is not so urgent yet. First the landlord or the government agency has to have organised a house in which the Jews are accommodated, and I am not worrying about that as yet, especially because Edith will hopefully come out soon …*

The brief sentence '*Jews are to live in Jewish houses*' is another chilling, coded message: a new racial ordinance meant that all Jews had to move to

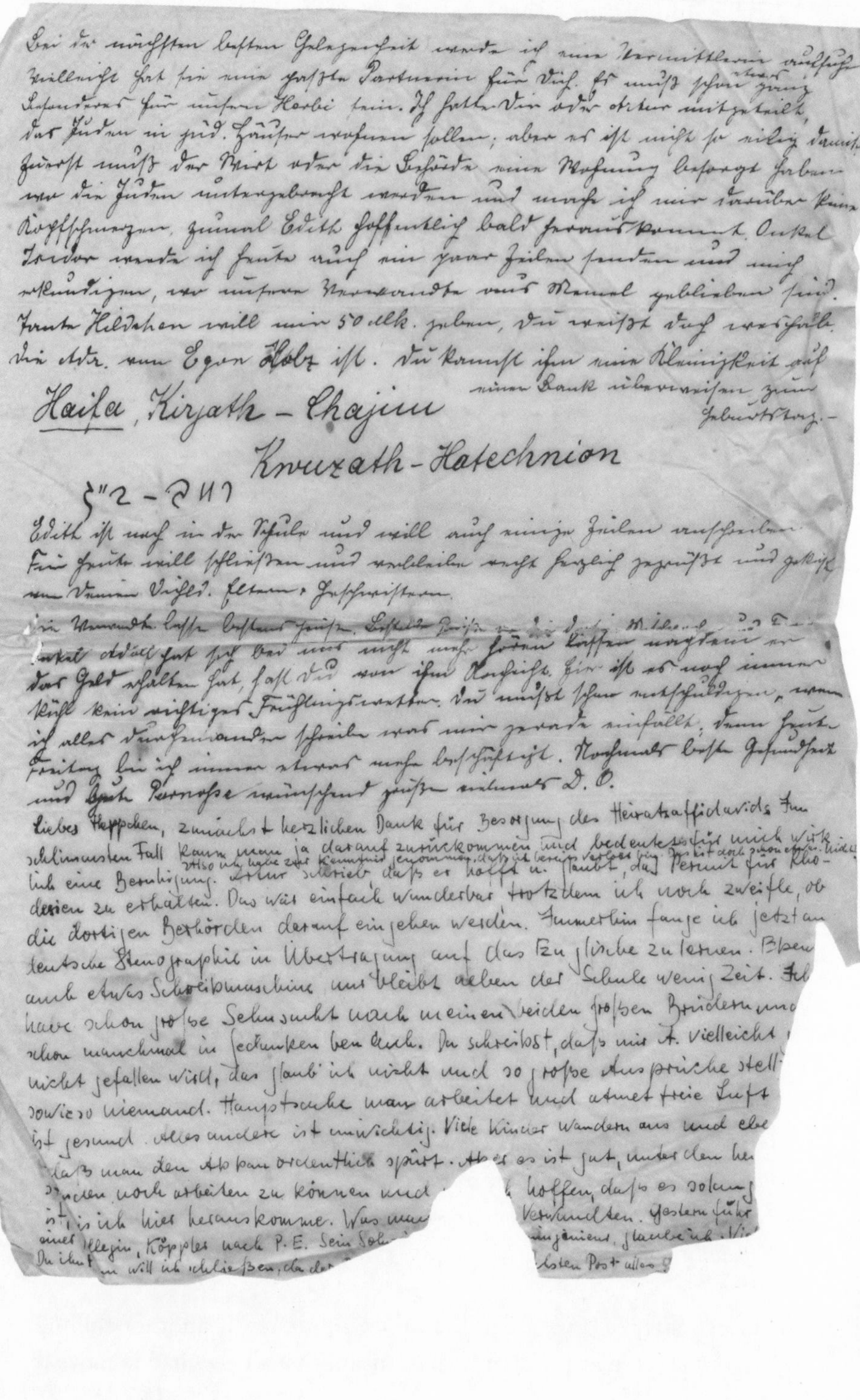

Bei der nächsten besten Gelegenheit werde ich eine Vermittlerin aufsuchen
vielleicht hat sie eine passende Partnerin für Dich. Es müsste schon etwas ganz
Besonderes für unseren Herbi sein. Ich hatte Dir oder Ditter mitgeteilt,
daß Juden in jüd. Häuser wohnen sollen; aber es ist nicht so eilig damit
zuerst muß der Wirt oder die Behörde eine Wohnung besorgt haben
wo die Juden untergebracht werden und mache ich mir darüber keine
Kopfschmerzen, zumal Edith hoffentlich bald heraus kommt. Onkel
Isidor werde ich heute auch ein paar Zeilen senden und mich
erkundigen, wo unsere Verwandte aus Memel geblieben sind.
Tante Hildchen will mir 50 Mk. geben, du weißt doch weshalb.
Die Adr. von Egon Holz ist. Du kannst ihm eine Kleinigkeit auf
einer Bank überweisen zum
Geburtstag.-

Haifa, Kirjath-Chajim
Kwuzath-Hatechnion

Edith ist noch in der Schule und will auch einige Zeilen anschreiben.
Für heute will schließen und verbleibe recht herzlich gegrüßt und geküßt
von Deinem Dich l. Eltern u. Geschwistern

Onkel Adolf hat sich bei uns nicht mehr sehen lassen [illegible]
das Geld erhalten hat, hast Du von ihm Nachricht. Hier ist es noch immer
kühl kein richtiges Frühlingswetter. Du mußt schon entschuldigen, wenn
ich alles durcheinander schreibe was mir gerade einfällt, denn heute
Freitag bin ich immer etwas mehr beschäftigt. Nochmals beste Gesundheit
und gute Parnosse wünschend grüßt Deine D. O.

Liebes Happchen, zunächst herzlichen Dank für Besorgung des Heiratsaffidavits. Im
schlimmsten Fall kann man ja darauf zurückkommen und bedeutet es für mich wirk-
Also ich habe zur Kenntnis genommen, dass ich bereits verlobt bin. [illegible]
lich eine Beruhigung. Arthur schrieb, dass er hofft u. glaubt, das Permit für Kho-
dessen zu erhalten. Das wär einfach wunderbar trotzdem ich noch zweifle, ob
die dortigen Behörden darauf eingehen werden. Immerhin fange ich jetzt an
deutsche Stenographie in Übertragung auf das Englische zu lernen. Eben
auch etwas Schreibmaschine uns bleibt neben der Schule wenig Zeit. Ich
habe schon grosse Sehnsucht nach meinen beiden grossen Brüdern und
schon manchmal in Gedanken bei Euch. Du schreibst, dass mir A. vielleicht
nicht gefallen wird, das glaub ich nicht und so grosse Ansprüche stell
sowieso niemand. Hauptsache man arbeitet und atmet freie Luft
ist gesund. Alles andere ist unwichtig. Viele Kinder wandern aus und ebe
dass man den Abbau ordentlich spürt. Aber es ist gut, unter den he
[illegible]den noch arbeiten zu können und [illegible] hoffen, dass es so lang
ist, bis ich hier herauskomme. Was ma[illegible] Verwandten. Gestern fuhr
einer Kollegin, Köppler nach P. E. Sein Soh[illegible] Ingenieur, glaube ich. Vi
Du [illegible] will ich schließen, da der [illegible] nächsten Post alles [illegible]

Jewish-only accommodation. My grandmother would have understood the implications of what this meant for her family, but instead of dwelling on it, she chose to hope that Edith would get out safely and that their landlord would protect her family, at least for a while, from being evicted. In spite of everything she had already seen and experienced, Cecilie needed to believe there were still some decent Germans left and that goodness would ultimately prevail. I try to desist from reading my grandmother's words with my knowledge of what is coming, but it is difficult not to see the warning signs, and the encroaching menace, in every word she writes. Whether she truly believed that these good Germans would help them in their time of need is another question, but she probably knew that if she didn't, all would be lost.

The letter gives information about members of the wider family, some of whom have received money from my father. Cecilie ends by apologising again that her writing is in disarray.

> *Today I will still send a few lines to Uncle Isidore and will ask where our relatives from Memel are. Aunt Hildchen wants to give me 50 marks, you already know why. The address of Egon Holz is*
>
> *Haifa, Kiryath Chajim*
> *Kvuzath[?] – Hatechnion*
>
> *You can transfer a small amount for him to a bank for his birthday.*
>
> *Edith is still in school and also wants to write a few lines. I will end for today and greet and kiss you with all our hearts your loving parents and siblings …*
>
> *We have not heard from Uncle Adolf since he has received the money, do you have news from him? Here it is still cool, no real spring weather. You must excuse if I write everything in disarray whatever just comes to mind, because today is Friday when I am always busier. Once again good health and wishing good parnose and greetings …*

A week later, Cecilie wrote to my father again.

Brl. 19.05.38 [sic]

My dear boy! Today is the day on which dear Artur will receive a letter from us, but as your letter came this week with the announcements, I must send you some lines today. Have you received what was sent to you? You surely know that Aunt Hildchen does not want a present from us. Please send something small to Egon, I have given you his address. The boy wants to save some proof money ('Vorzeigegeld') for himself. I have already told you in my previous letter that Uncle Hermann will give 50 mark for your things, he can make good use of them. How do matters stand with your new branch, is something going to come from this? Your expenses are really enormously high, I think your staff is better off than you are and they do not have to suffer your headaches. Have you acquired a vehicle or are you still going to wait until you will fetch us together with G.H. [God's help] by car? Is there hope for approval of the applications? Edith is already waiting with yearning for information from Artur. Meanwhile she is quite well here, over there she will not be able to earn money so easily. There are holidays all the time but she is a very dissatisfied person and thinks that luck will come flying towards her elsewhere. Today for example the Pentecost holidays are beginning again; because we have Shavuot already on Wednesday. How quickly time passes. This time 3 years ago you have crossed the great ocean with the hope of visiting us in peace one day. But the times have changed. Well, hopefully we will see each other in peace, but over there. I am always worried when the post from dear Artur does not arrive on time. After all, he does not have any close relatives in the vicinity. May the Almighty only grant him a constant good health, all the other good things will then follow. Your congratulations on father and Hildchen's birthday arrived precisely on time and they were very happy about your attention and your congratulations and have asked me to express to you on their behalf their heartfelt gratitude. We have celebrated the festival right on time. Father invited his skat friends and the celebration was closed with card games. In honour of the day he won 1,75 mark. As presents he received from one of the gentlemen a pack of cards and the medical councillor brought a big box of chocolates and said straightaway that I should consume them with a healthy appetite, Edith 1 bottle of honey, Hilde 1 pair of suspenders (braces), so that he would not lose his pants whilst playing, and I have contributed to the celebration with coffee and cake. Not to forget Siegfried's razor blades, Bethy [?] Israel brought cigarettes.

The brothers are in London and are waiting there for the continuation of their journey. Do you always send my letters on to dear Artur? Because he still receives news from me [only] every 14 days. How long does it take for a letter from you to Ndola? Why don't you send the letter to Segal, after all, the postage is cheaper. Manfred has already got married; but he does not like the girl. Anyway, he is now on the way to Eretz. Today I will write to Aunt Minna and will ask for the address of the boys from England. Otherwise everything here is as usual. Tomorrow (Saturday) I am going again to the aunts, last week I took along Hildchen, for her to pick up her birthday present. Each of the aunts gave her 5 mark. I am having my teeth seen to and have replaced them with an old set of dentures for which I paid 25 mark. Saturday will be Mother's Day and then I will be given sweets, and for that good teeth are required. How do matters stand with regard to your stomach troubles? I hope that everything is in order again and that it [your stomach] has ended its strike.

Do you not go much to the relatives? I am certain that they would be very happy if you would go there and then you would have a bit of diversion … I hope that everything is well with you again and we remain in old love and in new, your loving parents and siblings.

The relatives also send their best regards, and in the same way we send regards to the mishpoche over there.

A few months later, with war on the horizon, Siegfried writes one of his few letters to my father, updating him about his immigration efforts.

Berlin, 2 June 1939

My dear Herbert
Today I wish to write to you instead of dear Mutti. We received two letters after each other; one dated the 19th and the other dated 24th of the same month. We also received a letter from dear Artur yesterday. These letters always trigger great feelings of joy, hope and confidence – your last letter in particular gave rise to these feelings. I am eternally grateful for all your help and effort. It is true that it is difficult to make any arrangements from here, which is why, dear boy, we are so thankful that you are supporting us with the process of emigration. I wish to talk about the matter of Chile. You are aware that I have already initiated the plan to immigrate to Australia, but I have not yet heard anything back from them. However, I want to first wait for an answer

before you start the immigration arrangements for Chile. I do not want you to pay anything yet, because Australia is less costly than Chile. The money paid for Australia is also less likely to get lost. Dear mother has probably already told you that dear Edith [Siegfried's wife] works at a welfare society. Edith has enquired about the living situation in Chile and was told that, both from an economic as well as a climatic point of view, things are very good. Under the pledge of discretion, she was also given the following addresses: Dr Fritz Chodziesner, Montevideo in Uruguay, Feliciano Rodriguez 2668. This person could organise the entry permit needed, and I urge you to contact him as soon as possible. You will also have to give him our details: S R worker, 8.8.05. E R, born Urbanski, shorthand typist and housekeeper, 30.3.06. Dt Eylau [Germany].

Herbert must have asked his brother about the situation regarding accommodation for Jews, because Siegfried replies:

Now I want to come back to your question with regard to the apartment. A new law was implemented, which states that Jews are only allowed to stay in Jewish houses. The landlord can, however, only terminate an existing lease if alternative accommodation has been found. It is, of course, only for a limited amount of time that we will be able to remain in our present apartments. Yesterday Mr Völker visited the parents, and he said that the West [of Berlin] will be the first to be affected by the law. He said he would only terminate the lease if compelled to … Our present landlord does not seem to have any intentions to evict us …

Our Etsch [their sister Edith] is very agitated about your suggestion to leave and would like to jump onto the train immediately. The dear parents would also love to get rid of the nuisance, because sometimes she is truly unbearable.

We are in the middle of summer here and mother visits Aunt Frieda daily to lie in the sun on her balcony. Also dear father goes to the park to relax when he does not have a skat day.

I believe I have now reported on everything that is worth knowing. I am also tired from writing, which I have discovered is not one of my strongest qualities.

Warm regards, your brother Siegfried.

Three months before the outbreak of the war, Siegfried still seems optimistic as he considers immigration options for Australia or Chile if South Africa and Northern Rhodesia do not work out. But, without artisanal certification, he stands little chance of success. Perhaps he even knows this. He then makes what at first seems to be a criticism of his sister, referring to her as an unbearable nuisance. But on closer reflection, it is probably meant to be tongue in cheek, as he refers to her endearingly as 'Etsch'.

In an undated letter, Edith writes:

> *Dear Herbert,*
> *From Artur I received the information yesterday that permission to immigrate as a typist was declined, which is due to the general anxiety regarding refugees [in Northern Rhodesia]. A. wants to try again for a position as 'house helper', but also here one has to predict a negative result. I do not know what to do. The need to emigrate is pressing, as far as rumours are reliable. So no time is to be lost any more, on the other hand, I would like to circumvent the issue of marriage, because I presume that I will have to wait for two years until completion of the transaction, or is this not necessary?*
>
> *It will be best if I went to England for the time being, to do household work. If I would obtain a position there, I would come out soon, but I do not know whether Herbert [Reisner] will be successful, I will write to him today. Perhaps I could obtain a position pro forma, because once in the country, I would find something, there are enough jobs there.*
>
> *I have unfortunately only now taken the initiative ... There are difficulties to be expected, also in Rhodesia, but I will attempt to find temporary employment there. I hope I will succeed. From my colleague I can report to you that he had a position in Cape Town as cantor and [Hebrew] teacher, but that he was not granted permission by the government. On this one can therefore not place any hope. It is difficult today to get accommodated anywhere.*

Edith is hesitant about waiting any longer for the marriage that Herbert and Artur are arranging for her with a man in Northern Rhodesia. Her words betray a growing sense of despair and hopelessness. She already knows that a cantor and Hebrew teacher was denied entry into Northern Rhodesia, even though he had a job waiting for him there – so what chance did she have? Nevertheless, she is willing to work in England, South Africa or Rhodesia as a typist or a housekeeper.

In the months before the war started, most Berlin Jews who had the financial means had already left the city. The Robinski family were, unfortunately, not well off, which made their emigration much harder to accomplish. Most countries outside Germany were unwilling to open their doors to them, and, if they were, Jews who were not wealthy could rarely pay the onerous immigration taxes. In an earlier letter, dated 10 March 1939, Cecilie informs my father that his Uncle Bernhard and Aunt Minna Rubenstein had managed to get all five of their children to safety and that they were 'envied' by many. Cecilie then expresses her hope that all the children will be successful and that their parents will get much joy from them. She had probably come to the realisation by then that it was too late for her own family.

Britain and other European countries did open their doors to young Jewish children through the Kindertransport, but for adults it was more difficult. One of the countries least likely to accept 'ordinary Jews' such as my father's family was the United States, as a result of their 1924 Immigration Restriction Act which made it nearly impossible for German and Eastern European Jews to gain entry. Yet this was the same country that only a couple of decades earlier had celebrated itself as a sanctuary for refugees and poor immigrants. By the late 1930s, as Hitler's intentions became clearer, the US only accepted exceptionally gifted or wealthy Jews. Those who were aided by well-connected Americans had to be distinguished scientists, artists, writers and intellectuals such as Albert Einstein, Marc Chagall, Max Ernst, Franz Werfel, Lion Feuchtwanger, Heinrich Mann and Hannah Arendt. This system of sifting out more desirable Jewish refugees from the rest had been playing out in other countries too. In September 1933, a month before he fled Europe for the US, Einstein himself had entreated the Turkish president Ataturk to give refuge to forty German Jewish professors who he affirmed 'could prove very useful' to any country that accepted them. Ataturk acceded to Einstein's request, and these forty professors went on to make significant contributions to the development of Turkey's university system.[2] However, without money, exceptional talent or useful connections, there was little hope for the remainder of Germany's Jews. A perverse form of triage, this time state-driven, was taking place here.

At the more mundane level of kinship, a different type of triage played itself out among Europe's Jews – in Herbert and Artur's case, it was the tragedy of being forced to prioritise the rescue of their siblings. They had managed to escape to safer lands, but now had to decide who should leave and who should remain in the same country from which they had fled. Even though they could not have possibly imagined the death camps – and that racial discrimination could go to such extremes in 'civilised Europe' – from local newspapers, BBC radio broadcasts and information disseminated by the Jewish Board of Deputies, they would have been all too aware of how unbearable life had become for German Jews since 1933.

As I write, I am acutely aware that similar scenarios must be playing themselves out now, as hundreds of thousands of desperate refugees from Syria, Afghanistan and other war zones flee to Europe. Should they manage to safely cross the Mediterranean and find refuge in an increasingly hostile fortress Europe, their thoughts will immediately turn to the loved ones left behind. Should they not be able to rescue them, they too will have to live with the guilt.

As my own family history shows, once the international community absconds from its moral responsibilities, it is usually those who managed to flee to safety that end up living the rest of their lives with guilt. I fear that this may have been my father's fate. I wish I could have told him what I know now: that scientists, politicians and policy-makers had colluded in ways that preordained his failure to rescue Edith and the rest of his family.

In her seminal 1951 study of totalitarianism,[3] Hannah Arendt discusses how, in the period between the two world wars, European nationalist responses to displaced and stateless populations contributed to the lethal othering and criminalisation of refugees and non-nationals. Reflecting on the consequences of this statelessness of Jews and other refugees, Arendt concludes that human rights depend on national rights – that is, rights that constitute and protect one as a citizen of a nation-state. Without national rights, she insists, talk about human rights was 'hopeless idealism'. These hapless European refugees of the inter-war years were left in a desperate predicament: 'Once they had left their homeland they remained homeless; once they left their state they became stateless; once they had been deprived of their human rights they were rightless, the scum of the earth.' This condition of statelessness enabled the SS newspaper, the *Schwarze Korps*, to print in 1938 that 'if the world was not yet convinced that Jews were the scum of the earth, it would soon realise this when unidentifiable beggars, without nationality, without money, and without passports crossed their frontiers'.

Arendt also notes that the solution to the Jewish question in the aftermath of the Shoah merely created a new category of rightless and stateless refugees: the Palestinians. Israeli historian Ilan Pappé makes a similar point in *The Ethnic Cleansing of Palestine*, his account of the displacement of an estimated 700 000 indigenous Palestinians during the Israeli War of Independence, or what the Palestinians called the Nakba (Catastrophe). These Palestinian refugees were, as the late Palestinian scholar Edward Said put it, 'the victims of the victims'.

SIXTEEN

Doors Slam Shut

Before the start of the war in September 1939, Jews' freedom of movement in Germany continued to be systematically restricted as they were prohibited from a larger number of public spaces, institutions and occupations. Jews could only sit on yellow-marked park benches at Bayerischer Platz in Berlin; they could not enter the public service; they were forbidden from universities and barred from professions; and they could no longer own or run retail shops or mail-order businesses, or work as independent craftsmen. They also had to declare their incomes and property 'to ensure that these assets are used in the best interest of the German economy'. Jewellery made of gold, silver, platinum or pearls had to be handed over to the state, and these and other valuables could not be taken out of the country. Later, Jews would not be able to own radios, pets or receive ration cards for clothing. This was an impossible and unbearable way to live, and the letters from Berlin at this time are full of details about family members' desperate efforts to emigrate, as in this letter to Herbert from Cecilie dated 9 June 1939.

Berlin, 9.6.39

My dear good boy! This week we have received 2 letters from you and we are very happy that you are well thank God, health wise and also with regard to your business. Our good God should just help you to further good, that your wishes may be fulfilled and that we can still be together in joy for a few years. We have received the affidavit yesterday and dear father [visited] the Israels to gather information [about immigration to South Africa]. The Israels will probably leave here [for Port Elizabeth] in 8 days, should they get a place on the English ship ... The papers from the Tiergartenstrasse [the South African consulate in Berlin] have to be requested in writing and we have already written to them. Then the medical examination is to follow ... Hopefully everything will work out. I will notify you continuously about the further developments. About us, my dear Herbi, you do not need to have any great anxieties, neither with regard to the apartment, nor with regard to livelihood. Mr Völker is very decent and has not yet mentioned anything about giving notice, etc. Also there is rent control for every Jew, no Jew remains without lodging…

Cecilie continues to reassure her sons in Africa that the family are coping, but her words constantly betray her: '*Hopefully everything will work out,*' she wishes, after informing Herbert of the family's emigration developments, indicating that she is becoming less confident that they will all be able to leave. In her reference to a possible eviction ('*Mr Volker… has not yet mentioned anything about giving notice*') she puts a dent in her previous argument that Herbert does '*not need to have any great anxieties*'.

I have visited the South African consulate in Berlin's fashionable Tiergartenstrasse, now reconstructed into a large, modern, concrete and glass building. At the time it was a much more modest nineteenth-century structure, and it was here that the Robinskis submitted their immigration documents, medical certificates and photographs. This space would have occupied a significant place in their minds as their lives depended on the decisions made there, and in offices in Pretoria.

In the middle of June, with clouds of war gathering on the horizon, Cecilie writes a letter to Herbert that seems to mirror the freneticism around her; she jumps from topic to topic in no specific order, and combines darkness and despair with lighter and almost frivolous subject matter.

Berlin 15.6.39

My dear Herbie! This week I have not received a letter from you and assume that within the next few days post will arrive. I do not have much news to impart to you today. We had applied for the questionnaires at the consulate and received them the next day. As dear father has caught a cold this week we want to try to undergo the [medical] examinations next week, and if the results in father's medical certificate are positive, then we will obtain the other necessary papers. Tomorrow we want to visit the Israels, as they will now depart from here this coming Sunday, and we want to keep ourselves informed about various matters. Uncle Hermann should be discharged from the hospital today, as he was operated on the bladder eight days ago. Hopefully everything will go well with him, and I will visit him tomorrow. Last Sunday I visited him in hospital and at the same time did a detour to Meta [Cohen], as her flat is also in the hospital. There is little hope that she will be able to emigrate and they are already very despondent. But many others are in the same boat. Also Hanny does not know where to go. Next week Albert will start work at the building site, he must earn a livelihood. Meta wants to send you a picture of her little daughter. She is a sweet child …

This is another letter riddled with repressed anxieties. '*Everyone is in need of care [and] everything is barred*,' she writes further on. The more desperate things become, the more demands pile up for my father. He is asked to assist the two Holz brothers, Manfred and Egon, who have escaped to Palestine but who are without money. The question of whom to help is becoming increasingly fraught. Again, Cecilie is doubtful that Siegfried will get out: '*Like the thousands of other young people, we must wait for something to happen with regard to his emigration*.' Later in the letter she writes, '*Siegfried has also not made any progress and we can only hope for the best*.' But what is she hoping for? The miracle she is praying for is not coming, and I wonder what the limits are to her faith and optimism.

This is a deeply disturbing letter. Everyone my grandmother refers to seems vulnerable and despondent. It is less than three months before the start of the war, and Siegfried, like so many others, has no escape plan. Cecilie still tries to reassure my father: '*About us you do not have to worry. For the time being we are still living undisturbed*.' But this is unconvincing, proven in the change of topic: '*Soon the holidays will start but one has nowhere to go. The schoolchildren will spend the holidays on the school grounds, there is no place anywhere outside*.' A racial ordinance enacted in 1935 had prohibited excursions by Jewish children and youth groups of more than twenty, a development Edith has already alluded to in earlier correspondence. But, predictably, my grandmother switches tack: '*Yesterday was skat day in our house, and [your father] lost 1,05 mark; but last time he won 1,65 mk*.' She also enquires about my father's health and his business: '*Now enough about us. How are you my dear boy? Hopefully you are well and the new branch will develop*.' Then, after this dizzying flight between so many varied subjects, she turns her attention to Artur's predicament in Northern Rhodesia:

This week we also received post from dear Artur. Thank God he is feeling well, which is always the most important thing. Today I have sent off the tablets which he requested and the collar stiffeners as samples without value. I feel so sorry for the poor boy, that he has to live so alone there, without any relatives. He was so used to family life, I am thinking of him all the time with the hope of seeing him again in joy. He should only stay well then everything will be fine again.

Artur is still unmarried and living in Ndola, where he has no relatives. Cecilie considers him more vulnerable than his older brother, who has established his business in Port Elizabeth and has his cousins, Eugen's three daughters, as a source of comfort.

In her letters, Cecilie displays a great amount of concern for Artur's well-being and his being on his own in Northern Rhodesia. She refrains from burdening him with requests for help while expecting Herbert to provide financial support to the family and to organise their rescue. Ute notes: 'Your father was under tremendous pressure. Your grandmother never asked anything of Artur. She would say "poor Artur" – so she was worried about him. But to your father she said, "Send this one something for his birthday." It's a command. She shares more with him, and she puts more pressure on him.' This pressure intensified when life for the Robinski family in Berlin drastically began to deteriorate in the late 1930s. The weight on my father's shoulders must have been incredible.

Despite this, Cecilie again reassures Herbert, '*About us, you do not have to worry.*' Then, towards the end, she writes: '*Edith has enclosed a few lines; but what she has written is so very inconsequential.*' Edith writes:

Dear Heppchen! I cannot tell you anything of significance. At school, children are leaving daily, and after the holidays classes will be amalgamated because 50% are Pol[ish] children who must leave [Germany] within a very short space of time. On Tuesday I will go to the women's [employment] agency to try and get a job in England. If someone organises a position from E. [England] then it works out faster. Many jobs are available if one makes the effort on one's own over there; from here not much can be done. Next week the long holidays begin but I am not participating in the [school] holiday outing because one is not even allowed to be out in the fresh air. Our children do not have much here. Otherwise nothing new. Wishing you all the best, health and business success. Perhaps there will be a good outcome regarding the household job in N.Rh. [Northern Rhodesia]

More heartfelt greetings, your Edith

Why does Cecilie consider what her daughter writes to be inconsequential? There are clear tensions and frustrations playing out here in Cecilie's questioning of the 'significance' of her daughter's letter. Although Edith herself begins her message with the sentence '*I cannot tell you anything of significance*', I find what she has written of enormous importance. The number of children leaving daily in the Kindertransport, mostly to Britain, had intensified after April 1939, and by the start of the war in September, the majority of German youngsters had managed to get out, with 75 per cent of the Jews left in Germany over forty years old.[1] This naturally had consequences for Edith's career and livelihood; and life is equally bleak for the remaining schoolchildren who cannot go to the woods, lakes and parks of Berlin for their vacation. Cecilie's dismissal of Edith's despondent, but realistic, assessment of things is indicative of her unwillingness to acknowledge the truth of the reality her daughter sees so clearly. But Cecilie cannot completely submerge her anxieties, especially in the months leading up to the war. She does her best, however, to remain hopeful, which, along with her unwavering religious conviction, undoubtedly encouraged her family to withstand the continued indignities and threats to their existence. This burying of her own feelings would have placed immense strain on her.

Given the restrictions Jews were living under, letters from family members who had escaped must have meant the world to those who remained behind. Not only were they from relatives trying to get their families out of Germany, but they also offered reassurance from those safely outside the country. These letters were probably keenly anticipated and reread repeatedly, especially by my grandmother, who was so grateful that her sons were happy and beyond the reach of the forces gripping her family in Berlin. I would imagine that these letters were what kept Cecilie going during these dark times.

On 1 July 1939, Cecilie once more assures my father that the family are working hard on their emigration, and brings him up to date on their preparations.

Berl. 1.7.39

My dear Herbi! Today I must reply to two of your letters, as dear Artur received post from me and it is forwarded to you in any case. First of all, I want to tell you about myself, as you will by now be curious to know how far the necessary papers have progressed. So far everything went smoothly and we have got them together within one week. Health certificate, certificate of good conduct, testimonial of character and certificate of impecunity ('Mittellosenbescheinigung'). Next week the papers go to the translator and Edith has connections there. We still have to have photographs taken and in barely 8 days the papers can be sent to Pretoria, after first submitting them to the consulate. We have also settled our capital levy ... Now we must wait for the decision. This week Mrs Neumann was at the Aid Society (Hilfsverein) and she will also soon land in P.E. The Israels will probably arrive there during the next week. Now my dear boy, we thank you most sincerely for the little picture you sent. We were very happy about it and you look like a real boss in the midst of your staff. May God keep you in the best of health and give you happiness and His blessing on your undertakings, so that we will still have much joy in you as well as the other dear children. Do you drive a lot in your new car? Will it be big enough when you will fetch us at the harbour ——— Dear Artur probably waits with longing for Siegfried because of Edith. Nu, hopefully this time he will have more luck and Edith already has travel-nerves. Yesterday the long holidays started and she has gone to Strausberg for a holiday today. She needs this and I have my peace while she is away ... Siegfried comes here daily for lunch, Edith dines in the Aid Society in the canteen. The boy looks well thank God and he has not yet heard anything from Australia. Perhaps news will come one of these days. Now they are all stuck because they are not being accommodated anywhere, and they must wait with patience. Today I have nothing special to impart and it is time to eat as we do every Friday [Shabbat]. The family is getting smaller and smaller and we are today only 3 persons at the table, as Edith departed at midday. We further wish you the best of health and a very good business. Many tender regards and kisses from us all, your loving parents and brother and sisters ...

All the relatives send their regards. When you write to dear Artur, do not forget to send heartfelt greetings and kisses. Hopefully he will soon be able to send me good news.

It is unnerving to read this knowing what happened. Cecilie's tone is mostly cheerful, and she displays some confidence, even anticipation ('*Edith already has travel-nerves*') in having got nearly all the paperwork done. In her joking question whether Herbert's new car will be big enough for the family when he fetches them at the harbour there is a terrible poignancy.

Despite this optimism, Cecilie ends the letter with the lament: '*The family is diminishing more and more, and today we are only 3 persons at the table.*'

My father's family dutifully complied with all the paperwork requirements. Perhaps they had a blind faith in bureaucratic procedures, or maybe they were driven by my grandmother's belief in the magic-like outcomes of bureaucratic rituals – if you fill in the forms properly, salvation will follow.

In a letter dated 17 July, Cecilie tells my father that she joined Edith for a two-week holiday in 'Strausberg'. It is not clear whether this is Strasburg in France or the small Polish town the family originally came from.

Berlin, 17.7.39

My dear Herbi!
We have received your dear letter of the 17/6 and hope that you are well, which we can thank God also report about ourselves. You will probably have learned from dear Artur that I have been on holiday in Strausberg for 14 days together with Edith and returned yesterday evening. It was very nice there and I am thoroughly sunburnt. We slept in a living alcove and paid 9 mark per week. I cooked for the two of us and therefore the stay was cheap. Hilde also came there for the weekend, about which she was very pleased and in these 3 days turned as brown as a mulatto. Father cooked his own meals and he had fun ... Now, to another subject. We have the papers together so far, as we still have to wait for the [testimonial and character] reports, which are also necessary for this. Tomorrow dear Father will take all papers to be translated and we will then deliver them to the consulate, which will be sent from there to Pretoria for the decision. I hope that the expenses were not in vain.

Edith II will make an application today at the Aid Society with regard to Australia, which was opened for artisans without having to produce money, now one must wait and hope again. Yesterday evening Siegfried [visited] and found that I have had a very good rest, no wonder, resting and lazing around in the garden and forest air.

Uncle Hermann is not better and he is quite despondent, with pains and expenses adding to his problems. Uncle Isi [Robinski] from Königsberg came to Berlin yesterday and has visited us today. He looks very well; but he is very unhappy that he has not yet found the possibility to leave the country. He does have an affidavit to N. America but [there is] a long waiting period ... Uncle Max [Robinski] will go to Holland in three weeks ... I have already had 1 hour's lesson in English

... Tomorrow Siegfried wants to take a photo of us and we will then send you a picture. Now I will close, as father has just returned from the skat club and I must see to supper. Stay well, a good parnose and very heartfelt greetings and kisses from your loving parents and brothers and sisters as well as relatives. Today a letter arrived from Uncle Adolf that he hears nothing from Liesbeth Merkel, he should write again. One cannot always help everyone.

Cecilie once again flits from topic to topic in a vain attempt to appear calm and hopeful, but I detect a growing nervousness that she can no longer contain. Nonetheless, she refuses to collapse into a state of dejection, conveying a sense of purpose in her remark that she is learning English. But then she returns to despondent accounts of relatives who are not making any progress with emigration. She had already told Herbert on 1 July that he could not assist all his relatives, and she maintains this conviction, reminding him that '*One cannot always help everyone*'.

But it must have been difficult to turn down desperate calls for help. One such plea was conveyed in a distressing letter my father received from his cousin Egon Robinski, Isidore's son, in Kaunas, Lithuania.

Kaunas 7. ? 39

Dear Cousin
I have just received your address from my father and request the following from you: I am today in a terrible situation as I have lost my livelihood for the second time and will also in the foreseeable future lose my right of residence. So briefly: I am totally finished. But as I have heard, Artur has landed in Rhodesia, I am asking you now to send me his address so that he can send a permit for myself and my wife and also for my brother-in-law and his wife. We have money, he does not have to lay out anything. As you know I was employed as a dentist in Heydekrug in the district of Memel (East Prussia) [but] this has been terminated now.

Artur knows everything about me as he has visited me. So send the address of Artur by return post, sometimes only a letter from him would suffice, [in which he states] that he wants to have us with him, then we will get an entry visa.

So help us and write to us the address.
Egon Robinski
And Erna
Kaunas

In the months leading up to the war, the Robinski family were still exploring options in Australia, Bolivia, Chile, South Africa, England, Palestine, the United States and even China. They continued trying to navigate their way through the maze of bureaucratic red tape, but by the end of July, things looked hopeless. Yet, as always, Cecilie tries to be positive, even though options for her children seem to be diminishing daily. On 28 July she updates Herbert on the latest developments:

Berlin, 28.7.39

My dear Herbi! Today I want to reply to your last letter, because through my writing to dear Artur, each one of you receives post every 14 days, and we are always pleased if we hear that both of you are well, thank God … As already mentioned, our papers are arriving at the consulate at the beginning of the week, as they first must be certified by the expert. The school reports have delayed the submission very much … Werner has yesterday gone to Sweden on Hachshara with 20 children and the boy was completely happy. Aunt Frieda has equipped him like a bride. Perhaps she will succeed to get to Bolivia, for which 150 dollars is required, which she already has. Uncle Hermann is still sick and I will visit him tomorrow, perhaps he is already better. To go to Australia will probably be difficult for Siegfried, as only artisans with authorised trade examination [certificates] are considered. One can enter Chile with 300 dollars and we will write next week to father's relatives in Texas. Perhaps they will be of some assistance to us for his emigration …

In this letter Cecilie again advises Herbert to concentrate his efforts on helping his siblings:

Uncle Isi [from] Königsberg was here 14 days ago and told us that he has written to you, asking that you approach the relatives [in Port Elizabeth] on his behalf; that is a very tall order, as he knows that they do not want to give anything [financially] and that you still have siblings here, on whose behalf you will apply yourself. Lieselotte (Holland) has promised him money, Liesbeth Merkel has also offered him 10 pounds, and in addition he does not yet know where to go. He still has his house and he does not suffer deprivation; he is just afraid that he possibly will have to do compulsory work.

Writing to Artur three days later, Cecilie vents her frustration at Edith's fatalistic attitude and once more refers to Siegfried's diminishing prospects. Reports on the circumstances of other relatives are equally disheartening.

> *About Siegfried I am not able to write anything positive, since Australia only prefers artisans with trade examination [certificates]. Cilly Goldschmidt and family are still in the immigration camp in Argentina and were expelled. They will return to Chile, where they arrived after landing. Werner is now in Sweden on Hachshara. Jutta Kissmann is going to England this Saturday, to work as a domestic. And with our Edith nothing has been achieved as yet, because she does not try. You have always spoiled her and now she is missing your habit of excusing her from doing anything. I can't do anything for her and am letting everything take its course … Erving Schneter is in Belgium. He wanted to go to Czechoslovakia illegally but he was detained and had to go to prison for several months. Now he is sitting there in Belgium in the immigration camp. Finished for today, because I have to see to lunch and then I am going with Aunt Frieda to buy mezies [bargains]; because today the season sale begins. Father has bought himself a beautiful felt hat for 3,55 mark at Tietz [Hermann Tietz Departmental Store].*
>
> *Once again the best wishes for your happiness and blessings for your further well-being and heartfelt greetings and kisses from your parents who love you, and from your brothers and sisters. The relatives send you their congratulations. Best greetings and congratulations I send to your dear bride.*

Cecilie tries to end on a cheerful note by mentioning a shopping trip and sending greetings and congratulations to her son's future bride. But this letter is markedly different in tone to the earlier ones. It is less desperate than resigned. There are fewer signs of optimism, less chattiness, and very little upbeat trivia on family life. Instead, there are factual accounts of refugee camps and prisons. The illusions of rescue have been stripped down.

Two weeks later, on 14 August 1939, Cecilie informs Artur that the family are '*living here very peacefully*', but the sentence that follows is portentous: '*One does not know what the near future will bring us.*' The reassurance that '*Our papers have been handed in to the local consulate almost 14 days ago and we hope that they will soon go off to Pretoria*' seems

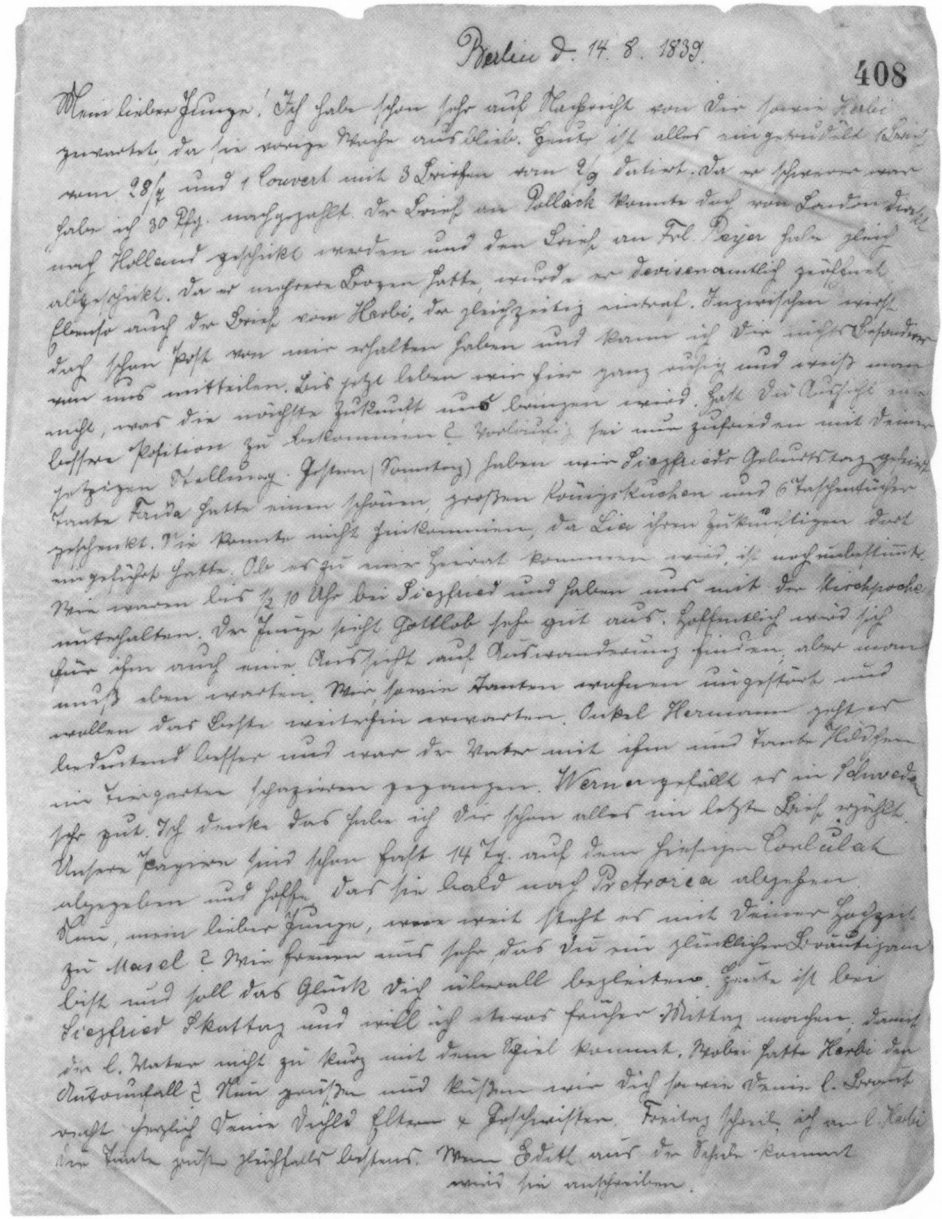
408

Berlin d. 14. 8. 1939.

mechanical. A fortnight later, the outbreak of war would render all of this paperwork pointless.

On 19 August, my grandmother writes to Herbert about developments at home, including Siegfried's birthday celebrations and, as always, emigration matters.

Berlin, 19.8.39

My dear Herbie!

We have received your dear letter this week, together with 2 letters from dear Artur, and Artur has received a letter on Tuesday, and today (Friday) you will receive a few lines from me. You already know that we sent the papers off 14 days ago to the consulate, and it takes time until they are attended to. It can still take a few months. Hopefully there will be no interference. Today we have received your letter from Walter, and Edith wants to find out tomorrow what papers she will require for this, and she will then inform you of all the details. Otherwise everything here is as usual. We have celebrated Siegfried's birthday very cosily. Aunt Frieda has baked a cake for the occasion and has given as a present a dozen handkerchiefs. I still had a beautiful morning jacket from Artur and your breeches with [long knee]-socks, that was our birthday present, and his mother-in-law brought pyjamas and new socks.

The boy looks, touch wood, very well, but with regard to his emigration there is little prospect. Uncle Hermann's health is at the moment quite satisfactory, but he also has no prospects of immigration anywhere, and he has to report daily [to the police]. Aunt Minna [Rubenstein] also writes without hope about obtaining a certificate. So everywhere one has to have patience and perseverance. Your last letter was opened officially. Now winter has come to you in Africa you should buy a warm pullover, previously it did not seem to have been that cold.

So the world has changed and the people as well. Here the days are still quite hot, but not for long any more; because in four weeks' time we will have Rosh Hashana and will go to the synagogue in the Heidereuter Street because in Kaiser Street no services are held any more … For you a wife will also be found, even if a bit later. You will not remain a bachelor forever, we will hopefully celebrate your wedding together in peace. How is the business and has the second business yet had any success? Today I do not have much to relate and the next letter will be longer. Good health and wishing you good parnose, greetings and kisses to you with all our hearts your loving parents and siblings.

Regards to all the relatives.

'*So everywhere one has to have patience and perseverance.*' But how can one persevere when there is no air to breathe? Her next sentence – '*Your last letter was officially opened*' – must have been especially disturbing for my father, but it is followed by a comment about winter in Africa and Herbert needing to buy a pullover. Then comes another chilling line: '*So the world has changed and the people as well*,' followed by a matter-of-fact report that services will no longer be held at the Kaiser Street synagogue.

It is disturbing what lies beneath these short, disjointed statements tucked in between the ordinary. Cecilie's words are saturated with sinister omens, and her letter conveys her growing weariness, even though she could not show any outward signs of succumbing to fear and despair. She had to be strong and hopeful at all times, and vigilant as well, watching every word she wrote. Her letters are written in a code that hides more than it reveals, but the patterns in her writing provide a glimpse into what she is feeling. Her habit of dropping a bombshell in a short sentence, and then immediately following it up with a mundane, light-hearted observation is her attempt at appearing strong to her sons, while also not revealing too much to whoever is reading her words. A lot remains unsaid. Yet, always seeking to comfort her children, she ends her letter to Herbert on an optimistic but wistful note: '*For you a wife will be found, even a bit later. You will not remain a bachelor forever, we will hopefully celebrate your wedding together in peace*.'

The war was now only days away and Cecilie would never see peace in Germany again. Reading the letters she wrote in the months leading up to the war, it is unclear whether she, and the rest of her family, could have anticipated what was coming. However, based on the fear and foreboding that permeated so many of her messages, she seems to have understood deep down that her family faced a dark future.

SEVENTEEN

The Photo Album

In July 2014, my cousin Cecilia found a photograph of our grandparents and Edith while cleaning her late mother's flat. The photo was probably taken in the late 1930s, in a park in Berlin, where the Robinskis are having a picnic, surrounded by trees. Edith's arm rests on her father's shoulders, and they look comfortable together, while my grandmother sits a little apart from them, somewhat excluded from this display of father–daughter intimacy. None of them is smiling, and my grandmother is not looking at the camera. To the right of the frame, near the tree behind them, is a briefcase. From the letters, I know that Edith and her parents would sometimes take a walk or have a picnic in the Tiergarten after dropping off their immigration documents at the South African consulate at Tiergartenstrasse 18. Again, I cannot help but sense the danger lurking in their surroundings, both in the space of the photo and outside it. I can almost see small shadowy figures moving between the trees, approaching my family with sinister intent. Blowing up the image on my computer makes the effect even more chilling. Like the haunting portrait of Edith that would stare at me from our dining-room table, this photo of an everyday family occasion holds a larger truth than what is seen on the surface. My family photos from Berlin are never innocent.

There is another photograph, apart from those of my family, that has followed me for most of my life. Taken by a Nazi soldier in 1943, the photo shows the violent rounding up and deportation of Jews from underground bunkers in Warsaw. In the foreground stands a young boy; he wears a peaked cap and knee-length socks, and his hands are in the air. Four German soldiers stand to the right, and one has an automatic pistol aimed at the boy's back. To the left of the boy is a group of women and children who are also raising their hands.

This photograph was originally included in a report compiled by Major General Jürgen Stroop, the commander of the operation that liquidated the Warsaw ghetto.[1] Titled 'The Jewish Quarter of Warsaw is No More', the report was eventually given to Himmler as a memento. The image of the Warsaw boy has appeared in countless films, novels, poems, paintings, photographs, installations, and on the covers of numerous scholarly texts. Advertising brochures for Holocaust histories, teaching aids and books have also used the image. These photos of child victims of the Holocaust, such as the Warsaw boy and Anne Frank, proliferate because they are so easy to identify with. I cannot remember where and when I first saw the photo of the Warsaw boy, but I have always noticed his uncanny resemblance to me as a boy of that age. He could have been me, or my two sons.

Marianne Hirsch, a professor of comparative literature at Columbia University, writes about how children of Holocaust survivors and exiles have a unique way of viewing photographs from this period. While attempting to forge stronger identifications with their parents through these images, they also continually look for the hidden, impending violence that resides outside of their contents, as if doing so can help them protect their loved ones. Hirsch calls us the postmemory generation. Some of us are artists and writers who compulsively concentrate our creative energies on iconic Holocaust imagery. We fixate on images of the Warsaw boy and Anne Frank in an obsessive effort to resurrect and remember the broken families and shattered worlds of our parents. Despite overexposure to these images, they still shock and pierce us as they stand in for the memories and losses that our parents cannot mention.

Like the image of the Warsaw boy, Edith's photographs survived the devastation. They now function for me as the ghostly remnants of an irretrievable past. My habit of perceiving the dangers lurking outside the tiny frozen worlds of these photographs is a way of forming a personal connection to Edith's past, and perhaps of changing it somehow. As Hirsch notes, these photographs 'enable us, in the present, not only to see and touch that past, but also to try to reanimate it by undoing the finality of the photographic "take"'.[2]

Family photographs promise to reduce the distance between individuals and periods of time, bridging divides and creating the possibility for identification and affiliation.[3] But, as Hirsch observes, those photographs that document lost past worlds and traumatic histories, while authenticating their existence, also reveal their insurmountable distance:

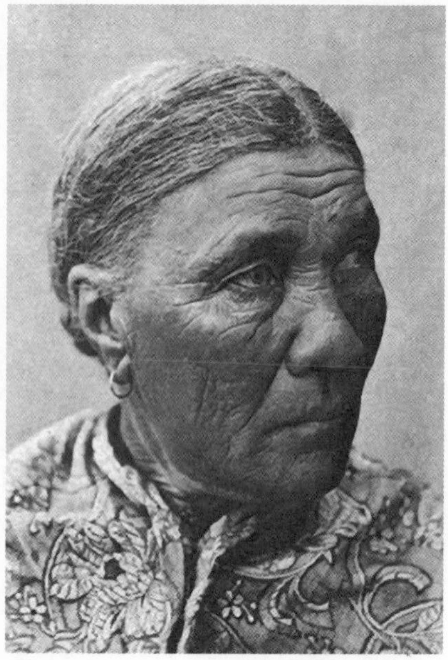

Photographs from Fischer's Die Rehobother Bastards*: Petrus Diergaart, Ellitie Koopman,*

> Small, two dimensional, delimited by their frame, photographs minimize the disaster they depict, and screen their viewers from it. But in seeming to open a window to the past, and materializing the viewer's relationship to it, they also give a glimpse of its enormity and its power. They tell us as much about our own needs and desires (as readers and spectators) as they can about the past world they presumably depict.[4]

In *Camera Lucida*, Roland Barthes discusses this ability of photographs to unsettle temporal, spatial and experiential borders.[5] But in complicating my sense of boundaries – between the past and the present; between South Africa now and Germany then; and between Edith's experiences, my father's and my own – I inevitably and repeatedly come up against the fact that they can never be crossed. The feelings of powerlessness that result from this inability to bridge such distances can then give rise to even more unsettling emotions and harsh responses. Michael André Bernstein, for instance, warns against a retroactive foreshadowing of historical events, whereby 'the shared knowledge of the outcome of a series of events by the narrator and listener is used to judge the participants in those events *as though they too should have known what was to come*'.[6] But I could never blame Edith and her family for what they suffered at the hands of the Nazis.

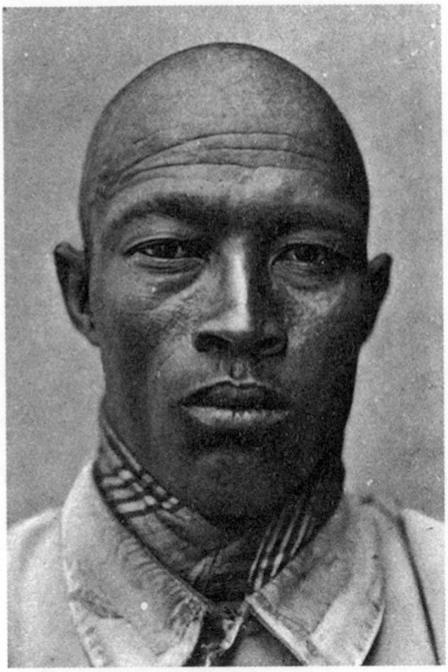

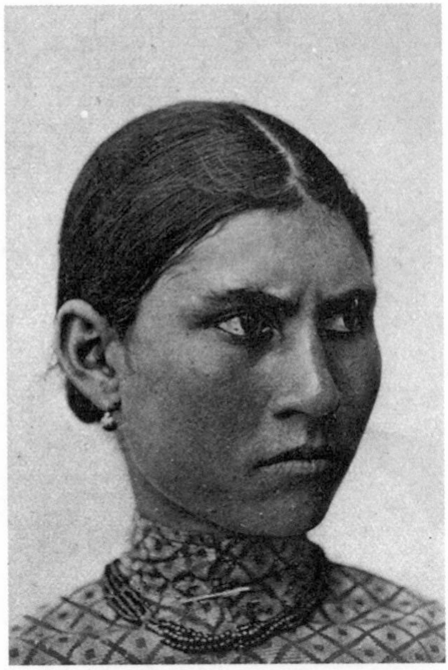

David Engelbrecht and Irma G.

They tried their hardest to save themselves, but their efforts were stymied at every step. Instead, my obsession with Edith's image inspires the seemingly implacable fantasy that, by reliving the past, I can somehow save her, or retrieve a relationship with her and other family members that I never had.

When I look at Eugen Fischer's cold and clinical anthropometric photographs of unsmiling Rehoboth Basters taken in 1908 in the aftermath of the Herero and Nama genocide, I cannot help but engage in retroactive foreshadowing. I am tempted to judge the Rehobothers for allowing themselves to become submissive subjects of an ethnographic study that would launch Fischer's career and later bolster his status as the Nazis' most senior racial scientist. But of course they could not have anticipated Fischer's scientific trajectory or how such eugenics studies would lead to Auschwitz. My knowledge of all of this does not prevent me from projecting onto the Rehobothers' faces expressions of anger and hostility towards the scientist who viewed them solely as racial specimens. I cannot help but look beyond the frame.

In *The Black Photo Album*, South African photographer Santu Mofokeng also looks beyond the frames of photographs to seek out the hidden intentions and identities of his subjects.[7] He focuses on family studio portraits, taken between 1890 and 1950, of ten black South African families from the working and middle classes. These photographs were found in

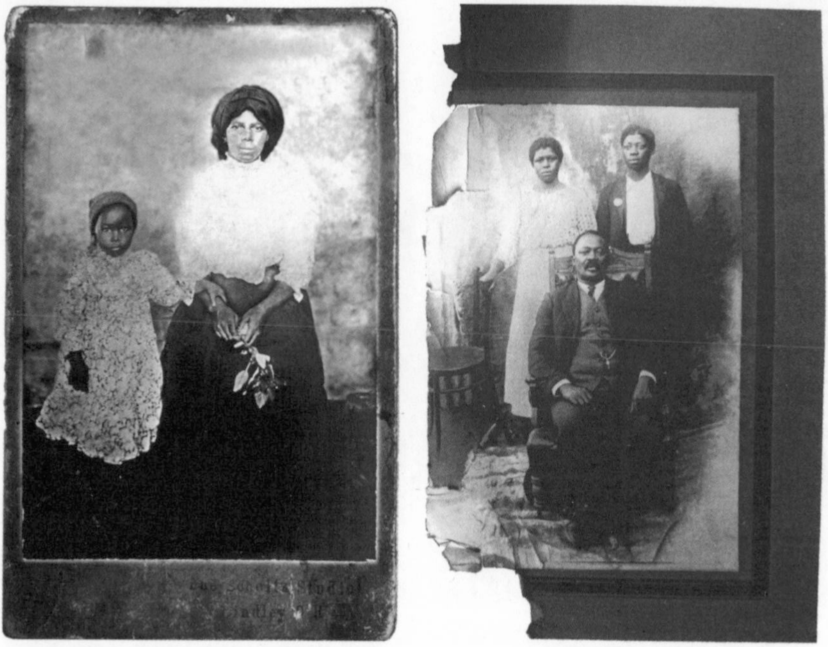

Photographs from The Black Photo Album*: Ouma Maria Letispa and her daughter Minkie; Joel Manyesane (seated), Titus Manyesane and an unidentified relative*

various homes, where they were hidden away or abandoned, and left to rot in cupboards, cardboard boxes and plastic bags. Having 'rescued' them, Mofokeng self-consciously created a fictive family photo album with these images of urban, educated, Christian Africans.

When these portraits were taken, their subjects were already being subjected to colonial racial classification and discrimination. Mofokeng, by considering events taking place outside the frame of the photographs, emphasises how context can inform our assumptions and understanding of the portraits' subjects.

> The significance of the images lies outside of their frames, i.e. in the realm of the political. They were made in a period when the South African state was being entrenched and policies were being articulated toward a people the government designated 'Natives'. It was an era mesmerized by the newly discovered life sciences, such as anthropology, informed by social Darwinism. [It was] a time which spawned all kinds of 'experts' (so dearly loved by politicians), who could be conjured up to provide 'expert knowledge' on any number of issues, including

'A present from ... P.G. Mdebuka – Location School, Aliwal North ... to Jane Maloyi'

matters of 'race'. Race thinking was given scientific authority in this period and was used to inform state policy on 'the Native Question'. Officially, black people were frequently depicted in the same visual language as the flora and fauna, represented as if in their natural habitat for the collector of natural history. Invariably they were relegated to the lower orders of the species, especially on those occasions when they were depicted as belonging to the 'great family of man'.[8]

Notwithstanding such brutal colonial realities and racialised representations, Mofokeng is intrigued by how these self-styled family portraits seem, momentarily, to have transcended such prejudices. The subjects of the portraits present themselves as well-groomed and dignified Victorian citizens, rather than primitive and subjugated victims of the colonial state. Mofokeng refuses to dismiss these self-representations as misguided and naïve attempts to participate in a bourgeois sensibility ingrained in ideas of racial domination, exclusion and subjection. Instead, he celebrates the agency of these Africans who have tried to hold onto their humanity despite the colonialist's persistent efforts to erode it.

Mofokeng's portraits resonate with me in their similarity to the photographs of Edith and her family from the late 1930s. When the Robinski family were photographed in Berlin, they too were victims of a form of racial classification that tried to undermine their existence, before eventually eliminating it. Susan Sontag reminds us that photographs are already always about loss – about lives and events that have passed. Perhaps Edith, Cecilie and Hildegard hoped the portrait they had made in 1937 would become a record for posterity. They seem to implore the viewer to remember them even while expressing their apprehension that, like their own lives, the photograph would not survive. But just as the subjects of Mofokeng's portraits undoubtedly learnt, the Robinskis, in their lifetimes, would never be able to reclaim their place in a universal idea of a common humanity. As South African art critic and journalist Matthew Krouse observes in his review of *The Black Photo Album*: 'looking at the images of [black African] tennis players, pipe-smoking dandies, gentlemen in riding breeches, ladies clutching parasols, brides and grooms and, later, flapper girls in collars and ties, one is reminded of the identity shift of Jews in Germany on the eve of the Nazi Holocaust. Somehow history would soon teach them that prejudice does not bow to assimilation.'[9]

The portrait of Edith, Cecilie and Hildegard was taken when this lesson began to hit Jews hard, and in the most devastating of ways. By then, the Robinski family would have had no illusions about being able to fit into German society. Once the war began, the Nazis would take unthinkably extreme measures to purge Jews from Germany and the other territories they occupied.

EIGHTEEN

War

On 1 September 1939, Hitler invaded Poland. Britain and France responded by declaring war on Germany two days later, and the Second World War had begun. In South Africa, Prime Minister Hertzog assumed that the United Party cabinet would support his call for neutrality. But the cabinet was divided, the call to side with Britain being led by Hertzog's coalition partner and deputy prime minister Jan Smuts, himself a former prime minister and, like Hertzog, an old Boer general from the South African War. Parliament voted for war by a narrow margin, spurring Hertzog to resign. Three days later, Smuts formed a new government and South Africa declared war on Germany.[1] By then my father must have known that his chances of rescuing his family were slim.

The Robinskis in Berlin would have realised as well that there was virtually no chance of them leaving Europe after the war started. Mark Roseman paints a dark picture of life for Jews in the city at this time:

> By the first winter of the war, one in four depended on Jewish welfare. The city authorities were vicious. Minor traffic offences, an infringement of the blackout or curfew, crossing the street at the wrong place or shopping at the wrong time could lead to very high fines of 40 marks or more, imprisonment, concentration camp or even death. Berlin was often the first to promulgate anti-Jewish legislation later adopted for the whole Reich.[2]

It must have seemed inconceivable to the Robinski family that the cosmopolitan city they had moved to after the First World War could have come to this.

The war also made it almost impossible to send letters to countries that were at war with Germany, as South Africa and the British colony of Northern Rhodesia were. Letters were replaced by twenty-five-word telegrams sent through the International Red Cross Committee. The instructions are clear: 'ENQUIRER: Message to be sent to recipient (not over 25 words; news of strictly personal character). REPLY: Message to be returned to enquirer (not over 25 words; news of strictly personal character).' The first of these was from my grandfather to Artur in November 1939.

Person making enquiry: D. Robinski, Wallnertheaterstr. 7, Berlin
Your parents and siblings are well. Please send news by the same channel about your state of health and that of Herbert.
8 Nov. 1939
Recipient: Artur Robins, Box 20, Ndola, Northern Rhodesia, East Africa.

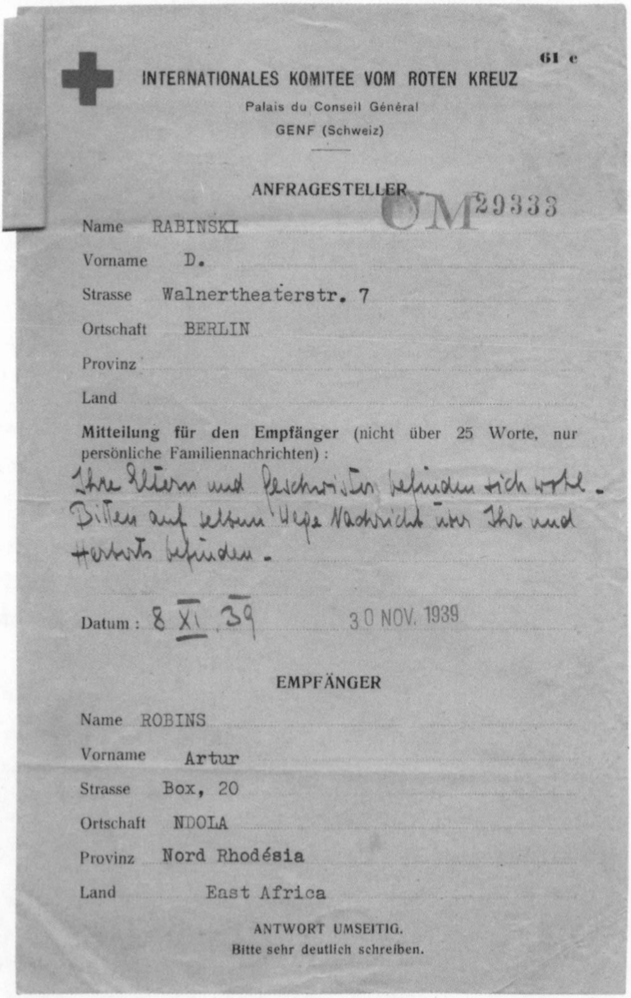
61 e
INTERNATIONALES KOMITEE VOM ROTEN KREUZ
Palais du Conseil Général
GENF (Schweiz)

ANFRAGESTELLER
OM 29333

Name RABINSKI
Vorname D.
Strasse Walnertheaterstr. 7
Ortschaft BERLIN
Provinz
Land

Mitteilung für den Empfänger (nicht über 25 Worte, nur persönliche Familiennachrichten) :
Ihre Eltern und Geschwister befinden sich wohl. Bitten auf selbem Wege Nachricht über Ihr und Herberts Befinden.

Datum : 8 XI. 39 30 NOV. 1939

EMPFÄNGER

Name ROBINS
Vorname Artur
Strasse Box, 20
Ortschaft NDOLA
Provinz Nord Rhodésia
Land East Africa

ANTWORT UMSEITIG.
Bitte sehr deutlich schreiben.

The paring down of the Robinskis' humanity and livelihoods was now mirrored by the restraints placed on their communication to their loved ones. But it would have been difficult for them to convey what they were really going through even if they were not limited to only twenty-five words as the censors were scrutinising all correspondence.

It was through their cousin Rudi Robinski (the son of their uncle Isidore) that the Robinski brothers in Africa would learn about their relatives' plight. On 31 December Rudi wrote to Artur:

Stockholm, 31.12.1939

Dear Artur
Thank you for your letter that I received on 26.12.1939. Sadly, it was not possible for me to write to you, because I was unaware of your whereabouts. I would be interested in discovering more about your journey to Rhodesia and … about your life in your new home and your contact with relatives. Because everything is unstable, I hope that my letter will reach you soon.

I am still not able to write everything to you as I would like, in spite of the so-called democratic freedom. You have probably read in the newspapers that the USSR has 'invaded democratic Finland', which brought the Scandinavian countries into the spotlight … Be that as it may, nobody knows what this means for Sweden; one can already sense an enthusiasm for war in bourgeois circles, which they are trying to spread to the middle and working class. The social-democratic government has been superseded by an interim government and our social-democratic movement, with the exception of a few elements, is now also calling for war. Maybe now you can see that my [comrades] and I are faced with great difficulties, even if we are not yet at war. Just as I started settling in, new problems arise … What the future holds, we do not know. The new situation will also sadly mean deterioration for our lifestyle (the same with all workers and employees). We have a small modern one-bedroom apartment, which my wife with her home-grown taste has decorated. Radio and telephone are taken for granted here. You see, it could be worse. But enough of our personal [problems].

Less pleasant things are to be told about [Egon]. After he went to the Memel territory [in Poland] and then fled to Lithuania, he sent letters repeatedly in which he asked for my help. I advised him some time ago to try to immigrate to a country overseas, to which he has not replied, until I received yet another letter after the mishap. Unfortunately it was impossible for me to arrange something for him from here. The best thing I could do was organise a transit permit. Eg[on] did not have the appropriate documentation ... A few months ago I received yet another letter, this time from his wife, who told me that Eg[on] spent four weeks in a jail in Riga because of inadequate documentation ... Eg[on] had a mental breakdown and his letters reflect his gloomy state ... In regards to the parents, I did all I could to get them to Sweden. I was unable, however, to meet the economic requirements ... The parents are, as I have said, still in Kaliningrad. I have sent them some butter [cash?], and will do so again, when I receive permission, for it is not simple to export certain items ...

Now, dear Artur, best wishes for you from my wife and me. Happy New Year, Rudi.

It is four months into the war, and Rudi's brother Egon is stateless and without refuge. Rudi, who had been active in the German Social Democratic party before fleeing to Sweden in the mid-1930s, starts his letter with a political analysis of the war, a style of writing strikingly different from Cecilie's in its worldliness. He ends his message with a short statement on his failure to rescue his parents from Nazi-occupied Kaliningrad (previously known as Königsberg, the East Prussian city from which Eugen Robinsky had fled). I initially found it strange that Rudi could mention this in such a matter-of-fact manner, but I now know that such responses were not uncommon. Rudi, like so many others, could probably not find the words to convey the grief and loss he was feeling, and, like my father, could not afford to peer too closely into this abyss.

A Red Cross telegram dated 19 February 1940 is addressed to Artur in Ndola:

Person making enquiry: David Robinski, Wallnertheaterstr. 45, Berlin, Germany
Parents and siblings are well. Everything as usual. Heartfelt greetings
19 February 1940
Recipient: Artur Robins, 20, Ndola, Northern Rhodesia, Africa

Artur replied:

> **Herbert and I are well, in good health. We did not have news from you for a long time, neither from Edith, Aunt Frieda. Have you sent letters to Liesbeth? Received none. Heartfelt greetings your Artur.**
> 20 April 1940

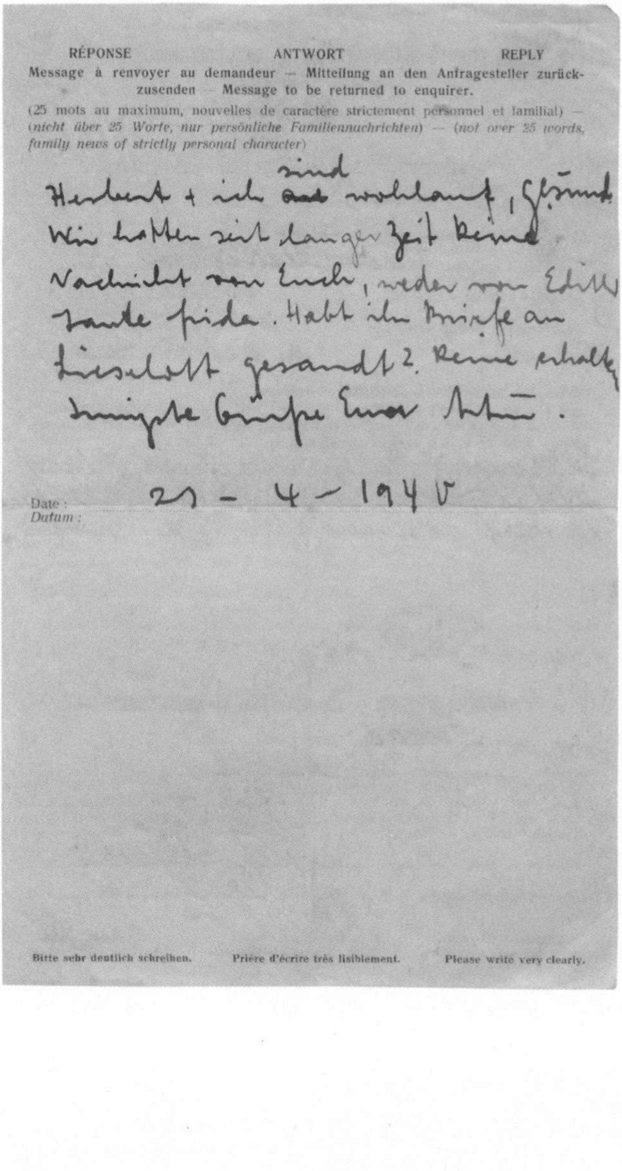

RÉPONSE ANTWORT REPLY

Message à renvoyer au demandeur — Mitteilung an den Anfragesteller zurückzusenden — Message to be returned to enquirer.

(25 mots au maximum, nouvelles de caractère strictement personnel et familial) — (*nicht über 25 Worte, nur persönliche Familiennachrichten*) — (*not over 25 words, family news of strictly personal character*)

Herbert + ich ~~aus~~ sind wohlauf, gesund. Wir hatten seit langer Zeit keine Nachricht von Euch, weder von Edith Tante Frida. Habt ihr Briefe an Lieselott gesandt? Keine erhalten. Innigste Grüße Euer Artur.

Date : 21 – 4 – 1940
Datum :

Bitte sehr deutlich schreiben. Prière d'écrire très lisiblement. Please write very clearly.

Another was sent to Herbert seven months later:

> Sender ('applicant'): David Robinski, Wallnertheaterstr. 45 II, Berlin C.2.
> Recipient: Herbert L. Robinski, 1 Westbourne rd., Port Elizabeth, South Africa
> **Parents and siblings in good health, otherwise everything unchanged. Request news.**
> 9 September 1940

Although Cecilie wrote nearly all the correspondence to her sons, something has changed here; suddenly all the communication via telegram is seemingly written by David. In one of the telegrams, sent on 22 August 1942, the 'sender' is noted as David Robinski, yet the message reports that 'father's health is satisfactory'. If David was the writer, he would surely have stated: 'my health is satisfactory'. This suggests it was Cecilie who had penned these reassuring words. Perhaps the Red Cross required that telegrams be sent by the male head of the household; or, given that the streets were so unsafe for Jews, it might have been considered wiser for David to go to the post office.

I do not know how my father responded to his family's situation, or his reaction to receiving news about them in these brief, indirect telegrams; but he must have been incredibly anxious and frustrated, especially since he could do nothing about any of this. His health began to deteriorate at this time. From 1939 he suffered from tuberculosis and hypertension, and in 1942 he contracted diabetes.

Artur was in an equally fraught and distressing predicament. Not only was he anxious about his family in Berlin, but his identity as a German Jewish refugee was coming under intense scrutiny in Northern Rhodesia. On 7 August 1940, Artur wrote a letter to the editor of *The Northern Rhodesia Advertiser* responding to the newspaper's questioning of German Jews' loyalty to Northern Rhodesia, and to the war against Germany:

> Sir – Since a few months your paper has questioned the loyalty of the German Jewish Refugees to this country. A few days ago some local groups have adopted the same outlook, and I would appreciate the courtesy of giving some space in your paper for removing some misapprehension likely to confuse and distort the facts. Your paper calls us 'Germans' and 'enemies', implying that we are the same brand of

> Germans who are out to destroy the British Empire. This is the first fallacy. We have been the first and foremost enemies of Nazi-Germany, fighting for the principles of democracy and liberalism, with the result that we became the first refugees from that country. How can a sensible man believe us to be all of a sudden enemies of a British country?... No – the refugees do not belong to the fifth column. They do not throw [bombs] into crowded buildings and streets, they do not attack the British Empire in newspapers and meetings, they do not clamour for peace with the Nazis and Fascists. They are those who know best what Fascism means. They have been at war with Hitler since 10 years, and must necessarily be friends with everybody who fights against the same enemies ...

The suspicion of Jews in Northern Rhodesia echoed events in Britain, where fears of a 'fifth column' led to the indiscriminate internment and deportation of European Jews from both Britain and the British Protectorate of Palestine. Artur was forced into refuting such accusations at the same time he and his brother were desperately awaiting news about their family, who were victims of fascism in Germany. His letter reveals a sophisticated understanding of politics and current events, and it seems that living outside of Germany has afforded him an outsider's viewpoint of the position of the Jews, as it has his cousin Rudi. This was not possible for those, like the family in Berlin, who were caught in the storm, and whose mindsets were focused towards surviving it.

Apart from his brief telegram, Artur's letter to the *Northern Rhodesia Advertiser* is the only wartime correspondence I have from the brothers in Africa. Artur comes across as assertive, courageous and dignified, in stark contrast to Cecilie's portrayal of her youngest son as 'poor Artur', a boy all alone in Africa. Artur proves that he is an articulate and educated young man who can speak his mind and stand up for himself and the Jewish community. His letter confirms what I remember about Artur, who would constantly prove how worldly and politically savvy he was in our debates. The Holocaust had been a catalyst for his embrace of Zionism, and while I generally disagreed with him on his stance on Israel, I always respected and enjoyed his intellect, humour and humanity.

Although the correspondence from his parents and siblings in Berlin had dried up, Herbert did receive letters from Cecilie's sister Frieda, who had fled Berlin for La Paz in Bolivia in late 1939. Written from the safety of that city, Frieda's letters pull no punches in what they divulge, as shown in a letter to Herbert dated 12 July 1940: '*It is truly sad that so far no real news concerning Auntie Dorchen's and Hertha's whereabouts were received. It actually is unthinkable that in the 20th century people just get deported and no one can figure out where they have been sent to.*' She later adds: '*Unfortunately at the moment nothing can be done about the immigration request. But I can tell you one thing: When the time comes I will move heaven and earth to get Siegfried out. After all, it could be worse here, and I wish all my loved ones were here [in Bolivia].*' In another letter to Herbert during the war years, Frieda writes: '*By now it will be difficult to find out how your relatives in Holland are doing … Most likely they will have been detained just like the others.*' She is probably referring to Lieselotte, who lived in Amsterdam, and who I suspect was Max Robinski's daughter. Siegfried visited Max in Elbing in late 1938 to ask for Lieselotte's address in Holland, and Max was due to join her there in August 1939, according to Cecilie's letter of 17 July. In May 1940, the Netherlands was invaded by the Nazis.

On 21 April 1941, Frieda tells my father that she is soon to be reunited with her son Werner, and that she has received news about my grandparents. She has written to assure them that they will receive monthly payments of money – money presumably being sent by my father, as Frieda requests financial help from him too.

La Paz, 21 April 1941

Dear Herbert

Unfortunately you did not reply to my last letter, and it's been a long time since I last heard from you. I hope you and Artur are well, which I can luckily say about myself.

I think I got quite used to the climate and also have no other health problems. By now I've been here for more than a year. How fast time passes despite all trouble.

I also would like to tell you some happy news: Werner is on his way down here. I received a telegram from him from Moscow and now I am waiting desperately for him to arrive. You can think how thrilled and excited I am! It took lots of effort, money and legwork – but thank goodness it was worth it.

Now I just want him to be here. Everything else is less important; but with some patience this time too shall pass quickly.

I received news from your parents 14 days ago. Thank God everything

Werner and Frieda

is fine back there – that's the most important. [That] all of them should stay healthy – that's my only wish. I wrote to them again that they'll receive some money monthly [so that] they will not be short of money and not have to worry.

Dear Herbert, it would be a great favour if you could also send me some money. I opened a guest house but that turned out not to be profitable. Everything is too expensive and I could not cover my expenses. So I just closed the guest house down. Work isn't easy here ... and to have a job that doesn't pay off does not make any sense. I then opened a kiosk but that also does not bring enough money. I want to look for something else but first I need to sell the kiosk and keep [myself going] until then. I hope I can sell it. It's the wrong business for one person because one needs to buy everything by [oneself] which means I have to close the kiosk for hours – it's not the right thing. You need to be present to grasp the conditions.

Finally I received my things as well. It took me lots of effort and money. From Genoa they were sent to New York and then here. I had to send another $125. The Friendship Society paid it in advance, as well as the delivery from Africa to here and a lot of custom fees. It felt like the paying never stopped. In the end the best things were still missing. But I lost so many things in my life – I now have to deal with this loss. I cheer myself up with the thought that other people lost even more. The most important thing is that I stay healthy; and that I can make a living for myself and for him [Werner].

I did not hear from Manfred and Egon in a long time. And your parents ...

How are you and Artur and your business? I just wished the terrible war would soon come to an end so that everybody could be reunited with their loved ones ...

Send my warmest regards to Artur.
Sincerely,
Auntie Frieda

Herbert must have felt overwhelmed by Frieda's pleas for help. He was, after all, struggling with his business, his health and the seemingly insurmountable obstacle of rescuing his family in Berlin.

Frieda says that she '*received news from your parents*' but '*I did not hear from ... your parents*', an apparent contradiction. It is likely that the news from Cecilie came not directly from her but from her sister Hildegard, who was also in Berlin. This is confirmed in a letter that Frieda soon received from Cecilie.

Berlin, 17.04.1941

Dear Friedel

I have received your letter from Hildchen [their sister] and I am so glad that you – thank God – are healthy and are proving yourself well, which I never doubted. I hope that Wernerle has arrived safely in the meantime. I can imagine what joy it must be to see each other again after almost 2 years. The dear Lord does not abandon us, and I hope that He will be at our side in the time yet to come. You receive regular mail from Hildchen, which is why I do not write to you that frequently, because she tells you everything anyway. This evening the last days of Pesach will commence and up until now, we missed nothing – praise the Lord! We did not have that much Mazzen [Matzos], but we still managed quite well. On Zeider [Passover Seder], Siegfried and Edith visited us, along with the tenant and her daughter, and it was very pleasant. Our two sons were missing though. I received a letter for my birthday from Herbi through the Red Cross. He still has the old address. I received wishes from Artur via Stockholm. Our daughter-in-law still works at a community project, and Siegfried has found a little work 2 months ago at Zeiss-Ikon. He likes it there and he earns well. Our Edith has found a position at a hostel, but only for 2 months. She will also find something that suits her ... Hildchen [Cecilie's daughter] has been working at the Bergmann laundry in Moabit [a district of Berlin] for 7 weeks now and she is very happy. She earns 17 to 18 mark weekly, which is nice. She brushes the stuff which has been chemically handled.

Now I have told you everything that is noteworthy and I will end now to ensure that the letter will not be too long.

Frieda must have forwarded this letter from Bolivia to Artur in Northern Rhodesia or to Herbert in Port Elizabeth. Cecilie suggests Artur sent an

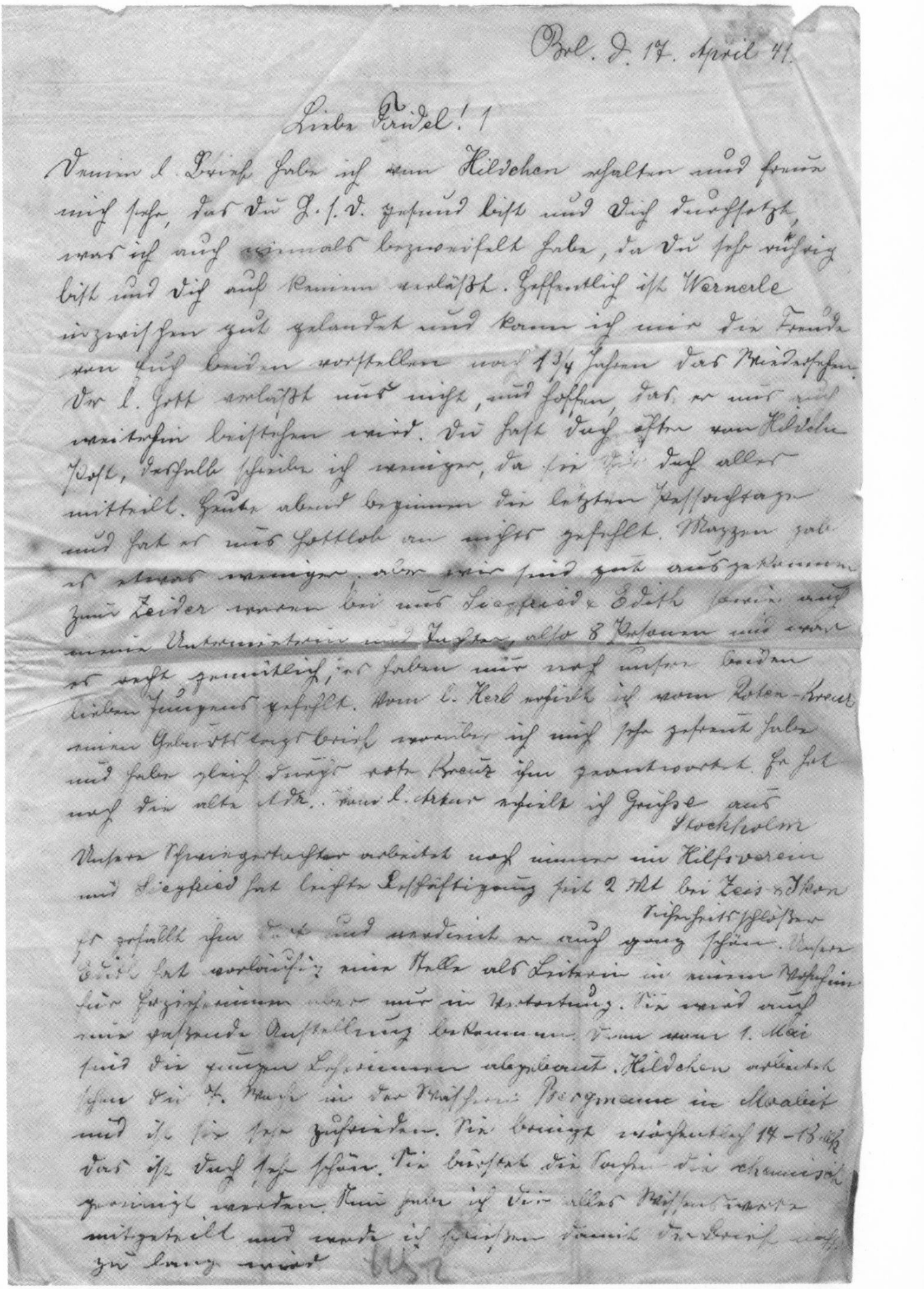

Bln. d. 17. April 41.

Liebe Trudel!!

Deinen l. Brief habe ich von Hildchen erhalten und freue mich sehr, daß du G.s.D. gesund bist und dich durchsetzt, was ich auch einmals bezweifelt habe, da du sehr rüstig bist und dich auf keinen verläßt. Hoffentlich ist Wernerle inzwischen gut gelandet und kann ich mir die Freude von Euch beiden vorstellen nach 1 3/4 Jahren das Wiedersehen. Der l. Gott verläßt uns nicht, und hoffen, daß er uns auch weiterhin beistehen wird. Du hast doch öfter von Hildchen Post, deshalb schreibe ich weniger, da sie Dir doch alles mitteilt. Heute abend beginnen die letzten Passachtage und hat es uns Gottlob an nichts gefehlt. Mazzen gab es etwas weniger, aber wir sind gut ausgekommen. Zum Seider waren bei uns Siegfried & Edith sowie auch meine Untermieterin und Tochter, also 8 Personen und war es recht gemütlich, es fehlen mir noch unsere beiden lieben Jungens gefehlt. Vom l. Herb erhielt ich vom Roten-Kreuz einen Geburtstagsbrief worüber ich mich sehr gefreut habe und habe gleich durch's rote Kreuz ihm geantwortet. Er hat noch die alte Adr. Vom l. Artur erhielt ich Grüße aus Stockholm.

Unsere Schwiegertochter arbeitet noch immer im Hilfsverein und Siegfried hat leichte Beschäftigung seit 2 Mt bei Zeiss-Ikon Sicherheitsschlösser es gefällt ihm dort und verdient er auch ganz schön. Unsere Edith hat vorläufig eine Stelle als Leiterin in einem Wohnheim für Jugendliche aber nur in Vertretung. Sie wird auch eine passende Anstellung bekommen. Denn vom 1. Mai sind die jungen Lehrerinnen abgebaut. Hildchen arbeitet schon die 7. Woche in der Wäscherei Bergmann in Moabit und ist sie sehr zufrieden. Sie bringt wöchentlich 14–15 Mk das ist doch sehr schön. Sie besorgt die Sachen die chemisch gereinigt werden. Nun habe ich Dir alles Wissenswerte mitgeteilt und werde ich schließen damit der Brief nicht zu lang wird.

earlier letter to Rudi Robinski in neutral Sweden, who then forwarded it to the family in Berlin. In this way, it may have been possible to avoid the Red Cross's twenty-five-word restrictions, as well as Nazi censorship.

Hidden in Cecilie's letter is a disturbing development, in her seemingly innocuous comments about the family's working arrangements. I know from the documents I found in Washington and Berlin that by 1941 Edith and Siegfried were conscripted into slave labour (*Zwangsarbeit*) at the Zeiss Ikon factory in Zehlendorf (a suburb of Berlin) manufacturing optical instruments for the German war machine. Hildegard had been working since February as a slave labourer at a laundry in Berlin. Later, in early 1942, she would sort paper at a Berlin waste-recycling depot. Yet my grandmother describes their slave labour in the most innocent language imaginable: '*Siegfried has found a little work 2 months ago at Zeiss-Ikon. He likes it there and he earns well.*' Hildegard, she says, is '*very happy*' at her work. I cannot imagine what slave labour must have been like for Hildegard. If her mother was so protective of her because of her mental frailty and felt she couldn't be sent anywhere on her own, how then did she cope?

By March 1941, almost all Berlin Jews of working age had been conscripted into forced labour where they had to endure the humiliation and exhaustion of doing unfamiliar work as well as long journeys to and from the factories. Their wages, after all the tax deductions, barely covered the most basic needs.[3] But it was well into the war by then, and Cecilie would have known full well that censors were systematically scrutinising all letters sent abroad; she had to be vigilant at all times.

In February 2013, on a freezing winter's day, Mark Kaplan and I visited the Zeiss Ikon factory where Edith and Siegfried once worked. The Zeiss factory was now, in partnership with a Swedish company, producing lenses and security locks. We filmed there on a Saturday afternoon when there was nobody around, except perhaps for the ghosts. The building is surrounded with barbed wire and security fences and is reminiscent of a military camp. I tried to imagine what Siegfried and Edith had to endure inside those walls. On the same visit I met Margot Friedlander, a former slave labourer who had lived underground in Berlin in the early 1940s. Margot confirmed to me that Siegfried and Edith's work conditions and pay would have been abysmal.

The stranglehold on Jewish life in Berlin intensified in other ways during 1941. It became illegal for Jews to take trips to the woods around

Berlin, and the only remaining place for Jewish children in schools to play and exercise was the Jewish cemetery.[4] Evictions began in the early months of 1941, with more than a thousand Jewish apartments required to be vacated within five days in March. In July and August, Berlin Jews lost extra rations granted for heavy work or long hours. And by autumn, virtually every business on the Kurfürstendamm, Berlin's centre of leisure and nightlife with its upmarket shops, hotels and restaurants, had the sign 'NO ENTRANCE TO JEWS'.

From 1 September 1941, all Jews over the age of six were required to wear a yellow star on their clothing. Mark Roseman observes that this proclamation had a much greater impact in Berlin than elsewhere in Germany as Berlin's large size had allowed for small evasions of regulations, which were now more difficult and dangerous to carry out.[5] The yellow star also attracted further ostracisation, stigmatisation and isolation. After 11 September, Jews could no longer receive relief from Jewish organisations when the Jewish Kulturbund was banned. Then in early October came a fresh round of evictions, accompanied by the harrowing order that those affected ought not to seek out alternative accommodation. The deportations followed soon afterwards.

In September, Jewish men and women between the ages of eighteen and forty-five were prohibited from emigrating, a decision by the Nazi government that seems absurd on the face of it. Jews' social and human rights had been all but eradicated in Germany, so by allowing them to emigrate, the Nazis could have rid the country of those they blamed for having stolen its former glory, power and wealth. Taking everything away from Jews – their property, citizenship, dignity and humanity – therefore became their tormentors' means of avenging supposed Jewish crimes against Germany and, through this, restoring its national sovereignty. The racial laws from 1933 onwards were the vehicle for these symbolically charged rituals of humiliation.

But of all the racial laws she had witnessed and experienced, the one forbidding emigration would have made Cecilie's heart sink the lowest. It seems unlikely that she, or Herbert and Artur, could have sustained any hope of getting Siegfried and Edith out after this. It is especially poignant, then, that in her last surviving letters she mentions nothing about efforts to get out. Instead, she writes to Artur to try to allay his fears about the family's financial predicament. She also provides the surprising news that Edith was supposed to get married, but that her plans had fallen through.

Berlin, 5.1.1942

My dear Artur

We have not heard from you for a long time and we hope that you are doing well and that you are healthy. I cannot tell you anything new from our side. Everyone on our side has found employment; even our old father has found a little work. But he has caught a cold and was thus unable to work for a couple of weeks. Thank God that he is doing better now. The skat club was at our place yesterday and Siegfried has 1 mark. Edith II, Mrs Stein and I did some needlework and so the day passed quite comfortably. Siegfried is busy in the office and looks, thank God, quite well. Edith [II] has recuperated and was able to make a profit of 108 pounds. Our Edith was about to get married and is still waiting for a document. The young man has changed his working location in the meantime and now she has to wait until he returns. Hildchen is still working for a company that sorts paper and she earns as much as Edith.

I received a long letter wishing me happy birthday from Herbert about which I was very happy. Why does he not let us know whether he has started his own business, as he had mentioned something of this in his last letter. We have not heard anything from Aunt Minna since June. Do you have the address of her children? Aunt Hildchen sends her best regards. Helmut [Cohen] now works in the hospital and they are well… For today I want to close, I will write more in due course. Best greetings and kisses from us all…

I interpret the reference to the postponement of the marriage as meaning that '*the young man*' has either been deported or recruited into slave labour. Or perhaps he was the Rhodesian man Edith was to marry as part of her escape plan before Jewish emigration was prohibited. Again, so much is left to conjecture, with Cecilie unable to reveal that her children are doing slave labour barely covering their basic needs and accompanied by humiliation, exhaustion and illness. Even the sixty-three-year-old David Robinski has '*found a little work*' and '*caught a cold*' because of it.

My grandmother still reports on the *skat* club, but this time there is no mention of laughter and a cosy atmosphere. She seems dispirited, and has clearly lost all hope of getting her remaining children out of the country.

Written at the top of the page are a few lines from Rudi Robinski and

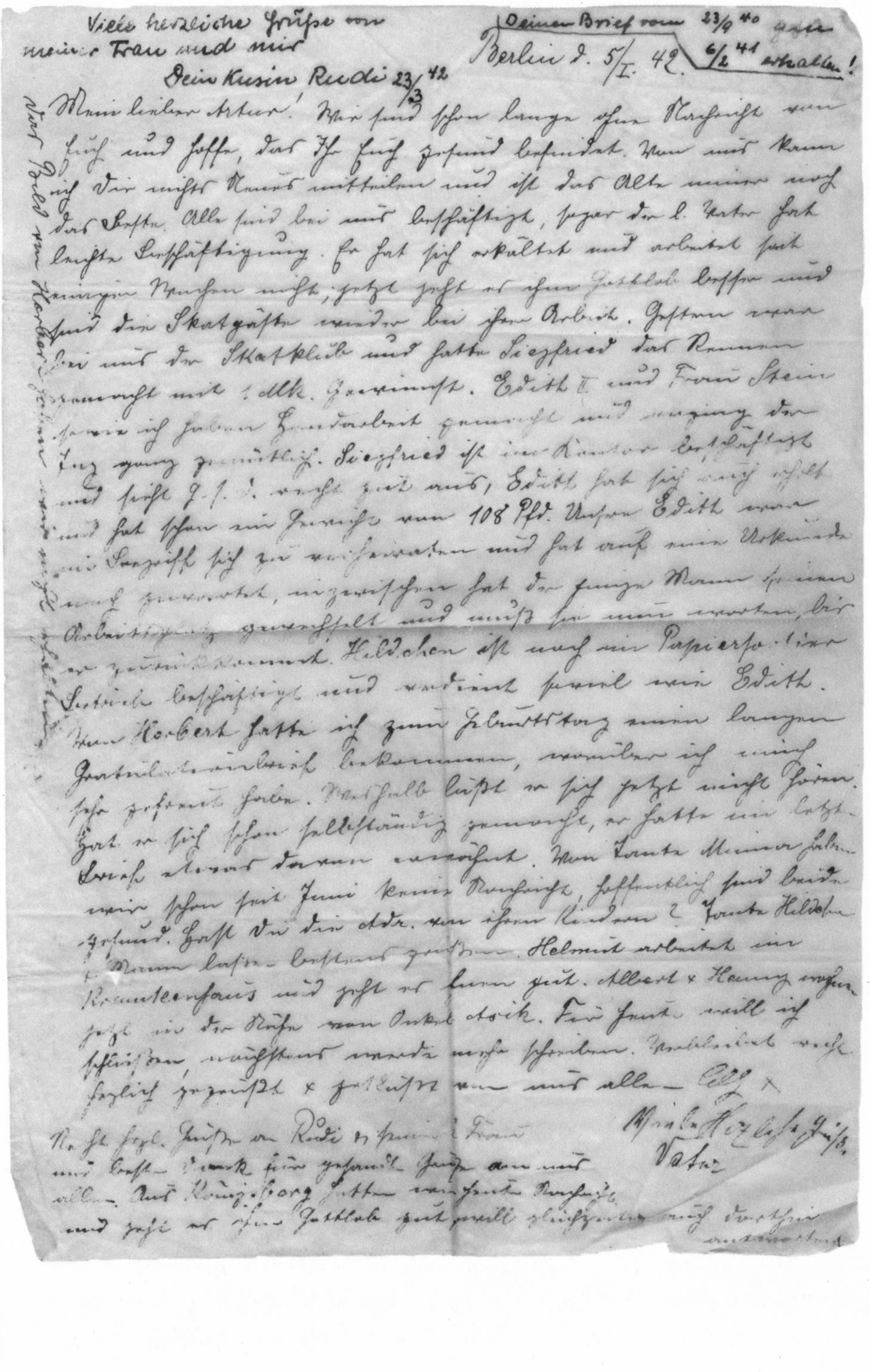

Viele herzliche Grüße von meiner Frau und mir
Dein Kusin Rudi 23/3 42

Deinen Brief vom 23/9 40 und 6/2 41 erhalten!

Berlin d. 5/I. 42.

Mein lieber Artur! Wir sind schon lange ohne Nachricht von Euch und hoffe, daß Ihr Euch gesund befindet. Neues kann ich Dir nicht viel mitteilen und ist das Alte immer noch das Beste. Alle sind bei uns beschäftigt, sogar der l. Vater hat leichte Beschäftigung. Er hat sich erkältet und arbeitet seit einigen Wochen nicht, jetzt geht es ihm Gottlob besser und sind die Skatgäste wieder bei ihrer Arbeit. Gestern war bei uns der Skatklub und hatte Siegfried das Rennen gemacht mit 1 Mk. Gewinnst. Edith II und Frau Stein sowie ich haben Handarbeit gemacht und verging der Tag ganz gemütlich. Siegfried ist im Kontor beschäftigt und sieht G.s.D. recht gut aus, Edith hat sich auch erholt und hat schon ein Gewicht von 108 Pfd. Unsere Edith war im Begriff sich zu verheiraten und hat auf eine Urkunde noch gewartet, inzwischen hat der junge Mann seine Arbeitsstelle gewechselt und muß sie nun warten, bis er zurückkommt. Hildchen ist noch im Papiersortierer Betrieb beschäftigt und verdient soviel wie Edith. Von Herbert hatte ich zum Geburtstag einen langen Gratulationsbrief bekommen, worüber ich mich sehr gefreut habe. Weshalb läßt er sich jetzt nicht hören. Hat er sich schon selbständig gemacht, er hatte im letzten Brief etwas davon erwähnt. Von Tante Minna haben wir schon seit Juni keine Nachricht, hoffentlich sind beide gesund. Hast Du die Adr. von ihren Kindern? Tante Hildchen [illegible] Helmut arbeitet im Krankenhaus und geht es ihm gut. Albert & Henny wohnen jetzt in der Nähe von Onkel [illegible]. Für heute will ich schließen, nächstens werde mehr schreiben. Unterdessen recht herzlich gegrüßt & geküßt von uns allen Elly

Meine herzlichsten Grüße
Vater

Recht herzl. Grüße an Rudi & seine Frau und besten Dank für gesandte Grüße von uns allen. [illegible] Nachricht und geht es ihm Gottlob gut [illegible]

Das Bild von Herbert [illegible] erhalten

his wife, as the Robinski family's wartime correspondence was being sent via Rudi in neutral Sweden. Rudi signs off his brief note with the date 23 March 1942. He also writes that he received a letter from Artur almost nine months after it was posted.

> *Many warm regards from my wife and myself. Your cousin*
> *Rudi (23/3/42)*

> *Received your letter of the 23/9/40 on the 6/2/41!*
> *We did not receive the photo of Herbert*

Cecilie wrote to Artur again in late July. (The letter is not dated, but Cecilie says she is writing fourteen days before Siegfried's birthday, which was on 8 August.) Again, she makes no mention of immigration plans.

> *My dear boy! I hope you have received my letters and I want to take this opportunity to write to you a few lines again. Nothing has changed here and everything is running its old course. Hildchen had a holiday for 8 days and I was with her and Edith in Woltersdorf [a municipality in the Oder-Spree district of Brandenburg]. It was a nice change, 3 hours ride with the steam boat. Her salary has unfortunately not increased yet, still 5 mark per month, but no one can accommodate her anywhere else and I am pleased that she is occupied throughout the day and does not have reason to be on the street. Otherwise she is quite sensible and I go out with her every Saturday and Sunday. Edith also is on holiday and she is going out of town almost daily. Are your friends Belitzer and Pollack still in Holland?*
>
> *Miss Peiser has received a letter from Mrs Schindler in New York who wrote that her father passed away in Eretz. I am very sorry about that, but he was already very ailing here. Are you still employed in the same position? How is our Herbi? Why does he not let us know anything at all? I miss his sweet letters very much. I expect news from you and greet and kiss you with all our hearts your loving parents and siblings. Siegfried looks well thank God and he also feels well. He also sends his warmest regards and kisses. Send regards to all the relatives. In 14 days' time Sige [Siegfried] has a birthday and I will give him a lovely birthday cake. I am going to him every week and then we chat a lot about you and your well-being. I am still busy learning to draw*

[dress] patterns. Perhaps I will put it to use one day, either here or there. ———

I would have liked to send you a photo but at the moment being this is not possible.

This was probably the last letter the brothers received from their mother. After this, the only correspondence I have from their parents is a Red Cross telegram dated 22 August 1942 and addressed to my father.

We received your message from December. With us all still the same. All siblings have work and are content. Father's health is satisfactory. In love with a kiss.

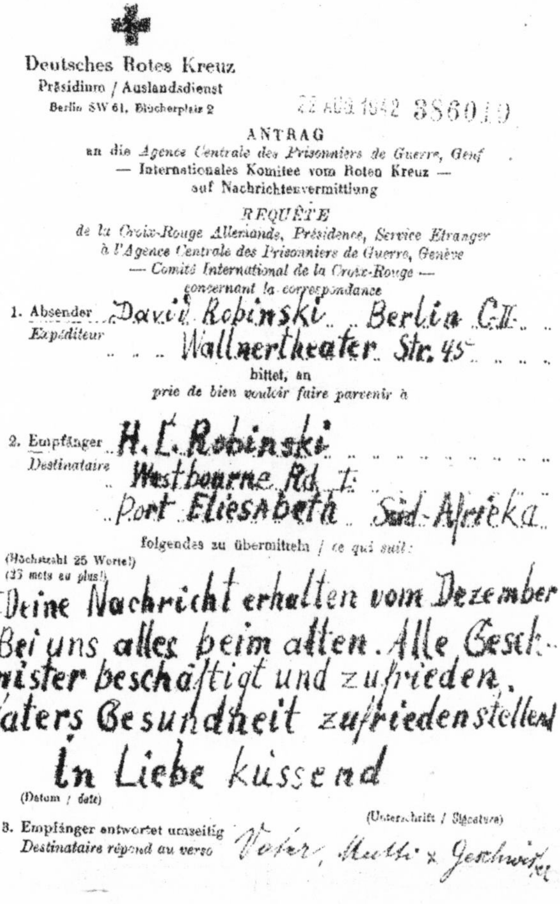

Deutsches Rotes Kreuz
Präsidium / Auslandsdienst
Berlin SW 61, Blücherplatz 2

22 AUG 1942

ANTRAG
an die *Agence Centrale des Prisonniers de Guerre, Genf*
— Internationales Komitee vom Roten Kreuz —
auf Nachrichtenvermittlung

REQUÊTE
de la Croix-Rouge Allemande, Présidence, Service Etranger
à l'Agence Centrale des Prisonniers de Guerre, Genève
— Comité International de la Croix-Rouge —
concernant la correspondance

1. Absender / *Expéditeur*: David Robinski Berlin C.II.
Wallnertheater Str. 45

bittet, an
prie de bien vouloir faire parvenir à

2. Empfänger / *Destinataire*: H. L. Robinski
Westbourne Rd. 1.
Port Eliesabeth Süd-Afrika

folgendes zu übermitteln / *ce qui suit:*
(Höchstzahl 25 Worte!)
(25 mots au plus!)

Deine Nachricht erhalten vom Dezember
Bei uns alles beim alten. Alle Geschwister beschäftigt und zufrieden.
Vaters Gesundheit zufriedenstellend
In Liebe küssend

(Datum / date)

(Unterschrift / Signature)

3. Empfänger antwortet umseitig / *Destinataire répond au verso*

Vater, Mutti u. Geschwister

* * *

The first major wave of deportations from the Third Reich had begun in October 1941, with Jews being sent to Łódź in Poland. These were followed in November by deportations to Minsk and Riga in Latvia. In January 1942 the Wannsee Conference was convened in Berlin to establish the responsibility and procedure for the murder of Europe's Jews. By 1942, for the Jews who still remained in Germany, life must have been one long miserable wait for deportation under steadily deteriorating circumstances.

On 16 October 1942, my grandparents' deportation process began with the filling in of forms, such as the declaration of assets (*Vermogenserklärung*), which are now filed with millions of others in the Landesarchiv Berlin. On 19 October, two months after sending the telegram to their son, my grandparents were deported on the 21st Transport to Riga.

NINETEEN

Underground

On 17 February 1943, a few months after her parents were taken away to Riga, Hildegard was arrested and sent to Gestapo headquarters. She would have been suffering tremendously by this stage given how dependent she was on her mother, who had always been averse to leaving Hildegard on her own or with strangers: '*To leave her here with strange people would be terrible for me, as she is also not so independent.*' Hildegard's arrest is documented in the Nazis' 'proof of delivery' which was unearthed in the Landesarchiv Berlin in 1996, and which catalogues Hildegard as a mere item of property. At the end of the sixteen-page 'declaration of assets' (*Vermögenserklärung*) form, most of which is left blank, is Hildegard's signature. As she did not write or contribute to any letters, this is the only trace I have of her handwriting. On 19 February, Hildegard was deported to Auschwitz.

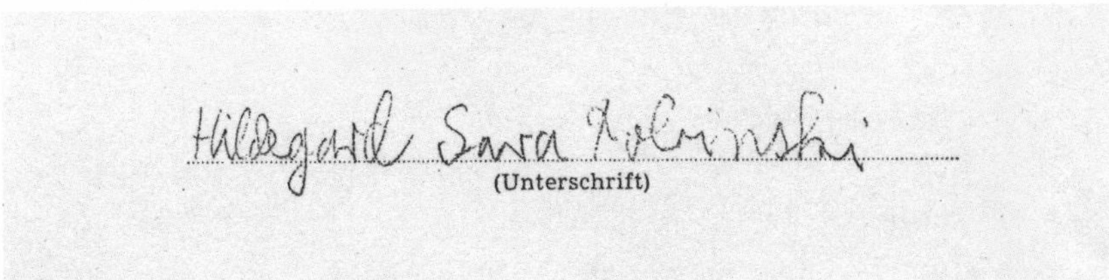

Siegfried and his sister Edith continued working as slave labourers at the Zeiss Ikon factory, but in late February rumours began circulating that all Jewish slave labourers were going to be replaced with prisoners of war and deported east. Siegfried was arrested on 27 February, the day of Adolf Eichmann's *Grossaktion Juden* (Major Action on Jews), or what its survivors came to call *Fabrikaktion* (Factory Action). That day, the Gestapo and SS rounded up 75 800 Jews working in arms factories throughout Germany, and those arrested in Berlin were transported to six detention centres before being deported to Riga and Auschwitz. Siegfried was sent to Auschwitz on 1 March, on the 31st Transport, and his wife followed on the 35th Transport five days later.

In the Landesarchiv Berlin is an inventory of the apartment at 45 Wallner-Theaterstrasse. The home that my grandparents and aunts inhabited, the domestic world into which my grandmother retreated, is subjected to the cold scrutiny of the Nazis, as every item is given a value in Reichsmarks.

		room no 1		Value in RM
1.	1	wash basin, with marble top		20
2.	1	VERTIKO, 1 table		30
3.	1	metal bed frames, with mattress		30
4.	1	white wardrobe, 1 mirror, 1 chair		60
5.	1	bedding, 1 pillow		30
6.	1	suitcase with workwear		40
7.		some menswear		40
8.	1	grey travel blanket, 1 electric iron		20
		room no 2		
9.	1	old couch, 1 ladder	)	30
10.	8	chairs, 1 hanging lamp, 1 storage compartment	)	
		room no 3		
11.	1	kitchen sideboard, light oak	)	
12.	1	sideboard "	)	275
13.	1	extending table	)	
14.	5	chairs	)	
15.	1	wardrobe		60
16.	1	storage compartment, 2 metal bed frames with mattress		65
17.	1	mirror, 1 armchair, 1 suitcase		30
		shelf:		
18.		a set of tableware and pots		20
		room no 4		
19.	1	old armchair, 3 beddings, 1 old couch	)	10
20.	2	window curtains	)	
		kitchen		
21.	1	kitchen buffet, 1 sideboard, 1 table, 3 chairs		70
22.	1	refrigerator, 1 small table, 1 stool		20
23.		kitchen ware, pots, washing sink		50

D.R.70.4.43. 43/19580

Akt.-Z. d. OFP

lt. Straßenliste 43/ 25387

Schätzungsblatt Nr. ....

(Gehören zu einer Wohnung mehrere Schätzungsblätter, so sind diese laufend zu numerieren.)

Zur Beachtung!

Zwischen dem Oberfinanzpräsidenten Berlin-Brandenburg und dem Oberbürgermeister der Reichshauptstadt Berlin ist vereinbart worden, daß bei der Bewertung der zu schätzenden Sachen ein **vernünftiger mittlerer Preis** auf der Grundlage des **Vorkriegspreisniveaus**, und zwar unter Berücksichtigung des allgemeinen **Vorkriegsverkehrswertes** der Sachen gelten soll.

Berlin- O.2, **Straße:** Wallnertheaterstr. **Nr.** 45 **Lage:** v.II.r.

Früherer Mieter bzw. Untermieter: (Früherer Eigentümer der Gegenstände) Robinski, Hildegard Sara

65

Ungezieferfrei! — Nicht ungezieferfrei! (Nichtzutreffendes bitte zu streichen!)

Schlüssel sind abgegeben bei: Hauswirt Völker, v.II,1

Inventar und Bewertung

Jeden Raum gesondert aufführen und mit Überschrift versehen (z. B. Schlafzimmer).
Nur zusammengehörige Sachen gemeinsam bewerten. — Kleinigkeiten als Sammelposten aufführen.

Lfd. Nr.	Stück	Gegenstand	Nähere Kennzeichnung	Bewertung in RM	Bemerkungen
		Zimmer Nr1			
1	1	Waschkommode, mit Marmorpl.		20	
2	1	Vertiko, 1 Tisch		30	
3	1	Metallbettstelle mit Aufl.		30	
4	1	weisser Schrank, 1 Spiegel, 1 Stuhl		60	
5	1	Oberbett, 1 Kopfkissen		30	
6	1	Reisekoffermit Arbeiterkleidung		40	
7		etwas Herrengarderobe		40	
8	1	graue Reisedecke, 1 elektr Plätteisen		20	
		Zimmer Nr 2			
9	1	altes Sofa, 1 Stehleiter,	}		
10	8	Stühle, 1 Hängelampe, 1 Schrankteil	}	30	
		Zimmer Nr. 3			
11	1	Büfett - hell Eiche -	}		
12	1	Anrichte "	}	275	
13	1	Ausziehtisch (vierzug)	}		
14	5	Stühle	}		
15	1	Kleiderschrank		60	
16	1	Schrankteil, 2 Metallbettstellen mit Aufl.		65	
17	1	Spiegel, 1 Sessel, 1 Koffer		30	

zu übertragen Seitensumme: RM 730,–

HWi 242a. Mat. 12066a. Din A 4. 10000. 3. 43

Lfd. Nr.	Stück	Gegenstand	Nähere Kennzeichnung	Bewertung in RM	Bemerkungen
—	—	Übertrag		730	
		Hängeboden :			
18		ein Posten Geschirr u.Töpfe pp.		20	
		Zimmer N4			
19	1	alter Sessel,3 Bettstücke,1altes Sofa }			
20	2	Fenster Gardinen }		1o	
		Küche :			
21	1	Küchenbüfett,1 -Anrichte,-1 Tisch, 3 Stühle		70	
22	1	Eisschrank,1 kl.Tisch,1 Hocker		20	
23		Küchengeschirr,Kochtöpfe,Abwaschwannen pp.		50	
			Sa	900,-RM	

Zuschlag auf 900,– RM
ab 10% 90,– "
bleiben 810,– RM

Gebührenberechnung :

Objekt : 900,-RM

Gebühren 18,-RM

Schreibgebühren 2,- "

Fahrgeld 1,- "

Sa 21,-RM

Runge I
Obergerichtsvollzieher
b. d. A.-G. Berlin
in Berlin-Friedrichsfelde
Alt-Friedrichsfelde 86
Telef. E5 Lichtenberg Nr. 2615
Postscheckk. Berlin 13174
Sprechstunden 5-7 Uhr
außer Sonnabend

Berlin,den 22.April 1943

Runge

Obergerichtsvollzieher.

810 RM — Rpf. (Jd. 43)
vereinnahmt im Titelbuch I
Teilband E Lfd. Nr. 757/12...
Berlin, 20.1.44
Der Oberfinanzpräsident Berlin-Brandenburg
Vermögensverwertungsstelle
Im Auftrag.

Not. 6/4.44

zu übertragen Seitensumme: RM ......

The form is dated 22 April 1943, and it states that the keys have been handed in to landlord Völker.

Siegfried's sister Edith was one of about 4000 Berlin Jews who escaped *Fabrikaktion.* Only around 1500 would survive the war. Following her escape, Edith lived underground for close on five months, until she was arrested in July. She would have known that Berliners had names for those who refused to wear the yellow star and hid in plain sight; they called them *die Taucher* (the divers), or U-Boats. Edith probably also knew how slim her chances were of eluding capture.

Before the war, many young Jewish women had disguised themselves as ordinary German girls, and had been able to walk freely through Berlin's neighbourhoods as a result. Some of the bolder girls even flirted with boys on the street. Until 1941, when the yellow-star law was enforced, it was possible, as Roseman has pointed out, for Jews to evade restricted access to public places in a big sprawling city like Berlin by looking confident and fitting in with the crowd. Edith generally comes across in letters as wary and nervous, but it is possible that, until the yellow star became obligatory, she too might have gone to cinemas and cafés and strolled through Berlin's streets.

* * *

Often, while visiting Berlin, I have tried to imagine Edith walking these same streets. I always end up in Naunynstrasse at the Kuchen Kaiser café, situated in the same building in which Siegfried and his wife lived from 1934 until 1943. In the 1920s and 1930s, Naunynstrasse was a busy section of the predominantly Eastern European working-class neighbourhood of Kreuzberg. Now it is mostly populated by working-class Muslims of Turkish origin, its streets swarming with people visiting the numerous stores, restaurants and coffee shops in the area. The neighbourhood would have been a hub of activity as well when Siegfried and Edith lived there.

Herr Ulrich Fluss Jr, the son of the former owner of Kuchen Kaiser, showed me photographs of the interior of the café in the early decades of the twentieth century. The décor has changed over the years, but one can still get a general sense of the atmosphere and what the café looked like in the 1930s and 40s. Edith and Siegfried would have had coffee and pastries there, just as I have since. As life became more dangerous for Jews, they may have seen the tall metal grids of the heaters next to the tables as barriers behind which they could hide.

Kuchen Kaiser (undated)

If Siegfried's sister Edith ever dared to visit Kuchen Kaiser during the months that she was underground, it might have been because she considered it one of Berlin's safer public places to visit, and, based on accounts from his son, Herr Hans-Ulrich Fluss Sr would not have informed on her or other Jews in his shop. He had helped two of his bakery assistants flee the country, and received compensation for assisting families who could employ his help in escaping. However, he would probably have refrained from helping Siegfried and his wife, who did not have the money to buy a passage to safety. As his son pointed out, Siegfried and Edith were Eastern European immigrants who lived in the low-rental garden flat, not in the main building with the rest of the tenants. Even with a more open-minded landlord, Siegfried and his wife were always at risk.

I imagine Edith sitting in a corner, hiding her face behind a newspaper. Now she was nobody, a young female fugitive on her own in a dangerous world. Where would she have got the money to buy food and a cup of coffee? If most public places were frequented by enemies, including the Gestapo and informers, she would probably have ventured out very rarely.

I can envisage Edith walking briskly through Kreuzberg's streets, along Naunynstrasse. Perhaps it is a warm day in the spring of 1943, the end of another cold Berlin winter, yet she is in no mood to celebrate. The blue sky and bright sun cannot lighten her thoughts, and she is oblivious to what is happening around her on Oranienplatz, where people are soaking up the first sunny weather of the new season. Instead, she is preoccupied with fitting in with the crowd. She might even have passed a homeless man sleeping on a bench in the square and related to him, feeling equally abandoned and adrift. The route she is walking would usually have taken her to Siegfried's place, but not any longer. She is on the run, and has to move from safe house to safe house.

I wonder if she and Siegfried talked about the possibility of living underground before he was arrested. If Siegfried had anticipated *Fabrikaktion*, he would have tried to prepare himself, and possibly Edith, for the consequences. Maybe he tutored his sister about surviving underground and living on the run: remove your star, destroy your deportation order, avoid contact with family and friends, and do not convey the slightest sign of fear in public spaces.[1] The U-Boats were instructed not to visit parts of the city where they were known and would be easily recognised, and Edith would have been advised to forget that she was Jewish; attending synagogue was over, as were any associations with fellow Jews.

Many U-Boats were caught by Jewish collaborators known as *die Greifer* (the catchers), who were recruited by the Gestapo to identify other Jews. Edith might have known about the notorious Stella Kübler, or 'the blonde poison', an Aryan-looking Jew who lived in Berlin and collaborated with the Nazis. Edith now lived in a world in which people

Postcard of Nazi event on Oranienplatz; view from Kuchen Kaiser (undated)

like Kübler committed such acts of betrayal to save themselves and their families from deportation.

My father told me that Edith did not look typically Jewish and this may have helped her to blend in with the non-Jewish population. Many Jews in Germany would actually have been able to pass as non-Jews because they did not conform to stereotypes promulgated by eugenicists about 'the Jewish look'. In 1940, the Nazis produced the viciously anti-Semitic propaganda film *The Eternal Jews*, which popularised the Jewish appearance as comprising a large hook nose and fleshy face in its film posters.[2] As a result of such stereotypes, former slave labourer Margot Friedlander decided to disguise her 'Jewish nose' before going underground, by having a Jewish doctor perform a clandestine operation on her in his living room.

Marianne Strauss, a Jewish woman in hiding during the war, also chose to mask her Jewish appearance by dyeing her black hair a fiery copper colour.[3] Her new look facilitated her metamorphosis into an 'Aryan-looking' woman which, along with her exceptional beauty and confidence, allowed her to move quite freely throughout Germany. Clearly looks could make the difference between life and death for the U-Boat.

I personally cannot see how Edith could have transformed herself to look like an Aryan-looking woman. Maybe she and Siegfried had deliberated on how she could accomplish this feat, with Siegfried persuading her that it would be easy to blend in with a few adjustments. He may have quipped, 'With your hair dyed you'll look like the most exquisite blonde in Berlin. You will be an Aryan princess, my dear sister.' Perhaps she had laughed at his tomfoolery. Cecilie's letters to Herbert and Artur intimate that Siegfried was a playful, free-spirited young man, evident in this line from the *Tafellied* composed for his marriage: '*Freedom! That is his ideal*'. Of all the members of her family, Siegfried was probably the one who could make Edith laugh, even during dark times. But now he was no longer at her side. For Edith, however, appearance alone was not enough. Even if she managed to look Aryan on the outside, she would no longer have felt German inside. Everything she heard on the radio, read in the newspapers and saw on the streets would have reinforced this feeling. The countless racial ordinances that had been passed since 1933 were a constant reminder that she was considered 'un-German' and undesirable by those who made the rules. Nevertheless, Edith had to keep up appearances at all times. She could never look unkempt, even if she was sleeping in parks or on trams or houseboats, as this would draw unwanted attention to her. An expression of fear might give her away as much as any physical feature.

Most importantly, U-Boats could not survive alone. Marianne Strauss's survival as a U-Boat was a result of the assistance given to her by an underground socialist organisation called the Bund. The Bund was able to give her access to safe houses throughout Germany because her father was a wealthy, influential businessman in Essen who had contacts with some of the Bundists. David Robinski was neither wealthy nor influential, and it is doubtful he had contacts who could assist his daughter in such a risky enterprise. Again, the tragedy of triage meant that those without wealth, social connections and power stood less chance of survival.

To have survived underground for five months, Edith would have had to find access to safe houses. The people who sheltered her must have felt she had a reasonable chance of evading the Gestapo and their catchers. And she could then only stay at a safe house for two to three weeks before moving on. Her life would have become like that of a pursued animal, always on the run from a tireless hunter. After going underground when Siegfried was deported, Edith would have known she was now one of the walking dead, a death-row prisoner waiting for her own moment to come.

But to have survived underground for five months, Edith must have had to muster an incredible amount of courage and fortitude. Public spaces had become treacherous to navigate, and she could not trust anyone, not even her former teacher colleagues, as anybody could be a 'catcher'. She would have had to avoid eye contact with people, which would not have prevented her from feeling as if their eyes were boring into her soul. Although she must have longed to make contact with someone from her old life – family, friends, or a work friend – any such move would have been extremely dangerous. She must have felt desperately lonely during this time.

Edith's life as a U-Boat followed a long and dispiriting process of trying to immigrate to South Africa and Northern Rhodesia, and she had also considered going to China, England and South America. All these efforts failed, including her attempt at being a U-Boat, and she was arrested on 29 July 1943. She was held at the detention centre at Grosse Hamburg Strasse 26, and after forms were filled in that stripped her of whatever possessions she might have had left, she was deported to Auschwitz on 4 August.

In February 2013, Mark Kaplan and I filmed at this former detention centre which functions now as a predominantly Jewish school. A tranquil Jewish cemetery with tall trees and inviting paths lies next to the school, and as I walked through it, I tried to imagine what it was like for Edith being detained in the building standing before me in 1943. But all I could see were her sad eyes staring back at me from a photograph taken in Berlin in 1937. In front of the cemetery, which is one of the oldest in Berlin, is a sculpture of inmates from the death camps, their anguished figures resonating with the despair in Edith's eyes and inscribed in her letters to her brothers. While we filmed the documentary, I could not speak on camera about what I was feeling; words seemed incapable of capturing my emotions. I walked through the cemetery silently, lost in my thoughts.

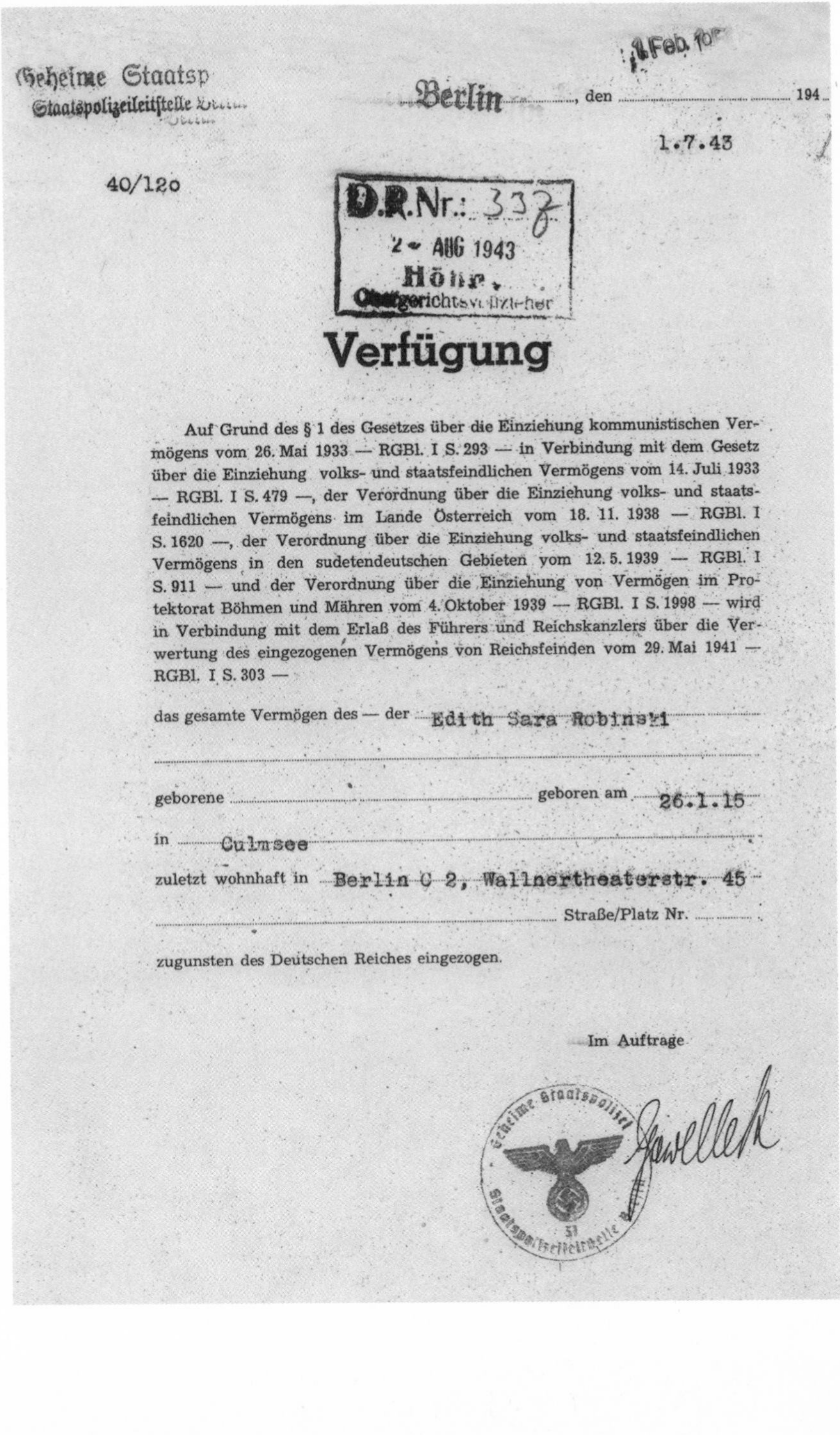

Geheime Staatsp
Staatspolizeileitstelle

Berlin, den 194

1.7.43

40/120

D.R.Nr.: 338

2 AUG 1943

Höhr.

Obergerichtsvollzieher

Verfügung

Auf Grund des § 1 des Gesetzes über die Einziehung kommunistischen Vermögens vom 26. Mai 1933 — RGBl. I S. 293 — in Verbindung mit dem Gesetz über die Einziehung volks- und staatsfeindlichen Vermögens vom 14. Juli 1933 — RGBl. I S. 479 —, der Verordnung über die Einziehung volks- und staatsfeindlichen Vermögens im Lande Österreich vom 18. 11. 1938 — RGBl. I S. 1620 —, der Verordnung über die Einziehung volks- und staatsfeindlichen Vermögens in den sudetendeutschen Gebieten vom 12. 5. 1939 — RGBl. I S. 911 — und der Verordnung über die Einziehung von Vermögen im Protektorat Böhmen und Mähren vom 4. Oktober 1939 — RGBl. I S. 1998 — wird in Verbindung mit dem Erlaß des Führers und Reichskanzlers über die Verwertung des eingezogenen Vermögens von Reichsfeinden vom 29. Mai 1941 — RGBl. I S. 303 —

das gesamte Vermögen des — der Edith Sara Robinski

geborene geboren am 26.1.15

in Culmsee

zuletzt wohnhaft in Berlin C 2, Wallnertheaterstr. 45

Straße/Platz Nr.

zugunsten des Deutschen Reiches eingezogen.

Im Auftrage

Gawellek

Geheime Staatspolizei
Staatspolizeileitstelle Berlin

TWENTY

Riga

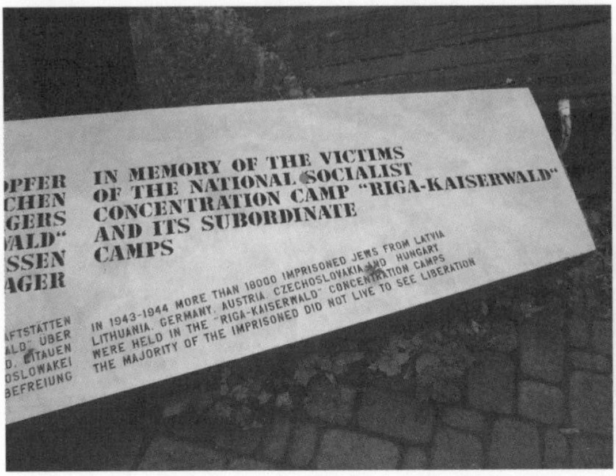

My older brother Michael, who moved to London in the 1980s and established himself in the film industry there, visited Riga in 2005 for a film shoot. He toured Riga's Salaspils concentration camp as well as Rumbula forest, where tens of thousands of Jews were shot and buried in mass graves in 1941 and 1942. Various monuments at these sites commemorate the Jewish victims, unlike the monuments erected elsewhere by the Soviets in the immediate post-war period, which made no specific mention of Jews, grouping them with the millions of other martyrs who died in the fight against fascism. At the time of his visit, my brother did not know that our grandparents were murdered at Riga. He recalled being told by our father that his entire family were killed at Auschwitz.

In 2010 Michael visited Riga again, this time with the knowledge of what had happened to our grandparents at that place. His trip happened to fall on 19 October, commemoration day for the 21st Transport – the transport that carried our grandparents in 1942. At a local Jewish museum, he saw their names on a list of the deportees and walked outside and cried. He also visited the forest, which is three and a half kilometres from the Skirotaba Railway Station. When he returned to London, he searched the internet and found an account of the events surrounding the 21st Transport.

> On 22 October, the next Berlin transport, which must have left the Reich capital three days earlier, reached the Skirotaba Station with 959 persons. The average age of this transport was 36,7 years. There were 264 people between 16 and 40 on this train; nonetheless, only some eighty persons were selected for labor, apparently only men. They were immediately put to work, unloading the coal cars attached to their transport. Shortly thereafter, they were sent to the Security Police athletic field in Mezaparks (Kaiserwald), where they relieved the Jews barracked there and continued with the levelling work. Individual survivors were taken to the barracking at the Security Police auto workshop on Petersalas St. (Peterholmsche St.). The final transport to come to Riga left on 26 October 1942, reaching Riga three days later. All 798 people, including the potential workers aged 16–40, were shot upon arrival.[1]

Again, I am struck by the fact that the Nazis would not even consider the potential of those they killed so mercilessly as workers, or even as slave labourers.

My brother and I now possess the barest facts of what happened to David and Cecilie Robinski at Riga in October 1942, but we still cannot begin to comprehend what they experienced. We will also never know how our father and Artur responded to the International Red Cross notice they received after the war.

For me, the mass murder of Jews at Riga is still too difficult to digest. One photograph, of the Einsatzgruppen (Mobile Killing Units) mass murders in 1941 in the forests of Babi Yar in the Ukraine, provides a

glimpse of the terrifying reality that my grandparents had to suffer at Riga. In the photograph, a woman uses her body as a shield to protect a child from a soldier whose rifle is aimed at them. On the right, a group of victims, including children, bend over as they wait for the soldier to kill them. I have seen similar photographs of groups of Jews standing naked next to open mass graves right before they were shot. But I always turn away before I can fully comprehend the horror of these scenes, creating a safe distance between myself and the black hole, that void that sucks in life and spits out ash.

* * *

A letter to Herbert from Frieda, dated 9 February 1943, captures the anguish of those who escaped and then had to learn of their relatives' deportations:

La Paz, 9 February 1943
Bolivia Poste Restante

Dear Herbert
I received your first letter after it travelled for almost nine months. I am also sending you airmail so that it arrives faster. Maybe you have some news from our loved ones. I did not hear anything from them for more than a year. Last July I inquired via the Red Cross but did not receive any reply. I also inquired via Cilly Goldschmidt [in] Santiago at the Red Cross, but they informed me that no news arrived. You probably can

imagine my worries, and I have only one wish: to see our loved ones again in fine form. Dear Herbert, if you have any news, please write me immediately – but also via airmail because otherwise it will take too long. It is horrible to know that everyone remained back there. It is impossible to imagine what they already have had to endure emotionally – and then the hunger and cold on top of that. If it wasn't for Hilde your parents would still have managed to get out, and Edith could have left for sure. Now there is nothing left to do. May God help all of them! Cilly also wrote that acquaintances informed her about Leo Leyde's deportation. I do not think that anybody is still there. All of them will be gone already …

Frieda blames Hildegard's mental disability for her family's fate. For Ute, Frieda's assertion that my grandparents would definitely have escaped had it not been for their daughter is particularly painful: 'Your grandmother couldn't send Hilda away or leave her behind. To me this is the opposite of what was happening in Germany. Here your grandparents remained ethical … They said they can't leave Hilda, then Hilda died in Auschwitz and they died in Riga.' Yet it is not certain that my grandparents

Frieda (right) outside her small café, 1943

would have escaped had it not been for Hildegard's condition. There were so many other obstacles in their path.

Frieda continues her letter on a more hopeful note.

Otherwise we are alright. I still run the guest house and make a living from it. It is anything but easy but at least it is quiet here and sufficient food is available. Werner still has the same job and he is one head taller than I. Hopefully he won't grow any more. I feel like a midget. I've been living here for three years now – how time passes despite all worries. Now there's hope that the horrible war will soon come to an end. Back then, after all, Auntie Minna and Uncle Bernhard escaped to Russia, and I am hoping that they moved further into Russia when the Germans entered.

From your letter I can tell that you are in quite good shape and follow a healthy diet. Do not worry if you lose your hair; most importantly one should be in good health. But please answer me immediately via airmail because we promised to stay in touch forever. Today I still want to write to Manfred and Egon; maybe they know something. As soon as I receive any news I will write to you, and you must do the same.

Last but not least I want to wish you a happy birthday. I can only wish you one thing: remain in good shape; and may God grant that you and dear Artur will be happily reunited with your dear parents and your siblings – all in good health.

Greetings and kisses to you and dear Artur. Best wishes.

Yours sincerely,

Auntie Frieda

Frieda was the only one of the Grünberg sisters who would survive the war. Historian Leo Spitzer, whose parents also found refuge in La Paz during the war, told me that it would have been futile for Minna and Bernhard Rubenstein to escape through Odessa to Siberia. To do this, they would have had to flee through Transnistria, where they would probably have been killed either by invading Einsatzgruppen or their Romanian allies. The Rubensteins had managed to get all their children out of Germany before it was too late. Norbert escaped to Liverpool, and Heinz, Horst, Irma and Margot settled in Palestine.

Among the letters and photographs found in my aunt Elsa's flat is a page from a newspaper with a photograph of a gravestone in Berlin's Weissensee Jewish Cemetery commemorating family members who died

in the war. I don't know who commissioned this tombstone, but it is possible that Frieda did it in commemoration of her sisters. Bernhard and Minna are listed there, as are my grandparents, Edith, Hildegard, Siegfried and Edith II. Also on the gravestone is Dora Wilk, born Grünberg, another of my grandmother's sisters, about whom I know the least. From the gravestone it appears that Dora was married to Alfred Wilk, and that Alfred's sister Hanna was married to Albert Wolff, and they had a daughter Judith. Also listed are Hertha Wilk and Arthur Wilk, who must have been siblings of Alfred. There are a few references to these relatives in Cecilie's letters: '*The Wolffs are also waiting for visas*', in January 1939; '*Albert, Hanny and child*' attended Frieda's birthday celebrations in March 1939; '*Today a letter arrived from Uncle Wolff and he misses news from all the relatives from Africa*', also in March; and, in June, '*Next week Albert will start work at the building site, he must earn a livelihood.*' Frieda laments in July 1940, '*It is truly sad that so far no real news concerning Auntie Dorchen's and Hertha's whereabouts were received.*' That is all I know about this wider circle of family members, and all of them died before the end of the war.

Handwritten in blue ink above the photograph of the gravestone are these words: '*Auntie Hilda Holz is mentioned on the front together with the name of Uncle Hermann whose grave is here. Arthur's grave no longer exists, so I had his name engraved too. Do you see the stones above? This is an old tradition; we were very surprised.'* I'm not sure who wrote these words, but they suggest that Cecilie's other sister, Hilda, and her husband Hermann Holz are not listed on the tombstone because they had already been buried in Weissensee Cemetery. According to the *Berliner Gedenkbuch*, Aunt Hilda was deported from Berlin to Auschwitz on the 30th Transport on 26 February 1943.[2] Hermann, who had battled with ill-health after being interned at Sachsenhausen after Kristallnacht, might have died in Berlin before this. I also found a mention of a Hermann Holz who went to Piešťany in Czechoslovakia and was deported from Žilina to Auschwitz on 17 July 1942,[3] but I cannot tell if this is the same man who was married to my grandmother's sister. The Holzs' sons, Manfred and Egon, survived the Holocaust, having escaped to Palestine before the war.

I also discovered that Harry Urbanski, the brother of Edith II, was murdered in Auschwitz.[4] Young Jochim Urbanski had escaped to England as part of the Kindertransport.

What happened to David and Eugen Robinski's brothers? Cecilie wrote in July 1939 that '*Uncle Max will go to Holland in three weeks*' – I am not sure if he managed to. Lieselotte, who I think was his daughter, had already settled there with her husband. But, as Frieda wrote to my father during the war: '*By now it will be difficult to find out how your relatives in Holland are doing … Most likely they will have been detained just like the others.*'

Isidore Robinski, who lived in Kaliningrad, was deported with his wife, according to a letter from his son Rudi in Stockholm. I don't know what happened to the other son, Egon. Rudi wrote in December 1939 that Egon had been detained in Riga for inadequate documentation and suffered a nervous breakdown. After that there is no trace of him in the letters. Rudi and Egon had a sister, also named Edith, who was deported along with her parents.

I don't know what happened to Adolf Robinski, my grandfather's brother who lived in Pirmasens in Germany. All I know from the family correspondence is that he received money from my father in May 1939 and that he wrote to Cecilie in July asking for help. There is no mention in the letters of my grandfather's sister Pauline.

While Frieda wishes in her letter of 9 February 1943 that Herbert and Artur will be reunited with their parents one day, Cecilie and David Robinski had already been murdered in the forests of Riga. Ten days after she wrote this letter, Hildegard was deported to Auschwitz, followed by Siegfried on 1 March, his wife Edith II on 6 March, and my aunt Edith five months later, on 4 August.

TWENTY-ONE

Auschwitz

During a trip to Germany in July 2015, I visited a newly established museum in the former premises of Topf & Söhne, the Erfurt company that manufactured the crematoria at Auschwitz, where the bodies of more than a million people were incinerated. While there, I came across a display of excerpts from the secret notes of Salmen Gradowski, an inmate and one of the Sonderkommando – prisoners at the death camps who were tasked with shepherding Jews into the gas chambers and disposing of their corpses. Gradowski – who was eventually murdered by the SS during a revolt in Auschwitz on 7 October 1944 – details the harrowing final stages of the dehumanisation of Jews, which started with the stripping away of their property and citizenship, and ended with the degradation and destruction of their bodies.

> We don't have the courage, we don't dare tell our precious sisters that they are to undress. For the clothes they are wearing are their last armour, the cloak in which life still reposes. The moment they take off their clothes and are naked, they will have lost their last defence, the last hold, the last anchor to which their life is tied. That is why we do not have the heart to tell them that they are to undress quickly. They should stop a moment, remain in their armour for one more instant ... But the delay is not tolerated for long. The presence of the murderous brutes makes itself felt. The air is filled with the screams of the drunken bandits whose bestial eyes feast on the nudity of my beautiful, my precious sisters. The blows of clubs rain down on their backs, their heads, everywhere, and their clothing falls quickly from their bodies.

* * *

Auschwitz was a cluster of concentration camps in Nazi-occupied Poland, including Auschwitz I, the original camp, Auschwitz II-Birkenau, which combined the internment and extermination of prisoners, and Auschwitz III-Monowitz, a labour camp for inmates and slave labourers who worked

at the nearby IG Farben factory, constructed in 1942 to produce synthetic rubber for the war. In addition, there were another forty-five satellite camps.

Auschwitz I was built to intern Polish political prisoners who arrived there in May 1940. The first exterminations began in Auschwitz II-Birkenau in September 1941, and from early 1942 until late 1944, over one million prisoners were murdered in gas chambers from exposure to the pesticide Zyklon B. Ninety per cent of the victims were European Jews; the others included Poles, Roma and Sinti, Soviet prisoners of war, homosexuals and Jehovah's Witnesses. Those who were not killed in the gas chambers died of starvation, disease, exhaustion from forced labour, execution and medical experiments, and their bodies were incinerated in the crematoria designed by Topf & Söhne's engineers. This was murder on an industrial scale, requiring scientific and technical expertise to design and manufacture efficient killing machines. But it was in the field of eugenics that some of the most barbaric science imaginable took place at Auschwitz.

In 1942, the sixty-seven-year-old Eugen Fischer retired as director of the Kaiser Wilhelm Institute for Anthropology, Human Genetics and Eugenics (KWI-A), after receiving news that his son Hermann had been killed in action on the Eastern Front. He was succeeded by his colleague Baron Otmar von Verschuer, who executed his predecessor's scientific ambitions with zeal. In 1943 Verschuer obtained Heinrich Himmler's permission for his promising former doctoral student, Dr Josef Mengele, to do post-doctoral research at Auschwitz, where he was later appointed as Executive Camp Physician in the 'Gypsy camp' (Section B Auschwitz II-Birkenau). Mengele's name has become synonymous with unthinkable atrocities perpetrated in the name of science.

Hans-Walter Schmuhl notes that the involvement of eugenics research in Nazi atrocities was a slow and cumulative process that unfolded in gradual stages. Fischer's scientists first used mental asylums and prisons, such as the Sachsenhausen camp north of Berlin, as their testing grounds, where they did research on inmates without their consent. By the time the war started, their studies were also taking place in prisoner-of-war camps. Mengele's Auschwitz medical programme, which involved gruesome experimentation on people, was the culmination of this slide into scientific barbarism. In the name of human improvement, an international eugenics movement had unleashed the scientific monstrosity that underwrote Nazi ideology and policy.

Upon his arrival in Auschwitz, Mengele recruited numerous medical specialists in the fields of pathology, paediatrics, gynaecology, ophthalmology, ear, nose and throat medicine, and dentistry, as well as technical assistants, nurses, kindergarten and nursery-school teachers, and secretaries.[1] As the trains arrived at Auschwitz, laden with people who had been deported there, Mengele would look for subjects for his experiments. As Schmuhl explains:

> The selection of new arrivals on the platform gave him unlimited possibilities to access humans completely devoid of rights and protection. From the endless stream of deportation trains he could single out any human 'guinea pigs' he pleased – Jews, 'Gypsies' and other 'alien nationals,' people with physical anomalies, entire families and, best of all, twins.[2]

Mengele and his colleagues could therefore pursue their interests in physical defects, eye anomalies, chondrodysplasia and twin research without the inconvenience of considering how unethical their procedures were, and without any regulation. They were free to study a variety of disorders that Verschuer was obsessed with in order to determine whether they carried hereditary traits.

Mengele's research included pharmaceutical studies for IG Farben,

Josef Mengele

but his most significant partners were undoubtedly Verschuer and the KWI-A in Berlin-Dahlem. In 1943, a KWI-A researcher, Karin Magnussen, used eyeballs taken from prisoners at Auschwitz and sent to the institute by Mengele for experiments on the pigmentation of the human iris. Mengele also sent Verschuer around 200 blood samples procured from camp inmates. Miklós Nyiszli, the prisoners' physician, reported after the war that Mengele pursued his interests in growth anomalies ('dwarfism' or 'gigantism') or other physical defects by selecting such individuals on the platform at Auschwitz where deportees were dropped off, and then ordering his assistants to examine, murder and dissect them. Some of these specimens were then sent to the KWI-A.[3]

Mengele was particularly interested in twins, as he could investigate and compare the physical features and traits of genetically identical subjects. As Schmuhl points out, Auschwitz presented Mengele with the unprecedented opportunity 'to supplement the clinical and anthropological examination of twins with the pathological examination of their corpses, as Mengele could murder, or have murdered, *both* twins at any time'.[4] At least 900 children went through his 'twin camp'.

Mengele's twin research aimed to prove that heredity trumped environment, thereby demonstrating the racial supremacy of Aryans. Nyiszli reported that Mengele or his assistants would examine and measure the physical features of the twins on a weekly basis. Their experiments on twins sometimes involved amputations of limbs, infecting one twin with typhus or another disease, and transfusing blood from one twin to the other. These experiments often led to deaths, and some of the twins were murdered. Nyiszli recalled the night that Mengele personally murdered fourteen twins by injecting chloroform into their hearts. If one twin died, he would sometimes murder the other so that a comparative post-mortem report could be produced.[5]

Medical experiments happened at other camps too. Some of these sought to aid the survival of German soldiers, by investigating the effects of extreme cold and high-altitude conditions on inmates at Dachau. Others tested the effects of pharmaceuticals and other treatments on various diseases and injuries. Subjects at Dachau, Sachsenhausen, Natzweiler and Buchenwald would be treated after being infected with tuberculosis, malaria or yellow fever, or after being subjected to mustard gas or phosphorus burns. Other experiments explored racial hygiene and genetic make-up, and attempted to establish and advance the superiority of the Aryan race.[6]

At Sachsenhausen is a permanent exhibition titled 'Medical Care and Crime: The Infirmary of Sachsenhausen Concentration Camp 1936–1945',[7] which I visited with Mark Kaplan in 2015. Dr Robert Ritter, whose name I first encountered during my visit to the US Holocaust Memorial Museum in Washington DC two decades earlier, had established the Racial Hygiene and Biological Population Research Unit in 1936, which also operated at Sachsenhausen and fell under the Reich Public Health Office. Ritter's researchers drew up 'racial assessments' of Roma and Sinti people, on the basis of which they were compulsorily sterilised or deported to Auschwitz-Birkenau. As the exhibition revealed, Ritter and his colleagues would use eye-, hair- and skin-colour charts to examine Sinti and Roma from Sachsenhausen. Eugen Fischer's patented hair-colour chart was also on display.

A photograph shows one of Ritter's researchers, Eva Justin, using an eye-colour chart to examine a Sinti woman. In 1943, forty Sinti children from the Roman Catholic St Joseph's Children Home in Mulfingen were spared deportation because Justin needed them as subjects for her doctoral thesis, which involved her filming them while they played various dexterity games. Following the completion of her thesis, thirty-seven of these children were sent to Auschwitz-Birkenau, where thirty-three were murdered. As I watched Justin's 'ethnographic' footage of the children, I was again reminded of the complicity of my discipline in crimes against humanity.

Outside the walls of the Sachsenhausen infirmary where this research was taking place, tens of thousands of prisoners were killed, mostly through starvation, disease and torture. Although it was designed to be a detention and work camp, 12 000 Soviet prisoners of war were killed there in 1941 alone. This created the need for the construction of a small gas chamber and crematorium.

Sachsenhausen is in the sleepy suburb of Oranienburg, about one hour north of Berlin by train. Mark and I were both stunned by the camp's proximity to the area and became convinced that its inhabitants must have known what was happening within the camp's walls. The smoke from the crematoria would have been easily detectable, either by sight or smell. And on the nights of 20 and 21 April 1945, shortly before the camp was liberated, they must have heard the footsteps of the more than 33 000 inmates, including women and children, outside their homes as they were forcibly marched northwards. They might even have heard the screams of prisoners being tortured when the wind blew in a certain direction.

While a number of Jews were interned at Sachsenhausen, mostly before 1942, the majority of inmates were Roma and Sinti, foreign nationals, Jehovah's Witnesses, political and common criminals, 'asocials' (artists, playwrights, homeless people) and homosexuals. Jews were moved far away from German soil to camps such as Auschwitz, where they were to be obliterated as a race. Among them were my father's sisters, elder brother and sister-in-law, as well as several other relatives.

* * *

While I was writing this book, I decided to re-read Art Spiegelman's *Maus*. Spiegelman's graphic novel is a harrowing account of his father Vladek's experiences during the war, including his time in Auschwitz. As an older man, Vladek frequently exhibits strange or off-putting behaviour, such as miserliness and an obsession with hoarding things, which has caused him to become estranged from his son. However, as the story unfolds, it becomes clear that Vladek's experiences of Auschwitz have lived on in his eccentricities, and in his nightmares. While reading *Maus*, I found myself drawing parallels between Vladek and my own father, who would, in his later years, shoplift from department stores. Hoarding and thriftiness are probably common traits exhibited by those who have lived through wars, famine and poverty. Perhaps my father's pilfering was a symptom of a pain that could not find expression in any other way.

I often wonder what visiting Auschwitz reveals and what it conceals. The March of the Living is an international education programme falling on Yom Ha'Shoah, Holocaust Memorial Day (16 April), during which participants from around the world travel to Poland to march from Auschwitz I to Auschwitz II-Birkenau. On 22 April, the youth who have done the march go to Israel to participate in Yom Ha'Zikaron, Israel's Memorial

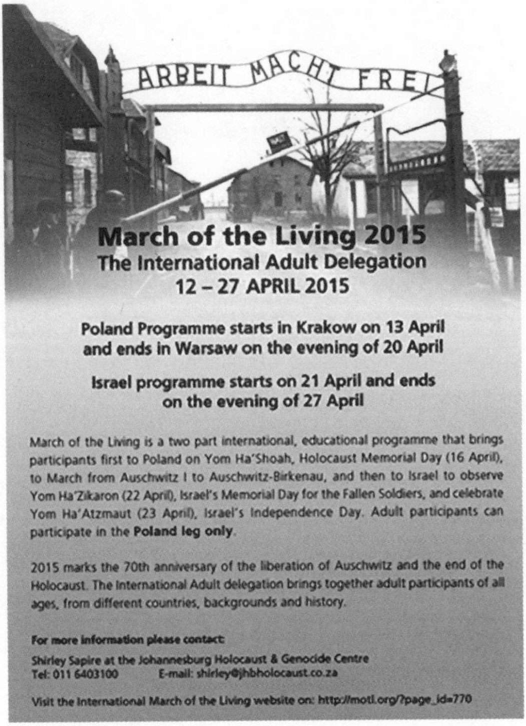

Day for the Fallen Soldiers. A day later they celebrate Israel's Independence Day, or Yom Ha'atzmaut.

These tours are tethered to a redemptive Zionist script about the formation of the Jewish state, but even without such ideological framing, it is unclear to me what one actually learns while walking through the remnants of this death camp. When I visited Auschwitz in 1999, I had known for three years that Edith, Hildegard and Siegfried were deported there in 1943, but there was a vast chasm between having this information and arriving at the place of their destruction. I had lived for so many years in the shadows and silences of the catastrophe, that when I finally came face to face with the place where it happened, I used my video camera, tightly strapped to my forehead, to shield myself from confronting the full horror of it. The visit taught me one thing about myself: whenever possible, I try to look away from the abyss, for fear of turning into stone.

I would not be the first to observe that language, understanding and conventional historiographic modes of representation break down at the gates of Auschwitz – all we can hope for are glimpses of what happened through the fragments that remain. There is a vast amount of scholarly literature on these limits of representing and comprehending the death camps. Today, the mere mention of Auschwitz is enough to elicit feelings and utterances of shock, outrage, grief, melancholy, despair, blame, guilt, moral fatigue, ethical indifference and even outright denial. People everywhere have encountered versions of the Shoah's history via affectively charged television documentaries, educational programmes, films, photographs, books, plays, museums, memorials, artworks and other media. Given this proliferation of responses, does it make any sense to claim that Auschwitz is shrouded in silence? Or, perhaps more to the point, what is there left to say in the wake of this cacophony of voices?

Historians, sociologists and philosophers insist that a fundamental question still remains unanswered: how could Auschwitz have happened in the heart of civilised Europe? Numerous perspectives and schools of thought have naturally clamoured to answer this question, and most pin all the blame on those figures from the Third Reich who have come to epitomise pure evil: Hitler, Himmler, Heydrich, Eichmann, Goebbels and Mengele. But such accounts tend to ignore the build-up to the Holocaust and the fact that anti-Semitism, ethnic nationalism and fascism in Europe didn't appear from nowhere. Instead, they were the result of a long history of racism and prejudice that sprang up in the heart of the continent.

Then there are those who believe that the Nazis' actions were the result of an inherent predisposition of all Germans to an irrational, uncontrollable hatred of Jews, which can be traced back many generations. American Jewish scholar Daniel Goldhagen falls into this category. However, for Polish-born sociologist Zygmunt Bauman, the Holocaust was caused by a kind of bureaucracy and technical rationality that was the culmination of the cold and potentially lethal logic of modernity itself. [8]

Bauman's argument about the character of modern states echoes that of Hannah Arendt, who proposes that the death camps were made possible by 'thoughtless' bureaucrats such as Adolf Eichmann. It was these unthinking officials who followed orders and created the tight train schedules that made the genocide possible. Arendt's 1963 book *Eichmann in Jerusalem: A Report on the Banality of Evil* emphasises the horrifying banality of Eichmann's personality, which made him a mindless cog in the bureaucratically driven, industrial murder machinery of Auschwitz. Arendt also asserts that Nazism and Soviet totalitarianism were the endgames of the brutality of empire and colonial rule and the methods of racial extermination they conceived. These processes found their way back into Europe where they were utilised by the Third Reich for their own gruesome purposes.

According to Moishe Postone, the Holocaust was a catastrophic form of modern anti-Semitism that itself was a product of the logic of capitalism, whereby Jews came to signify the dangerous, antisocial and abstract quality of exchange value. Jews were seen as being part of an extraordinarily powerful, international conspiracy responsible for the destructive consequences of capitalism and socialism, the decline of Europe's traditional values and institutions, as well as the rise of a vulgar market culture. It was Jewish participation in modern capitalist developments that supposedly made them so dangerous and destructive to the health of society.

Yet another perspective on the Shoah insists that it is ultimately futile, and perhaps even perverse, to search for reasons for such an incomprehensible human tragedy. For French philosopher Jean-François Lyotard, Auschwitz has become the paradigm of historical catastrophes that cannot be represented by usual forms of language and representation. In fact, any explanation of the Holocaust will always be inadequate as nobody can truly understand or testify to what happened in the gas chambers and crematoria. Even a survivor – one of 'the saved', as Primo Levi refers to them – would be disqualified as a witness to what actually happened in Auschwitz's dark abyss by virtue of having lived. Modes of modern discourse such as language, films and books are thus rendered mute by the unspeakable nature of this catastrophic event. For figures such as Claude Lanzmann, the acclaimed French director of the epic documentary film *Shoah*, any attempt to interpret or explain the Holocaust becomes sheer obscenity.

The problem with such arguments is that they set up the Holocaust as a limit event, a unique and exceptional case that reduces all other genocides – those in Armenia, German South West Africa, Cambodia, Indonesia and Rwanda – to secondary cases. A hierarchy of genocides and human suffering is thus created that restricts our capacity to understand and commemorate other catastrophes.

Saul Friedländer, the pioneering historian of the Holocaust, takes a less extreme and judgemental position than Lyotard and Lanzmann, arguing that such an insoluble dilemma forces us to confront the inadequacy of traditional ways of historical representation while being compelled to provide as reliable a narration as possible. If historians are unable to provide convincing and accurate accounts of this event, Friedländer stresses, Holocaust denialists will step into this breach.

* * *

In December 2012, I met Miriam Lichterman, an Auschwitz survivor who lived in Cape Town. I had been thinking about contacting her for a few years, but inchoate feelings of dread prevented me from setting up an appointment. I was fearful of a face-to-face encounter with someone who had lived through the nightmare of Auschwitz, but another part of me really wanted this meeting. The documentary finally provided me with an opportunity to overcome my ambivalence. Mark Kaplan and I met Miriam at the comfortable Sea Point beachfront flat of Marlene Silbert, the education director at the Cape Town Holocaust Centre.

Miriam described to us the notorious selection processes she frequently had to participate in at Auschwitz. During one of these, she was ill with typhus, almost a walking skeleton, and was convinced, as she stood in front of Mengele, that she would be selected for the gas chamber.

> Mengele, the camp commandant and an assistant were standing in front and we would file past him naked so that he could assess quickly by the movement of his baton. Then you went to the table that was standing at the side of him. Behind the table a woman prisoner from a privileged barrack, a sort of an officer, would write down the numbers of those whom Mengele showed left. Those that Mengele showed right would go back to the barrack.

Miriam describes surviving this selection as a miracle. Despite being close to death, she was not sent to the gas chambers. Miriam had noticed that the woman sitting at the table had given her a furtive glance of recognition and believes she must have placed a secret mark next to her number to indicate to the office workers who typed up the selection list to spare her.

> She lifted her face and looked into my eyes as if to give me some message. Otherwise there was no need to look into my eyes. All she had to do was to look at my number and write it down … The following morning when the woman in charge of the whole barrack came around the barrack with a list of numbers, my number was not called out. Now that girl removed my name from that fateful list. She was not my friend, relative, or anybody who should have cared about me

> enough to save my life ... At the risk to her own life she did it. She did it simply because she was somebody obviously that had a heart, that saw an opportunity to save a human being. This is what made me there and then, and even today, made me believe in humanity ...

Miriam also survived another ordeal: the death march following the evacuation of Auschwitz in early 1945 as the Russians approached from the east. It was Miriam's testimony of surviving the camp that helped me continue to chip away at the silences about the atrocities perpetrated on my own family.

Miriam often recollects a late summer's day in August 1944 when she heard beautiful singing coming from the barracks of Polish-Ukrainian women and the effect this had on her:

> They were singing and it was such beautiful singing, such beautiful harmonising. It went right through my soul. So, I kept my head up and I listened. That barrack was here, my barrack was in front of me there, and as I lifted my head to listen to this beautiful singing, I saw the sun, this big orange red ball of sun going down on the horizon and in the distance, the chimneys were smoking. It was the time of the Hungarian transports 1944, they were still sending people and that dark smoke was filling the air with that acrid smell.

Miriam's husband was also an Auschwitz survivor. One day, while walking along the Sea Point promenade with their youngest son, he smelled the sharp, acrid odour of burning meat coming from a nearby restaurant and started to panic. He immediately grabbed his son and ran along the promenade. For the teenaged boy, his father's behaviour was, of course, mystifying. 'So, when he, my husband, could catch his breath again,' Miriam recalls, 'then he explained to my son what that smell reminded him of, and I can still smell today and I can still see it.' Before then, Miriam and her husband had tried to protect their son from this past. Such silence about the Holocaust was prevalent in the decades after the war, when survivors felt that nobody wanted to hear about what they had suffered. It was only in the 1960s and 1970s, Miriam noted, that survivors began to speak openly and publicly. The televised reportage of Eichmann's trial in Jerusalem in 1961 helped to open up the space for survivors to begin to talk about their experiences in the camps. Miriam now regularly addresses schoolchildren and other audiences about her experiences in Auschwitz.

TWENTY-TWO

Finding My Father

During the war years, in Port Elizabeth, a small group of German Jewish refugees would gather at the home of Hetty Levy, Eugen Robinski's daughter, to play bridge. Hetty's son Harold recalls how the group of card players – which included my father Herbert as well as Ewald Nagel, the husband of Eugen's daughter Lily – would gather around the radio to hear news about the war. Harold remembers that Herbert would become agitated whenever one of Hitler's speeches was broadcast or a German military advance was reported. Ewald, a pessimistic man, believed that Germany's military superiority would lead to their victory in the war, but my father still had hope that the Allies would win. I try to imagine how he felt each time he heard of the seemingly invincible German army's victories. It is hardly surprising that his health took a turn for the worse in 1940.

Harold, a bright and precocious boy, was deeply influenced by this group of worldly European refugees. He learnt about and witnessed the effects of a war at a time when most boys from his world were preoccupied with rugby and cricket. Knowing what the Jews had suffered at the hands of the Nazis led to Harold's early conversion to Zionism, but he soon became disenchanted with the violent methods of militant Zionists in their struggle for a Jewish state. More inclined towards rational argument, his temperament would suit his later career as an attorney and Supreme Court judge. Harold's mother Hetty had worked tirelessly alongside Herbert to get Edith out of Germany, and Harold can vividly recall the day Herbert told her that he had received news that Edith had been deported to Auschwitz. My father must have been devastated, but he could not afford to dwell for too long in this space of inconsolable grief.

On 29 June 1943, soon before Edith's deportation, Herbert received an unusual letter from Rudi Robinski, his cousin in Stockholm, whose parents and sister had likewise been sent to their deaths.

Stockholm, 29.6.43
Bergsgatan 9 Stockholm

Dear Herbert!

You will perhaps be surprised to receive this letter from me. First of all, I can inform you that my sister Edith and my brother-in-law have also been deported a while ago, so I no longer correspond with Berlin. My parents have, as you perhaps already know, suffered the same fate. Should I, against all expectations, hear something about your relatives, I will inform you immediately.

The actual reason for this letter is of a business nature. I wished to request you to investigate, whether there are pelt firms (en gros or detail) over there who would wish to have a connection with Stockholm.

Either this could pertain to African furs sent here, or even the export of Swedish furs (red, silver-blue and platinum fox and mink). Should you be interested in this yourself or should you wish to work together with a firm, even better.

As these are plans for the future, i.e. post-war plans, we could arrange all the details here later. Thanking you in anticipation for all possible efforts I remain

Your cousin Rudi

P.S. I am a qualified furrier.

Rudi briefly mentions the deportation of his family with strikingly detached language before moving on to discuss a business proposition. In a letter sent a year later, on 25 May 1944, Rudi again cuts to the chase: '*As I have to be brief, I will immediately deal with business matters.*' There is no reference at all to the war, or his parents; instead, he resumes his proposition to my father that they start a fur-trade business. Nothing ever came of this idea.

It is not difficult to understand why survivors like Rudi did not discuss the loss and hardship they had experienced. When faced with this kind of horror, it is a common reaction to turn away from it. Even though I am of the second generation, and therefore at much more of a distance from these experiences of loss, I too sometimes felt like doing the same while reading the letters. My cousin Cecilia still finds it too distressing to read them. During the translation process, Ute told me that she would go into denial whenever she read a particularly distressing letter and would try to forget its content. This reaction was even more true of the people who managed to escape but whose family members did not, such as Rudi and my father, and Aunt Frieda in Bolivia. They had no choice but to put the past behind them if they hoped to restart their lives in their new homes. It is also doubtful that they could have found the words to capture what they felt even if they were willing to discuss it, and it was probably easier to cope if the guilt and pain they carried remained buried within them.

* * *

I have none of the letters my father sent to his family in Berlin, and he never spoke to me about this period in his life, so I have no access to his state of mind at the time. But there is a medical history, recorded in correspondence and documentation that my father submitted to Berlin's United Restitution Organisation office at Helmstedter Strasse 5 in the 1960s, that testifies to the pressure and anxiety he endured.

In an enclosure attached to a letter to a Mr H. Bergheim in Port Elizabeth on 24 February 1967, my father provides details about his medical history. This information was probably needed to complete the forms that Bergheim submitted to Berlin's restitution office on his behalf. It summarises a number of medical conditions that are to be listed in the form:

> Catarrhal bronchitis in 1934 after release from prison in Erfurt; Tuberculosis in 1939 by extreme cough and haemorrhage; Hypertension in 1939 extreme nervousness & irritability; and Diabetes in 1942 [with] fainting spells.

This is followed by a short sentence: 'The fear for life and the spell in prison.' The document then provides a brief history of treatment: the bronchitis was treated in Erfurt in 1934 until he emigrated in 1936; TB treatment began in Port Elizabeth with a Dr Robertson; and in September 1944 my father was admitted to the TB sanatorium in Nelspoort in the Karoo. He spent the rest of the war there, and was eventually discharged in January 1947. Thereafter he was treated at the Donkin Hospital in Port Elizabeth until May 1950. In 1967, when this documentation was being prepared, his general practitioner, Dr Aaron Gordon, was taking care of his health.

In an undated letter, Dr Gordon (who happened to be the husband of Eugen Robinski's daughter Laura) testifies to my father's poor health in the 1940s:

> Mr H.L. Robins has been a patient of mine for the past fifteen years. He was treated for pulmonary tuberculosis in Port Elizabeth and at Nelspoort Sanatorium from 1940 onwards. At first he was hospitalized and had complete bed-rest. He also had streptomycin paz and I.N.H. Tablets. He still has a great deal of catarrhal bronchitis. Mr. Robins also suffers from diabetes and hypertension. As a result of all these conditions Mr. Robins health and normal expectancy of life have in my opinion been considerably diminished. I estimated that impairment of his working capacity to be more than 50%.

My grandmother never mentions my father's ill-health in her letters, so I assume he never told her about it at the time. Given the profound concern and protectiveness she always displays in her letters to her sons in Africa, I presume she would have been very worried about Herbert's health had she known. Herbert may have felt he had no grounds for complaint since he was safe in South Africa, and probably didn't want his family to worry about him. Like his mother, he too had to be silent and stoic.

He did mention to his aunt Frieda that his hair was falling out, as she writes in a letter to him in early 1943: '*Do not worry if you lose your hair; most importantly one should be in good health.*' I don't know if he was merely going bald at this stage, or if his hair was falling out because of extreme stress.

My father's poor health in the 1940s suggests that the relentless pressure he faced trying to get his family out of Germany was too great for his body to bear. When he was admitted to the sanatorium less than two years after his family's deportation, he must have felt even more helpless and distressed.

Fifty kilometres north-east of Beaufort West, the Nelspoort TB sanatorium was situated deep in the Karoo, where the dry air is suitable for curing chest ailments. It was set up after the First World War by the Cape's Society for the Prevention of Consumption, after a sizeable donation by John Garlick, a philanthropist and founder of one of South Africa's largest department stores, who was shocked by the lethal toll of tuberculosis in working-class 'Cape coloured' areas such as District Six. Garlick was inspired by Thomas Mann's novel *The Magic Mountain* (published in 1924), which tells the story of a sanatorium in the Alps. The Nelspoort sanatorium became internationally renowned from the mid-1920s until it closed down in the 1970s.[1]

I wonder if my father knew about this connection between the Nelspoort sanatorium and Mann, the illustrious German writer who won the 1929 Nobel Prize in Literature and who was a strident anti-Nazi essayist and public speaker. In May 1933, the Nazis burnt his brother Heinrich's books for being 'un-German', but exempted Thomas's because he was a Nobel laureate. Later in 1933, Mann and his Jewish wife fled Germany for Switzerland. The Nazi government revoked Mann's German citizenship in 1936 and, when the war broke out in 1939, Mann and his family moved to the US. During the war he gave anti-Hitler broadcasts on the BBC.[2] Perhaps Herbert listened to some of them.

By the time my father was admitted to the sanatorium in September 1944, his parents and siblings had already been deported. It would take him time to recover from these ordeals, and marriage and starting a family had to wait until a decade after the war ended.

Letters sent to my father from friends and relatives after the war suggest that what happened to him and his family had left him shattered. The South African researcher on Lithuanian Jewry, Claudia Braude, found Jewish Board of Deputies documents and letters from 1944 and 1945 that reveal that South African Jews were crushed when they received the Red Cross telegrams informing them of what had happened to their relatives. Suicides and depression were commonplace. Most South African Jews had their roots in Lithuania, where 90 per cent of the country's Jews perished during the war. South African Jews also feared for their own future in a country where so many Afrikaner nationalists had supported Germany's wartime campaigns, before Prime Minister Malan began his friendly overtures to South African Jews.

In 1957, a Mr T. Schraml, a former work colleague of my father's from Erfurt, wrote to him: '*I want to ask you not to hate the Germans. You get the good and the bad, and he who hates is not a good person. And I know you as a good person who has been, however, a little unstable.*' I am not sure what Mr Schraml means by the word 'unstable'. But who would not have been deeply disturbed by what had happened to my father? Yet he was also being called upon to forgive, forget and reconcile with Germans – a mere dozen years after the liberation of the camps. In another letter, a relative advises him that it would be good for his health if he were to start a family of his own; this would distract him from thinking about the past.

* * *

From left to right: Artur, Steven, Herbert and Michael Robins. This photograph was taken at Michael and Deborah Robins' wedding in Cape Town in 1983

In 2013, while writing this book, I visited my brother in London and we spoke about my father and how he responded to his loss. Reading the letters from Berlin had led me to conclude that he must have been a broken man, even though he tried his utmost to conceal this from his sons. I believed that behind my father's conviviality and charm, there was a man with a large gaping hole in his soul. Michael, however, saw things differently. In his opinion, my father and Artur had to get on with their lives because this was what their generation did whenever they experienced loss. Trauma counselling and our contemporary 'talk cure' culture were foreign to them, and they were unfamiliar as well with post-traumatic stress disorder. The brothers found their own ways of coping with catastrophe. For Herbert, living among English-speaking South Africans may even have caused him to acquire their stereotypical stiff-upper-lip approach to tragedy.

To Michael, our father's generation had learnt to accept the brutal realities of war. During the First World War, millions of men had died on Europe's barbaric killing fields, and the Robinskis themselves had suffered loss when my father's little sister Erika died of malnutrition owing to food shortages. My grandfather had come back from the war shocked and disillusioned by the devastation it had wrought. Average life expectancy back then was low as well, and death was everywhere. As a result, those who had grown up in this world could accept mortality more easily than we do. Perhaps they were more fatalistic. Even so, I still suspect that my father hid away his sorrow in a black box in his unconscious. Now, as a second-generation survivor, I was warily prising open its lid.

My father became good friends with a couple named Rudi and Ruth Cohn. Rudi and Herbert were both German Jewish refugees who arrived in Port Elizabeth in 1936, while Ruth, who came from a very wealthy Jewish family in Altenburg, joined Rudi two years later. Rudi and Ruth had met in Germany in 1936, when her father, desperate to get his daughter out of the country, agreed that she should marry Rudi who was about to leave for Port Elizabeth. They married a few days after Ruth's arrival in 1938. Rudi and Ruth got on so well with Herbert that they invited him to stay with them. Rudi and Herbert would become inseparable.

Mookie Tabakin, the Cohns' daughter who was born in the early 1940s, remembers that Rudi and Herbert frequented the Sky Roof nightclub at the Marine Hotel in Summerstrand, where they enjoyed their whisky, chain-smoked, and played cards into the early hours of the morning. Before he got married, my charming, elegant and good-looking father was always seen at nightclubs in the company of attractive young women.

I am not sure who this woman is, or where and when the photograph was taken; I suspect it was taken in Port Elizabeth before my father married in 1955

Rudi, Ruth and Herbert lived together in a large house in Allen Street on the Old Cape Road. Two other German Jewish refugees stayed there too: Werner Lowenstein, the owner of a string of shoe shops, and an ambitious businessman named Henner Levy, who did not approve of the party-loving and nightclubbing pair of Rudi and Herbert. Despite this, Levy, along with the other men in the house, who were all involved in the rag trade, helped my father establish himself selling socks and stockings and, later, as a travelling salesman. Rudi had already opened an upmarket retail shop, Continental Fashions, and invited Herbert to join him there, which gave him a foot into the *smutter* (clothing) trade in Port Elizabeth.

Many of the people in the Cohns' circle were members of the Reform synagogue, a liberal form of Judaism with German roots that had recently been founded in the town. Though my father was not a member, he was exposed to their values. Jean Comaroff, whose parents were part of this group, remembers Werner Lowenstein as a sophisticated and educated man. 'I think that in his own estimation, he was always more than merely a businessman. He was a cultivated person, well-read and knowledgeable, who, if he had remained in Europe, would have been a professional.' To compensate for these lost opportunities, Werner and his friends had formed a small group that appreciated European music, art and literature. Port Elizabeth may have been an industrial, frontier city where one had to knuckle down to make a living, but these cosmopolitan Jews continued to valorise European culture. They bought imported German food from a delicatessen called Harris's – and I do recall that my father enjoyed his pumpernickel bread and overripe camembert cheese. Jean adds:

> In spirit, they were never merely salesmen. In their minds, their lives had been interrupted, though they never talked about that. I never remember any of them ever showing me pictures or talking about the families and the careers they left behind … You made a life here, a life of immediacy, security, comradeship, good food, making sure that your children were well educated and cared for. As they made money, they bought or expanded their homes, the quality of their lives. There was always good artwork, often good music … But as I recall it, there was rather little talk of South African politics, nor the German past – the details, or the loss. It was very much about investing in the present, in family, material security.

My father and mother on their wedding day in 1955

By the early 1950s, my father had become a relatively successful businessman. In 1955 he married a pretty young woman named Ruth Naomi Rom, who was born in Port Elizabeth in 1929 and, at twenty-six, was twenty-two years younger than Herbert. Her father Harry Rom was born in Lithuania and had arrived in South Africa in the early 1900s. He lived with his children in the mixed white and coloured working-class area of South End which, in the early 1960s, witnessed the forced removal of the coloured population under the notorious Group Areas Act. Harry Rom owned a small trading store, and my mother and her siblings would have to walk from house to house to collect the debt owed to their father's shop. Ruth, desperate to escape this kind of life, realised her dream when she married Herbert and could finally move out of South End and up the social ladder in Port Elizabeth's small Jewish community.

As an ultra-orthodox Jew, Harry was deeply suspicious and disapproving of this secular, assimilated refugee who wanted to marry his daughter. Herbert was much older than Ruth and, in Harry's eyes, his exploits as a handsome and dapper man about town made him untrustworthy. Harry's disapproval meant that whenever my family would visit my grandparents at their flat in Humewood, my father would stay in the car and do crossword

My mother in the middle with her parents, Sarah and Harry Rom

puzzles or read the newspaper. He would tell me and my brother, still children, that he found the two flights of stairs leading to their flat difficult to manage, yet he coped quite well with the long, daily walks he took with his dogs. I also cannot recall visits to our house from Harry, who could probably not stomach the thought of being in the company of my father in our non-kosher home at the same time. My cousin Paul once told me that upon hearing about the moon landing, an enraged Harry decided to speak to the rabbi about this arrogant intrusion of man into God's sacred territory above. My father's response to this event was very different, and I can remember him being in awe of this great scientific achievement. When it came to Harry's Great God of the Universe, my father would ask how it was possible for such a God to sit by idly and watch six million perish. No wonder he and Harry could not be in the same room.

When my father proposed to my mother, he told her that she would have to raise their children on her own as he felt that being forty-eight made him too old to be actively involved in his children's upbringing. When I started school, my friends would always assume he was my grandfather; and by the time I was a teenager, he had already retired to his daily routine of doing crossword puzzles, reading detective fiction and walking the dog. It was left to my mother to manage the household and me and my brother.

We lived in a large and comfortable house in a middle-class suburb, and my parents could afford to send my brother and me to good schools and to university, so, in many respects, things worked out well for us in Port Elizabeth. In his later years, my father seemed reasonably content with his life. He had lived a long and relatively healthy life, and died peacefully in a hospital bed on 26 May 1990 at the age of eighty-three.

I am comforted by Mookie's accounts of the frivolous fun my father had as a bachelor in Port Elizabeth and his adventures with Rudi Cohn. These moments of freedom must have served as a respite from the grief and loss he had experienced. In Port Elizabeth, my parents socialised with a band of South African–born Jewish *jollers* led by Boetie Berger, who, unlike the German Jews who took themselves too seriously, relished their music, drink, card games and revels at nightclubs. A colour photograph of my parents at a party in the 1970s or 80s shows them dressed in traditional Asian attire. In this double-exposure image, Boetie and his wife Lily are smiling spookily at the bottom of the photograph.

My father and mother hover above the spectral double-exposure image of Boetie and Lily Berger. The photograph was probably taken at a fancy-dress party in PE in the late 1970s or early 1980s

I have often tried to imagine what it was like for Artur and my father to have left their family behind in Germany. Did they speak to each other about it? Perhaps they kept their feelings to themselves so as not to burden each other or their families. Or maybe they feared that opening up the black box of repressed memories would precipitate an emotional and psychological collapse from the weight of trauma and grief that it carried. They certainly could not afford to be derailed as they had to rebuild their lives in new and alien countries.

I found a photograph of the two brothers and their wives, possibly taken at a restaurant in Port Elizabeth in the 1960s. The frostiness that characterised my mother and Aunt Elsa's relationship probably meant that they did not get on well on that night either. But, to me, the brothers seem satisfied with their lives; by then they both had their own families and reasonably successful businesses. Even so, they would always have had to live with the knowledge of what had happened to their loved ones in Berlin during the war.

On the left is my mother and next to her is my father; on the far right is Elsa with Artur sitting next to her

TWENTY-THREE

Fischer's Footprint, Again

As the end of the war approached in 1945, Baron Otmar von Verschuer, who had succeeded Fischer as director of the Kaiser Wilhelm Institute for Anthropology, Human Heredity and Eugenics, and who was closely linked to Josef Mengele's scientific experiments at Auschwitz, loaded a truck with the institute's files and bodily remains, and transported them to western Germany. He apparently did this anticipating a more favourable reaction from the advancing Allies than from the Soviet Army.[1]

On 13 May 1947 Verschuer was interrogated by the American military authorities about his knowledge of what had taken place at Auschwitz. He vigorously denied knowing anything about the exterminations but admitted to having heard rumours at the time. Verschuer claimed that when Mengele visited his institute he had spoken about the factories there, his camp hospital and the harmonious relations he had established with his patients. We will never know exactly how much Verschuer and his fellow researchers at KWI-A knew about the conditions under which the eye specimens and blood samples they received from Auschwitz were extracted. But it seems clear that they knew much more than they were willing to reveal to their American interrogators.

In 1951 Verschuer was awarded the prestigious professorship of human genetics at the University of Münster. Like so many 'racial hygienists' of the Nazi era, Verschuer was able to reinvent himself after the war as a leading German genetics scientist, and would establish one of the largest centres of genetics research in West Germany, with many of his students appointed to top academic positions. Fischer himself had retired in Freiburg, and died in 1967 at the age of ninety-three. Josef Mengele was the only scientist associated with Fischer's institute who was charged with Nazi crimes, and he managed to escape to South America, drowning in 1979 while swimming at a beach in Brazil. He was buried using a false name, and it was only in 1985 that a forensic examination identified his body.

In July 2015, Mark Kaplan and I visited the site of the former KWI-A on the campus of Berlin's Free University (formerly the Kaiser Wilhelm University), where we interviewed historian Annegret Ehmann. Dr Ehmann told us that earlier that year, during renovations to the former director's villa which is adjacent to the KWI-A building, bags of labelled human remains from the colonies and concentration camps were unearthed, having been buried there by Verschuer. The bones were sent to Berlin's Charité Hospital where they were scanned and then incinerated, apparently on instructions from the university's administration. This sparked public outrage at what was viewed as the destruction of further evidence of the transgressions of Nazi science.

Fischer, Verschuer and their colleagues had benefited from the post-war consensus that it was necessary to rebuild Germans' trust in science, and many of these researchers continued to be cited in international academic journals well into the 1960s. In response to the direction eugenics had taken in Nazi Germany, UNESCO insisted after the war that 'race' had to be understood as a social construct rather than a biologically determined essence. A leading author of such post-war treatises on race was the Jewish anthropologist and founding figure of French structuralism Claude Levi-Strauss. The work of Franz Boas, the German Jewish anthropologist who had directly challenged racial science of the pre-war period, was also influential. Boas, in his position as chair of the Department of Cultural Anthropology at Columbia University, ultimately won the battle by successfully refuting the findings of eugenicists such as Madison Grant, H.H. Goddard and Charles Davenport.

As a social anthropologist who studied at the University of Cape Town in the late 1970s and early 1980s, I was trained to be suspicious of anything that smacked of scientific racism or biological determinism. It was these very ideas that were also used to prop up apartheid ideology. Then, in 1996, during my visit to the US Holocaust Memorial Museum, I learnt about Eugen Fischer's contribution to Nazi racial science. At the time, I jotted down in my diary: 'An accomplice no doubt about it. Fischer's findings led to policy decisions that led to the killing of Jews and Gypsies.' Little did I know that I would stumble upon Fischer's footprint again while searching for traces of my ancestors in the Karoo – and that I would do so once more at the anthropology department at Stellenbosch University, where I taught.

* * *

In February 2013, during a visit to the Eugen Fischer Collection at the Free University's Max Planck Society archives in Berlin, I was shown the original prints of Fischer's photographs of the Rehoboth Basters. The photographs, taken shortly after the Herero genocide, contain dozens of images of sombre men, women and children. According to some, the devoutly Christian Rehobothers had steadfastly refused Fischer's requests to photograph and measure them naked, while others claim he never asked them to strip. I wondered, while I looked at the Basters' unsmiling faces, whether they could see through Fischer's cold science and foretell where it was headed. Maybe Fischer had simply asked them not to smile for the camera.

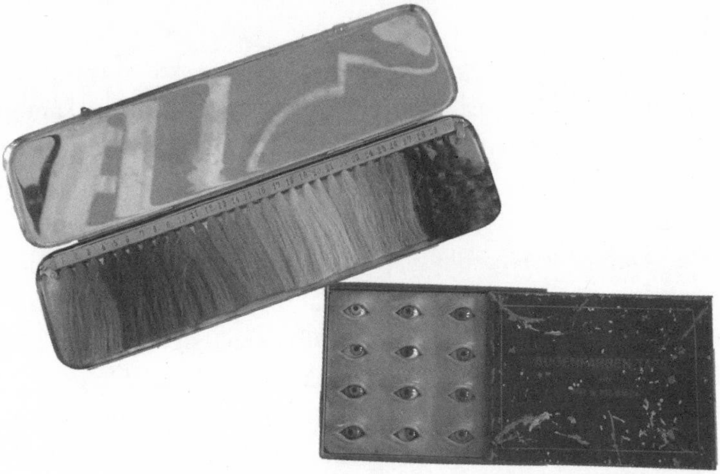

Eugenics instruments at the tip of Africa: the hair-colour table of Eugen Fischer and the eye-colour table of Rudolf Martin

A couple of days later I returned to Stellenbosch University where my research assistant, Handri Walters, told me about a cardboard box she had received from the university museum's curator. In the box was a skull, an eye-colour scale, and a hair-colour chart – with thirty different shades of hair from blonde to black – in a shiny silver case with Eugen Fischer's name engraved on it. The curator had been desperate to get rid of the skull since 1997, when the Volkekunde Department at the university closed and the box was handed over to her, so she was only too happy to relinquish it to my department.

The closure of the Volkekunde Department was inevitable given its embarrassing association with apartheid's policy of separate development, with its 'independent' ethnically based bantustans. One of apartheid's chief architects, Werner Eiselen,[2] was intimately associated with Volkekunde at the university, and he argued that South Africa's 'tribes' were biologically and culturally distinct and should live apart in ethnic homelands. In 1997, such a philosophy was completely at odds with Mandela's new Rainbow Nation. Yet, in spite of this purging of the Volkekundiges, there was still a literal skeleton in their cupboard.

We had little idea how the Volkekunde Department used Fischer's eugenics toolkit, and why it, along with the skull, had been hidden away for so long in a box in the university museum. They might have simply been the remnants of a discredited science; or perhaps Fischer had visited Stellenbosch and left behind this poisoned chalice for those who shared his interests.

After it was handed over to my department, the skull was immediately sent to a former Stellenbosch professor of anatomy and physical anthropology for forensic investigation. He found that it belonged to a female aged between thirty-five and fifty and of mixed ancestry ('not Xhosa, Zulu or Caucasian'), and that it had not been exhumed from a coffin or grave. Professor Alan Morris, a physical anthropologist at UCT, did his own investigation, identifying the skull as that of a man in his thirties or forties; its shape indicating a person of Khoisan ancestry who was probably a pauper.[3] The embalmed skull had apparently belonged to a designated anatomy facility and was acquired legally in terms of the Human Tissue Act. For the lawyers on the university's risk-assessment committee, this meant that the skull posed no legal threat to the institution. But some senior university managers were still concerned that the finding could undermine their efforts at creating an image of a transformed post-apartheid institution.

Professor Russel Botman, the university's first black rector, refused to bury these relics, however. After a press conference, at which my colleagues and I tried to explain the importance of further investigations into the history of racial science and Volkekunde at the university, Botman showed his own support for the idea: 'The researchers say they consider it their moral duty to pose critical questions about the context, focus, relevance and legacy of conducting science at their institution. I agree. We look our past squarely in the eye; similarly our future.' He added, 'As at key moments in the past, Stellenbosch University finds itself at a crossroads. We have long since left the *laager*.[4] We need to keep our momentum and face the future confidently.'

There followed a raging debate in the Afrikaans press, with sensationalist headlines implying that we were latter-day Simon Wiesenthals hunting for Nazis in a picturesque university town. The newspaper *Die Burger* published letters from outraged alumni incensed at the idea that the university could have had anything to do with the ideas of a Nazi scientist.

Professor Hermann Giliomee led the attack, claiming that Eiselen, his university colleagues, as well as Afrikaner nationalists, were in no way influenced by Nazism or German eugenics. In 1996, when the TRC was established, Giliomee asserted in his presidential address to the South African Institute for Race Relations that an analogy between apartheid and Nazism was mere anti-apartheid rhetoric and 'propaganda in a war in which the higher moral ground was decisive';[5] and he insisted that it was both historically inaccurate and politically opportunistic to claim that 'the NP [National Party] and the Afrikaner Broederbond were influenced by the Nazi Party'. He also rejected the United Nations General Assembly's 1973 resolution that apartheid could be understood as a 'crime against humanity'. Yet, despite the National Party distancing itself from Nazism after the war, many of the racial laws that shaped the lives of black people under their rule were remarkably similar to some of the racial ordinances my grandmother alluded to in her letters.

Giliomee remains adamant that apartheid drew its inspiration from Dutch Reformed Church theology and US Jim Crow segregationist laws, and that it was not influenced by German or any other school of racial science. But historians such as Andrew Bank and Saul Dubow suggest otherwise. The sympathies that Afrikaner nationalists such as Verwoerd and Vorster showed towards Nazi Germany signalled an affiliation with its racial programmes. And even after the war, when eugenics was repurposed and relabelled as genetic science, it continued to have a following in South Africa. Saul Dubow notes that 'although scientific racism was by no means the most important or determining ideological strand of apartheid, it was an indispensable component or trace element in apartheid discourse, an assumption that helped sustain the everyday assumptions of [racial] difference'.[6] He adds:

> The resurgence of scientific racism in the 1960s displays some clear continuities with prewar scientific racism but it also displays some distinctive features. Whereas obsessive fears of race mixture, white degeneration, and contamination marked the phase of apartheid's rise,

> this was no longer the case during apartheid's heyday ... The science of race that emerged in the 1960s was, on the one hand, directed outwards in order to position South Africa as part of the defence of western, Christian civilisation ... On the other, it was intended to reassure apartheid's internal supporters that the Bantustan policies of ethnic self-determination could be justified in biological as well as cultural terms.[7]

When most Volkekundiges and physical anthropologists at Stellenbosch University realised that eugenics was no longer a respectable science, they jettisoned their earlier obsessions with anthropometry and the measurement and classification of racialised bodies and began to focus on the innate cultural and ethnic differences between whites and blacks and between African 'tribes'. But, like Fischer's racial science, this was clearly not innocent scientific inquiry, with many of these studies treating cultural, tribal and ethnic differences as if they were biologically determined, and all in an attempt to justify apartheid's policies of separate development. Ideas about essential racial characteristics, inherited from eugenics, were therefore just transposed onto the more politically correct terrain of culture and ethnicity. Eugenics was dead, long live eugenics.

Just as skulls, skeletons and cadavers are all standard teaching objects in anatomy departments and medical schools, the 'race index' instruments found in the Stellenbosch museum were part of an internationally approved eugenics toolkit in the 1920s that could be found in almost every university around the world. While they had become anachronistic after the war, Namibian anthropologist Robert Gordon still recalls seeing these eye and hair tables in the late 1960s when he was an undergraduate student at Stellenbosch. C.S. 'Coert' Grobbelaar, a senior lecturer in zoology and physical anthropology at Stellenbosch, had also relied on Fischer's hair table for his 1952 study of the eye, hair and skin colour in male students at the university.[8] It is possible that the instruments found in the museum had belonged to Grobbelaar, a man who was clearly behind the scientific times.

The spectre of Eugen Fischer's scientific footprint in Stellenbosch suggested that the past was once again leaking into the present, and, while for some conservative alumni and professors the leak had to be plugged at all costs, for others it was a reminder of a misuse of science that we dare not forget.

* * *

In September 2014, Mark Kaplan and I drove 1500 kilometres from Cape Town to Williston, and then to Rehoboth, eighty kilometres south of Windhoek. We wanted to trace the lengthy journey undertaken by the Basters in the 1860s when they left Williston and trekked northwards, and to film the Rehoboth museum and document local stories about Eugen Fischer's 1908 visit.

As we travelled through the harsh Karoo desert, we tried to imagine the hardships the Basters must have endured on their trek. Despite the support they received from German Rhenish missionaries, they continued to be pushed further north until they were finally offered land in South West Africa. There they became allies of German colonial authorities in the wars against the Herero and Nama. Later, when the apartheid government took custodianship of South West Africa, they again aligned themselves with the powerful state. Like South African Jews after the Second World War, their liminal, in-between status – caught between the white colonial settlers and the indigenous peoples – had induced them to collaborate with both colonial and apartheid authorities. These alliances came back to bite them when Namibia became independent in 1990 and SWAPO, the former liberation-movement-turned-ruling party, would not look sympathetically on their history of colonial collaboration. It is therefore not surprising that the story of their Great Trek of the 1860s and their struggles to establish a Rhenish mission town in Rehoboth do not feature in Namibian school history books.

When Mark and I travelled to Rehoboth, we interviewed Basters about how they made sense of their complicated history. At the local museum we met the Baster *kaptein* John McNab, who, instead of discussing Fischer's objectification and dehumanisation of the Basters as I expected, provided us with a glowing account of Fischer's visit to Rehoboth. A seventy-five-year-old former teacher and seasoned politician, the *kaptein* portrayed Fischer as a man who had respected the Basters, and who had left them with an invaluable ethnographic archive. He said that Fischer measured and photographed every conceivable part of Basters' bodies, but that he did not disrespect them by asking them to strip naked. Fischer had also left the Basters with detailed genealogies and rich material about their history. Although Kaptein McNab had read that Fischer, after returning to Germany, became involved in the forced sterilisation of hundreds of 'Rhineland Bastard' children, he insisted that Fischer did no wrong during his time in Rehoboth. Kaptein McNab was not even born when Fischer was in the area, so I was perplexed by his narrative. I could not reconcile the *kaptein*'s seemingly authoritative local account of Fischer's 1908 research with my own research on his complicity with Nazi eugenics. So, was Fischer's research in Rehoboth as innocent as Kaptein McNab wanted me to believe, or was there a line of continuity between his early study and what was to follow?

The more I read about Fischer, the more complex his story became. But, with time, a shadowy image of the man began to appear. By 1933 he realised that if he was to attain power and prominence as a scientist in the Third Reich, he needed to adapt his scientific ideas to its political climate. He made no further public utterances on the 'hybrid vigour' of racial mixing among the Basters and the Jews, and, in this way, his publications and speeches could neatly align themselves with Nazi racial science. Like so many of his colleagues, he played the game and ensured that his science served the state.

Fischer became for me the link in a chain that connected Washington DC, Berlin, Williston, Rehoboth and Stellenbosch. These unanticipated connections between different times and places reflected the entanglement of the Robinski past with colonialism, racial science, Nazism and apartheid. When I first began my search for Eugen Robinski in Williston, I never imagined that scratching around its archives would take me to Rehoboth, only to send me back to Berlin, and, later, to my own university. Fischer's study of the Basters had set in motion a chain of scientific ideas that eventually boomeranged its way back to Europe. This looping story had come full circle, thoroughly blurring the lines between my personal, family and professional lives along the way.

TWENTY-FOUR

Optimism and Despair

In 1943, two years after she immigrated to the United States, Hannah Arendt reflected on her experiences as a German Jewish refugee. In her essay 'We Refugees' Arendt analyses the responses of refugees who had fled Nazi terror and were living in the United States in the early 1940s:

> Our optimism is indeed admirable, even if we say so ourselves. The story of our struggle has finally become known. We lost our home, which means the familiarity of daily life. We lost our occupation, which means the confidence that we are of some use in this world. We lost our language, which means the naturalness of reactions, the simplicity of gestures, the unaffected expression of feelings. We left our relatives in the Polish ghettos and our best friends have been killed in concentration camps, and that means the rupture of our private lives.[1]

For Arendt, this experience of loss is completely political, and she calls for a strict avoidance of the sentimentality of private feelings, melancholia, mourning, despair or optimism, all of which she regards, some would argue somewhat unreasonably, as a dangerous withdrawal from the world. This withdrawal, she insists, makes it impossible to respond politically to existing conditions. Arendt is particularly critical of Jewish refugees in the US who resort to 'false optimism' and forced happiness, which often give way to complete hopelessness and despair, and, in some cases, suicide. 'Their optimism is the vain attempt to keep their head above water. Behind this kind of cheerfulness, they constantly struggle with despair themselves. Finally, they die of a kind of selfishness.'[2] For Arendt, engaging in public political life is a far healthier response.

My grandmother's letters from Berlin convey a withdrawal from the world. She writes with a forced cheerfulness and does not respond politically to existing conditions, but instead retreats into the home. Arendt was of course writing about people who had escaped Germany, but my father's family could be seen as internal refugees, stripped of all citizenship until they were reduced to a state of bare existence. Forced into the private space of the home as the world outside became too hostile and dangerous, their seclusion was a survival strategy. Yet Jews like Cecilie Robinski were also determined to hold onto hope, and her optimism and fixation on the minutiae of daily domestic life became perhaps an expression of a defiant will to live. In her repeated references to the entertaining *skat* evenings, she sought to reassure her sons in Africa and to make her own fears, vulnerability and loss more bearable. They were also an attempt to stitch together the fragile fabric of family life that was being torn asunder. Cecilie had no choice but to turn to hope and the conviction that God would protect her family, and that they would ultimately survive the storm.

Through these actions, was Cecilie participating in the kind of 'reckless optimism' that Arendt questions? For Jewish refugees who found sanctuary in the United States, England or South Africa, more choices were available to them about how to respond to trauma and loss; but for my grandmother, survival required holding onto any hope, no matter how distant or futile. She had to keep believing that her remaining children would escape, as Herbert and Artur had managed to do. My grandfather's reaction to his situation might have been different, but my knowledge about his feelings is limited. All I have from him are a few lines at the end of one of Cecilie's letters and the brief wartime telegrams.

I doubt Arendt would have labelled Cecilie's responses as reckless optimism, or questioned her retreat into the sanctuary of the domestic domain. Her criticisms targeted Jewish refugees in the United States who, in the face of their loss, turned away from what was happening in the world. They feigned unbridled optimism in public while living privately in a state of deep despair. For Arendt, both hope and despair are inextricably tied to the loss of one's sense of self, and to the conditions that make life bearable in this world. To turn to 'blind optimism' or 'reckless despair' involves a denial of loss that inhibits interacting with the world: 'The less we are free to decide who we are or to live as we like, the more we try to put up a front, to hide the facts, to play roles.'[3] Arendt later expanded on this in the preface to her book *The Origins of Totalitarianism*: 'The central events of our time are no less effectively forgotten by those committed to a belief in an unavoidable doom, than by those who have given themselves up to a reckless optimism ... This book has been written against a background of both reckless optimism and reckless despair. It holds that Progress and Doom are two sides of the same metal; that both are articles of superstition, not of faith.'[4] Arendt had strong reasons for being frustrated with this façade of hope put forth by Jewish refugees in the US in the early 1940s, when fascism was still sweeping across Europe and the battle seemed far from over.

I am not sure how to interpret my father's response to his loss and exile. He did not speak to me about losing his parents, siblings, language and home. Even when I interviewed him in 1989 about his life, he made no mention of the emotional toll these deaths had wrought on him. I have often asked myself why he did so. Perhaps he thought that I or others would not be interested, or that he had no choice but to get on with his life. I don't believe he responded with blind optimism or reckless despair, either. Instead, he seems to have retreated into silence. No one asked him about his past, and he did not feel compelled to tell anyone about it. He might simply have not had the words to express the pain or suffering of such incredible loss. Maybe that is why he never told me who the three women in the photograph were on the table in our dining room. Unlike Arendt, who was a public intellectual, my father could not channel his private experiences of loss and exile into a politically engaged response. It is not surprising, then, that he turned away from the world and became a private man, committed to raising a family and remaking his life at the tip of Africa. He must have resigned himself to living under the shadow of despair, even if he did not show this to those closest to him.

There are of course other ways to interpret my father's response to what happened. Perhaps he accepted that there was an insurmountable gap between the realities of the world he had left behind before the war and the one he started thereafter. Or maybe he learnt to live with the profound sense of powerlessness that most people experience when confronted by political forces beyond their control. Mere survival – establishing a business and marrying and having children – was in itself an act of defiance of a certain kind. Arendt's insistence that Jewish refugees ought to have turned their private suffering into social and political action is perhaps asking too much of them. Sometimes just getting on with one's life in the aftermath of a catastrophe can be considered a victory over those who have tried to take away your life and dignity – although Arendt would probably not have recognised this as being properly political.

* * *

Among my parents' photographs is a picture of them taken on 14 June 1955 with Margot Rubenstein, one of the daughters of Aunt Minna and Uncle Bernhard, in Allenby Street in Tel Aviv. I don't know how much contact my father had with the other family members who survived.

My cousin Cecilia told me that Artur took his family to Israel in the early 1970s, where they met the Rubenstein children who had settled there. One of them, who had taken on the Hebrew name Zwi, was married with children and had settled at Kibbutz Givat Chaim, a few kilometres south of Hadera. The family later left the kibbutz and went to live in Hod HaSharon ('Splendour of Sharon'), a city in Central District of Israel. Cecilia found an old address book with the contact details of Zwi's daughter, Rut, and I managed to have a few Skype conversations with her son, but he seemed completely uninterested in discussing our shared family's past. Since his mother could only speak German and Hebrew, I enlisted an Israeli genealogist in Tel Aviv, Rose Lerer Cohen, to contact her. Rose emailed me after trying to talk to Rut: 'She kept on saying "It's 70-year-old history. I cannot remember anything."' And, later, 'Just called Rut ... she is unavailable to talk!!' I was frustrated, perplexed and angry about their responses. At the same time, I realised that my father had chosen to remain silent about this tragic past, and I too had once been indifferent to my family history. One thing Rose managed to squeeze from Rut was that Margot had married and had two sons, but I had no way of tracing them. I would soon discover more through another route, however.

In November 2015, two weeks before this book was to go to the printers, my editor, Robert Plummer, urged me to try to find out the surname of Aunt Frieda, my grandmother's sister who escaped to Bolivia with her son Werner. Robert was determined to find this missing piece of information. Going through the Robinski documents again, I came across an envelope with Bolivian stamps and addressed to my father. The back of the envelope indicated that the letter was sent by a Frau Finkelstein from La Paz, Bolivia. I instantly recalled that my father had spent a few unhappy years working as an apprentice salesman for an Uncle Finkelstein in Gumbinnen, East Prussia. This must have been Frieda's husband.

I then did a Google search with the names Frieda, Werner and Finkelstein and discovered much more than I could have imagined.

In 2002, Werner Max Finkelstein published a book (with his co-author Kerstin Emma Schirp) titled *Jew, Gringo, German: The Adventurous Life of Werner Max Finkelstein*,[5] in which he describes his childhood in Germany, his journey via Sweden to be reunited with his mother in Bolivia, and his life in South America thereafter. The book contains photographs of my family, including the first one I had seen of my grandmother with her parents and all four of her sisters, and many photographs of Frieda and Werner.[6] The journey of discovery seems never to end: finding Werner's book recalls the moment I learnt about my relatives' fates in documents at the Holocaust Museum in Washington DC and at the Landesarchiv Berlin, or when I first read the letters that they had written from Berlin.

Werner's book tells of a colourful life. He was a crocodile hunter, a prison warden, a miner, a jazz musician and a journalist. In 1948 he moved to Argentina and launched the last German-speaking immigrants' newspaper in Latin America. While working on this newspaper he met Kerstin Schirp, a woman forty-nine years younger than him, who would become his second wife (and who would later co-author his autobiography). In 1999, at the age of seventy-four, Werner returned with Kerstin to Berlin, where he received a prestigious journalism award from the German federal president Richard von Weizsäcker.

Werner was probably the last surviving member of my father's generation of family members: the children of the Robinskis and Grünbergs, who were young men and women at the time of the Nazis. He died on 24 January 2012, six months before I discovered my family's letters from Berlin.

I made email contact with Kerstin Schirp, who told me more about Werner's life. Frieda had already died when they met, but she had lived into her seventies after following him to Argentina. Werner had two children from a previous marriage, who still live in South America. He maintained strong ties with his German Jewish roots, but he was not religious like his mother. After his father's death shortly before his bar mitzvah and the horror of the Shoah, he had lost his faith. But a week before he died he called a rabbi to speak to him, and he was buried beside his father's grave in Berlin's Weissensee Jewish Cemetery, the same cemetery with the gravestone inscribed with the names of his mother's sisters – Dora, Cecilie and Minna.

Kerstin and Werner had divorced but remained best friends. 'He was the most charming man one could imagine,' she told me. 'I always described him as a man with whom every woman wants to go to bed and every man wants to have a beer with.' Her words reminded me of Mookie Tabakin's account of my father during his bachelor years in Port Elizabeth. I am sure my father and Werner would have got on well. Not only did they both have a good supply of charm, but they also knew what it was like to lose one's home and family and have to start a new life in a foreign land.

One of the photographs in Werner's book was taken in Israel in 1982 and shows Werner with Egon (Moshe) Holz, Manfred (Menachim) Holz and Heinz (Zwi) Rubenstein. For the first time I was seeing the faces of these people who I had read about in my grandmother's letters, although they were all now old men. I wonder what happened to them between their escape from Germany and the time of that photograph, and how they had dealt with their loss.

There is something encouraging in the fact that there are other people who survived the devastation and who led fulfilling lives. Werner, the Holz brothers and the Rubenstein children were all in the same position as my

Egon (Moshe) Holz, Werner Max Finkelstein, Manfred (Menachim) Holz and Heinz (Zwi) Rubenstein in Israel, 1982

father and Artur: they managed to escape Nazi Germany and settle elsewhere. They too lost their parents in the Holocaust. Unlike them, my father and Artur lost their siblings too: Siegfried, Edith and Hildegard.

* * *

I doubt that my father could comprehend how National Socialism's brand of barbarism had thrived in the heartland of 'civilised Europe'. His own father probably thought his family was forever leaving behind Polish anti-Semitism for hospitality and tolerance in modern, cosmopolitan Berlin. Although he was an intelligent and thoughtful man, my father never read scholarly and philosophical debates on the Shoah. Unlike me, he did not have the luxury of going to university, having had to leave school at the age of thirteen because of his family's financial circumstances. As far as I can remember, we never spoke about the Shoah, but we did see the film version of Günter Grass's *The Tin Drum*. I cannot remember whether we spoke much about the film afterwards. I missed out on so many opportunities to speak to him about his past.

I wish I could have told my father what I have learnt about what happened to his family. I wish I could have reassured him that I know he did all he could to rescue them. I would have explained to him that the cards were stacked against his success, and that my own discipline of anthropology, along with the decisions of Verwoerd and other Afrikaner Nationalists, were responsible for his family's fate. This book is my attempt to tell him this.

But what would I have told Edith? Her eyes have followed me, everywhere. They have constantly implored me to answer her plea, yet I have struggled to fathom what it is that she wanted. How could I release her restless spirit? In South Africa, Zulu people practise the *ukubuyisa* ritual to bring the spirits of their dead back home. I once visited a Jewish psychic who told me that the shattered souls of my father's family had to be 'treated' in a place resembling a trauma clinic before they could move on in the spirit world. But believing in such things does not come easily to me. My schooling in the modern, secular truths of scientific rationality inhibits me from entirely accepting such notions. However, my job as an anthropologist also requires that I take seriously alternative ways of seeing and being in the world.

After all these years of searching for remnants of my family in Berlin's archives and in the streets of Kreuzberg and Mitte, I still sometimes sense their presence, watching over me as I place flowers at their *Stolpersteine*, or when I read their letters and write about their lives. I think I have found my own way of appeasing their restless spirits. This has become my *ukubuyisa*, my way of breaking through the silence in my father's house and bringing my ancestors home. These days I look into Edith's sad eyes and they seem to recognise what I have done to remember her, and to love her.

HIER WOHNTE
DAVID
ROBINSKI
JG. 1878
DEPORTIERT 1942
RIGA
? ? ?
HIER WOHNTE
CECILIE
ROBINSKI
GEB. GRÜNBERG
JG. 1882
DEPORTIERT 1942
RIGA
? ? ?
HIER WOHNTE
EDITH
ROBINSKI
JG. 1915
DEPORTIERT 1943
AUSCHWITZ
? ? ?
HIER WOHNTE
HILDEGARD
ROBINSKI
JG. 1917
DEPORTIERT 1943
AUSCHWITZ
? ? ?

Acknowledgements

A book as a finished product hides as much as it reveals. Although the author typically appears to be entirely responsible for its creation, those who write and publish books know this to be a fallacy. I will try my best to acknowledge this insight.

First, I would like to thank my late father, Herbert Robins, and his brother Artur, whose story this is. Despite all they went through, they were both real *menschen* with big hearts and wonderful wit and charm. I am indebted to my cousins David and Cecilia for finding the family letters and allowing me to use them in this book. Other relatives who supported me over the years include my brother Michael, my mother, Ruth, my aunt Elsa Robins, Moonyeen and George Muller, Kathy Robins, Deborah Robins, Leslie Singer, Jonathan Shapiro and Karina Turok. During my search for the Robinski family in the Northern Cape I was also greatly assisted by my relatives Harold Levy, Merle Oddes, Jeffrey Racki, Colette Thorne, Jos Thorne, Jill Thorne and Deirdre van Tonder.

Since this project unfolded over a period of almost two decades, I need to thank numerous friends and colleagues. I am especially indebted to Brahm Fleisch and Bettina von Lieres for their friendship and intellectual camaraderie over the long haul. Heidi Grunebaum was both a friend and colleague on this journey of recovering buried pasts. Jean and John Comaroff have inspired me through their generosity, energy and scholarly brilliance, and Jean provided extremely insightful comments on an earlier draft of the manuscript. I thank Deborah Posel for her intellectual generosity and for creating a space where I could discuss this project with others. I am also grateful to Mark and Gabriella Kaplan for their creativity and belief in the film and the book. Martin Düspohl, the director of the Friedrichshain-Kreuzberg Museum in Berlin, has been a good friend and supporter of this project for almost twenty years. Kees van der Waal was another loyal friend and colleague while we were together in the Department of Sociology and Social Anthropology at Stellenbosch University.

Robert Plummer went well beyond the call of duty and provided exceptional editorial guidance. He encouraged me to dig ever deeper into the Robinski archive, and the manuscript improved immeasurably under his attentive watch. Alison Lowry also provided important editorial insights and expertise, as well as much-appreciated enthusiasm. Genevieve Adams, Monique van den Berg, Ryan Africa, Surita Joubert and the rest of the Penguin Random House team were exceptionally professional in their work.

I am especially indebted to Ute Ben Yosef, who not only translated the family letters from German to English, but was also my guide as I stepped into this unsettling spectral world of shadows and silences. Thank you to Miriam Lichterman, who generously agreed to meet with me to talk about her traumatic experiences in Auschwitz. Aubrey Herbst provided his historical expertise on Williston's complicated frontier past; Robert Gordon contributed his rich knowledge on Namibian anthropology and history; and Saul Dubow, Andrew Bank and Allan Morris offered important insights into the history of racial science and anthropology in South Africa. Others who contributed in various ways to the research process include Anni Beukes, Rose Lerer Cohen, Jan-Georg Deutch, Thorsten Egner, Hans-Ulrich Fluss, Richard Freedman, Marianne Hirsch, Rebecca Hodes, Godfrey Hollander, Thomas Kirsch, Kaptein John McNab, Isabell Schneider, Myra Osrin, Boike Rehbein, Hermann Simon, Marlene Silbert, Leo Spitzer, Hedley Twidle, Elsa van Schalkwyk, Handri Walters, Paul Weinberg, Harry Wels and Gerhard Werle. Klaus-Peter Kurz, Dietlinde Peters, Erika Hausotter, Frauke Erdmann and Judith Kehnscherper from the Friedrichshain-Kreuzberg Museum in Berlin also provided invaluable help in transcribing the letters from Gothic script into modern German script.

Some friends and colleagues may not even be aware of how important their gestures of support were in spurring me on. I am particularly grateful to the following: Ben Cousins, Thomas Cousins, Bernard Dubbeld, Sean Field, Harry Garuba, Carolyn Hamilton, Nadia Kamies, Achille Mbembe, Martin Miller, Ranjita Mohanty, Robert Morrell, Sarah Nuttall, Rob Pattman, Lindsey Reynolds, Pamela Reynolds, Richard Rottenburg, Nick Shepherd, Andrew Spiegel, Sally Swartz, Leslie Swartz, Stephen Symons, Marianne Thamm, António Andrade Tomás, Jane van der Riet, Jan Vorster and Cherryl Walker.

There are many accomplished writers and scholars to whom I owe my gratitude. Etienne van Heerden led an exciting series of workshops as part of the University of Cape Town's Creative Writing MA programme;

as convenor of this programme, Imraan Coovadia encouraged me to sign up at a time when I was still quite reticent; Margie Orford recognised the poignancy of Edith's letters for the overall narrative and inspired me to tell my aunt's story; and Antjie Krog's close reading of an earlier draft greatly assisted me in improving the manuscript. I would also like to thank my fellow creative-writing students for their insights and encouragement.

I would also like to acknowledge the generous support provided by the National Research Foundation during my research for this book.

I am most indebted to my life partner and comrade-in-arms Lauren Muller. Lauren and my sons Joshua and Daniel had to patiently, and sometimes not so patiently, wait for my attention as I pounded away on my keyboard. Lauren was at my side on this journey from its very beginning, including the moments I entered the gates of Auschwitz and walked through the streets of the small Polish towns my father grew up in.

Finally, I would like to pay homage to my father's parents and siblings who did not survive – David, Cecilie, Siegfried, Edith and Hildegard. It has been a privilege to be able to tell their story, and by writing this book I hope to keep memories of them alive.

STEVEN ROBINS
CAPE TOWN, DECEMBER 2015

Notes

CHAPTER 1

1. Cited in Marianne Hirsch, *The Generation of Postmemory: Writing and Visual Culture After the Holocaust* (New York: Columbia University Press, 2012), pp. 120–21.

CHAPTER 2

1. The surname is spelt inconsistently. My grandfather and his children generally spelt it with an *i*, although it is spelt with a *y* on his shoe shop in East Prussia – see p. 18. Other branches of the family more often spelt it with a *y*. For convenience I have used the spelling Robinski throughout, except when copying a document.
2. Richard Mendelsohn and Milton Shain, *The Jews in South Africa: An Illustrated History* (Johannesburg and Cape Town: Jonathan Ball Publishers, 2008), p. 134.
3. Ibid., p. 148.
4. Ibid., p. 150.
5. Ibid., p. 169.
6. Josette Cole, *Crossroads: The Politics of Reform and Repression 1976–1986* (Johannesburg: Ravan Press, 1987), p. 146.

CHAPTER 4

1. This is the Hebrew name of Waldemar Schapiro.
2. The *Duilio* began the Genova-to-Cape Town route in 1928 with Lloyd Triestino, and it was sunk after the Allied bombing of Trieste in 1944.
3. Mendelsohn and Shain, *The Jews in South Africa*, p. 105.
4. This letter from the Afrikaner Broederbond Archive in Pretoria was translated and sent to me by my friend and colleague Kees van der Waal.
5. Mendelsohn and Shain, *The Jews in South Africa*, p. 105.
6. Ibid., p. 112.

CHAPTER 5

1. Daniel Goldhagen, *Hitler's Willing Executioners: Ordinary Germans and the Holocaust* (New York: Alfred A. Knopf Publishers, 1996).
2. Hannah Arendt, *Eichmann in Jerusalem: A Report on the Banality of Evil* (New York: Penguin, 1963).
3. See Hans-Walter Schmuhl, *The Kaiser Wilhelm Institute for Anthropology, Human Heredity and Eugenics, 1927–1945: Crossing Boundaries* (Dordrecht: Springer, 2008), p. 235.
4. See Steven Robins, 'Silence in My Father's House: Memory, Nationalism and Narratives of the Body', in Carli Coetzee and Sarah Nuttall (eds.), *Negotiating the Past: The Making of Memory in South Africa* (Cape Town: Oxford University Press, 1998), pp. 120–142.

CHAPTER 6

1. http://en.wikipedia.org/wiki/Stolperstein.
2. Ibid.
3. http://www.stolpersteine-berlin.de/en/projekt.
4. *Stumbling Stones in Berlin: 12 Neighbourhood Walks.* Published by Aktives Museum Faschimus und Widerstand in Berlin e.V. Koordinierrungsstelle Stolpersteine Berlin Kultureprojekte Berlin BmbH, 2014.

CHAPTER 7

1. Today Königsberg is known as Kaliningrad, and is situated in an enclave belonging to Russia on the Baltic Sea and bordered by Poland and Lithuania. The city was destroyed during the Second World War and occupied by the Soviet Union.
2. I use the term 'Bushmen' even though there are differing views as to whether the term San is more appropriate. Some argue that both terms have derogatory connotations.
3. Milton Shain, *The Roots of Anti-Semitism in South Africa* (Johannesburg: Wits University Press, 1994).
4. Eugen Fischer, *Die Rehobother Bastards und das Bastardisierungsproblem beim Menschen. Anthropologische und ethnologische Studien am Rehobother Bastardvolk in Deutsch-Sudwestafrika* (Jena 1913, reprinted Graz 1961).

CHAPTER 8

1. A mischievous, naughty person (Yiddish).
2. Grete Fränkel uses the German formal, 'polite' form in all her letters to Herbert.

CHAPTER 9

1. This section is based on the 1959 essay on Hendrik Frensch Verwoerd by Stanley Uys, the late former political correspondent for the *Sunday Times*, http://www.politicsweb.co.za/news-and-analysis/stanley-uys-on-hendrik-verwoerd.
2. Cited in Roger Cohen, *The Girl from Human Street: Ghosts of Memory in a Jewish Family* (London: Bloomsbury, 2015), p. 126.
3. South African Jewish Board of Deputies, 15 December 1937.
4. Andrew Bank, 'Fathering *Volkekunde*: Race and Culture in the Ethnological Writings and Teachings of Werner Eiselen, Hamburg, Berlin and Stellenbosch Universities, 1921–1936', paper presented at the Indexing the Human Seminar Series in the Department of Sociology and Social Anthropology, Stellenbosch University, 12 February 2015. Although Meinhof, who died in June 1946, subscribed to prevailing cultural-racist ideas in Europe, historian of African linguistics Sara Pugach believes that, like Eiselen, Meinhof was more influenced by German missionary thinking on racial difference than Nazi eugenics.
5. A *minyan* refers to the minimum number of twelve adult Jewish men required to have a religious service.
6. A *machzor* is the Jewish prayer book for the High Holidays.
7. Mendelsohn and Shain, *The Jews in South Africa*, p. 111.
8. Ibid., pp. 120–1.
9. Saul Dubow, 'Afrikaner Nationalism: Apartheid and the Conceptualization of "Race"', *The Journal of African History*, Vol. 233, No. 2, 1992, pp. 209–37.
10. *Vorzeigegeld* refers to the amount of money Jews and other refugees had to pay the countries that received them.

CHAPTER 10

1. Mark Roseman, *The Past in Hiding* (London: Penguin, 2000), p. 86.
2. Ibid.
3. https://www.wsws.org/en/articles/2013/11/13/kris-n13.html.
4. Roseman, *The Past in Hiding*, p. 97.

CHAPTER 11

1. Giorgio Agamben, *Homo Sacer: Sovereign Power and Bare Life* (Stanford: Stanford University Press, 1998), p. 10.
2. Mahmood Mamdani, *When Victims Become Killers: Colonialism, Nativism, and the Genocide in Rwanda* (Princeton: Princeton University Press, 2001).
3. Jan-Bart Gewald, 'Mirror Images? Photographs of Herero Commemorations in the 1920s and 1930s', in Wolfram Hartmann, Jeremy Silvester and Patricia Hayes, *The Colonising Camera: Photographs in the Making of Namibian History* (Cape Town and Ohio: University of Cape Town Press and Ohio University Press, 1999), p. 118.
4. For detailed accounts of the Herero and Nama genocide see David Olusoga and Casper W. Erichsen, *The Kaiser's Holocaust: Germany's Forgotten Genocide and the Colonial Roots of Nazism* (London: Faber & Faber, 2010); George Steinmetz, *The Devil's Handwriting: Precoloniality and the German Colonial State in Qingdao, Samoa, and Southwest Africa* (Chicago: University of Chicago Press, 2007); Michael Mann, *The Dark Side of Democracy: Explaining Ethnic Cleansing* (New York: Cambridge University Press, 2004), p. 105; Raffael Scheck, *Hitler's African Victims: The German Army Massacres of Black French Soldiers in* 1940 (Cambridge: Cambridge University Press, 2006), p. 83; Helmut Walser Smith, *The Continuities of German History: Nation, Religion, and Race across the Long Nineteenth Century* (Cambridge: Cambridge University Press, 2008), p. 199.
5. See A. Morris-Reich, 'Anthropology, standardization and measurement: Rudolf Martin and anthropometric photography', *British Journal for the History of Science* 46 (3), 2013, p. 496, cited in the doctoral thesis of Handri Walters, Department of Sociology and Social Anthropology, University of Stellenbosch (forthcoming).
6. See Mahmood Mamdani, *When Victims Become Killers: Colonialism, Nativism, and the Genocide in Rwanda* (Princeton: Princeton University Press, 2001).
7. See Olusoga and Erichsen, *The Kaiser's Holocaust.*
8. This discussion of Fischer draws extensively from the work of Hans-Walter Schmuhl and Annegret Ehmann. See A. Ehmann, 'From Colonial Racism to Nazi Population Policy: The Role of the So-called Mischlinge', in Michael Berenbaum and Abrahm J. Peck (eds.), *The Holocaust and History: The Known and the Unknown, the Disputed and the Reexamined* (Washington DC and Bloomington & Indianapolis: United States Holocaust Memorial Museum and Indiana University Press, 1998), pp. 115–33.
9. Steinmetz, *The Devil's Handwriting*, p. 217.
10. Ibid., pp. 233–4. In 1865 Gregor Johann Mendel discovered laws of biological inheritance that were controversial at the time but had, by the early 1900s, come to be accepted in scientific circles.
11. Steinmetz, *The Devil's Handwriting*, p. 234.
12. Ibid., p. 217–25.
13. Cited in Hans-Walter Schmuhl, *Crossing Boundaries*, p. 120.
14. Ibid., p. 121.
15. Ibid., p. 120.
16. Ibid., p. 231.

17. Ibid., p. 231.
18. Ibid., p. 134.
19. See Handri Walters' doctoral thesis, Department of Sociology and Social Anthropology, University of Stellenbosch (forthcoming).
20. Erwin Baur, Eugen Fischer and Fritz Lenz, *Human Heredity*, translated by Eden & Cedar Paul (London: George Allen & Unwin Ltd; New York: The Macmillan Company, 1931).
21. Ibid., p. 192.

CHAPTER 12

1. This requirement of a letter of '*Unbedenklichkeitserklärung*' was introduced in December 1931 in the Weimar Republic as part of the *Reichsfluchtsteuer* (Reich Flight Tax) to avoid capital flight during the unstable period between the wars. After the Nazis seized power in 1933, the government used the tax to confiscate assets from Jews who attempted to flee. To emigrate legally, a 'letter of no objection' now had to be issued by the tax offices to confirm the payment of this tax.
2. https://en.wikipedia.org/wiki/Kindertransport.

CHAPTER 13

1. Mark Roseman, *The Past in Hiding*, p. 123.

CHAPTER 14

1. Keith Breckenridge, Chapter 2, 'Science of Empire: The South African Origins and Objects of Galtonian eugenics', in *Biometric State: the Global Politics of Identification and Surveillance in South Africa, 1850 to the Present* (Cambridge: Cambridge University Press, 2014).
2. 'Eugenics and the Jew: Interview for *The Jewish Chronicle* with Sir Francis Galton', *The Jewish Chronicle*, 29 July 1910, p. 16.
3. Theodore M. Porter, *Karl Pearson: The Scientific Life in a Statistical Age* (Princeton: University of Princeton Press, 2005), p. 283.
4. Ibid.
5. Ibid., p. 297; emphasis added.
6. Stephen Jay Gould, 'Science and Jewish Immigration', in *Hen's Teeth and Horse's Toes* (New York: W.W. Norton, 1983), p. 3.
7. Jonathan Peter Spiro, *Defending the Master Race: Conservation, Eugenics, and the Legacy of Madison Grant* (Burlington, Vermont: University of Vermont Press, 2009).
8. Gould, 'Science and Jewish Immigration', p. 8. See Gould, *The Mismeasure of Man* (New York: W.W. Norton, 1981).
9. Karl Pearson and Margaret Moul, *The problem of alien immigration into Great Britain, illustrated by an examination of Russian and Polish Jewish children, Part I* (published in the Annals of Human Genetics' archive of material originally published in print format by the Annals of Eugenics, 1925–1954).
10. Pearson, who believed he was simply following rigorous scientific methods of investigation, proceeded to recruit 600 alien Jewish children at the Jewish Free School in London. He measured the cleanliness of their hair and clothing compared to native Gentile children, and collected masses of data on education, literacy, language, physique, and diseases of the ear, eye, teeth and heart. His findings led him to conclude that the Jewish children were indeed inferior to native stock in height, weight, susceptibility to disease, nutrition, visual acuity and cleanliness. He subsequently advised that those Polish and Russian Jews whose physique or mentality

were proven to be inferior to the autochthonous white British race should not be allowed into the country.

11. Todd M. Endelman, *The Jews of Britain, 1656 to 2000* (Berkeley: University of California Press, 2002), pp. 212–14.
12. Ibid.
13. Ibid.
14. Ibid.
15. Edwin Black, *War Against the Weak: Eugenics and America's Campaign to Create a Master Race* (Washington DC: Dialog Press, 2003), p. 300. Also see Spiro, *Defending the Master Race.*
16. Ibid.

CHAPTER 15

1. Vinh-Kim Nguyen, *The Republic of Therapy: Triage and Sovereignty in West Africa's Time of AIDS* (Durham and London: Duke University Press, 2010).
2. I found this letter in Istanbul in 2015, in a seventeenth-century former Sephardic synagogue that had been converted into the Quincentennial Foundation Museum of Turkish Jews.
3. Hannah Arendt, *The Origins of Totalitarianism* (Florida: Harcourt Publishers, 1968), originally published 1951.

CHAPTER 16

1. Roseman, *The Past in Hiding*, p. 113.

CHAPTER 17

1. Marianne Hirsch, *Family Frames: Photography, Narrative and Postmemory* (Cambridge, MS, and London: Harvard University Press, 2012). See also Hirsch, *The Generation of Postmemory: Writing and Visual Culture After the Holocaust* (New York: Columbia University Press, 2012).
2. Hirsch, *The Generation of Postmemory*, pp. 36–37.
3. Ibid., p. 38.
4. Ibid.
5. cf Hirsch, *The Generation of Postmemory*, p. 63.
6. Michael André Bernstein, *Foregone Conclusions: Against Apocalyptic History*, cited in Hirsch, *The Generation of Postmemory*, p. 63.
7. Santu Mofokeng, *The Black Photo Album/Look at Me: 1890–1950* (New York and Göttingen: The Walther Collection and Steidl, 2012).
8. Ibid.
9. Matthew Krouse, 'Confounding Expectations? Thing of Beauty, *The Black Photo Album*', *Mail & Guardian* Arts Section, Friday, 22–28 November 2013, p. 3.

CHAPTER 18

1. See Mendelsohn and Shain, *The Jews in South Africa: An Illustrated History*, p. 119.
2. Roseman, *The Past in Hiding*, p. 123.
3. Ibid., p. 125.
4. Ibid.
5. Ibid., p.130.

CHAPTER 19

1. Roseman, *The Past in Hiding*, pp. 344–54.
2. Sara Lipton, 'The Invention of the Jewish Nose', *New York Review of Books*, 14 November 2014, http://www.nybooks.com/blogs/gallery/2014/nov/14/invention-jewish-nose/.
3. Roseman, *The Past in Hiding*, pp. 334–5.

CHAPTER 20

1. Andrej Angrick, Peter Klei, *The 'Final Solution' in Riga: Exploitation and Annihilation, 1941–1944* (Berghahn Books, 2009).
2. This information is based on a list of deportations in the *Gedenkbuch Berlins*.
3. Based on a deportation list found in the Slovakia Holocaust Jewish Names Project, Commenius University of Bratislava, Department of History, Bratislava.
4. Based on a list of deportations in the *Gedenkbuch Berlins*.

CHAPTER 21

1. Schmuhl, *Crossing Boundaries*, p. 367.
2. Ibid., pp. 367–68.
3. Ibid., p. 369.
4. Ibid., p. 368.
5. Ibid., p. 383; https://en.wikipedia.org/wiki/Josef_Mengele.
6. 'Nazi Medical Experiments', http://www.ushmm.org/wlc/en/article.php?ModuleId=10005168.
7. Astrid Ley and Gunter Morsch, *Medical Care and Crime: The Infirmary at Sachsenhausen Concentration Camp 1936–1945* (Berlin: Metropol Verlag, 2007). The information on the research done by Ritter and his colleagues at Sachsenhausen is from Ley and Morsch's excellent exhibition and catalogue.
8. Zygmunt Bauman, *Modernity and the Holocaust* (Ithaca, New York: Cornell University Press 1989).

CHAPTER 22

1. http://www.beaufortwest.net/index.php/explore/central-karoo/nelspoort/100-nelspoort.
2. https://en.wikipedia.org/wiki/Thomas_Mann.

CHAPTER 23

1. Interview with Annegret Ehmann, 2015.
2. Bank, 'Fathering *Volkekunde*'.
3. Alan G. Morris, *Report on the Human Skull from Stellenbosch Anthropology* (An1191), 1 May 2014.
4. A *laager* is an Afrikaans word for a defensive circle of wagons.
5. Hermann Giliomee, 'Liberal and Populist Democracy in South Africa: Challenges, New Threats to Liberalism' (Johannesburg: South African Institute of Race Relations, 1996), cited in Claudia Bathsheba Braude (ed.), *Contemporary Jewish Writing in South Africa: An Anthology* (Cape Town: David Philip, 2001), p. ix.
6. Saul Dubow, 'Racial Irredentism, Ethnogenesis, and White Supremacy in High-Apartheid South Africa,' unpublished, September 2015, pp. 3–4. See also Saul Dubow, *Scientific Racism in Modern South Africa* (Cambridge: Cambridge University Press, 1995).
7. Dubow, 'Racial Irredentism, Ethnogenesis, and White Supremacy,' pp. 3–4.

8. C.S. Grobbelaar, 'The distribution of and correlation between eye, hair and skin colour in male students at the University of Stellenbosch', *Annals of the University of Stellenbosch*, edited by Professor C. du Toit and co-editors Professors F.X. Laubscher, J.P.J. van Rensburg and R.W. Wilcocks, Vol. XXVIII, Section A, No. 1, 1952.

CHAPTER 24

1. Hannah Arendt, 'We Refugees', originally published in *Menorah*, 1943; reproduced in Mark Robinson (ed.), *Altogether Elsewhere: Writers on Exile* (Boston and London: Faber & Faber, 1994), p. 263.
2. Ibid., p. 268.
3. Ibid., p. 270.
4. Arendt, Hannah, *The Origins of Totalitarianism* (New York: Schocken Books, 1951), p. vii.
5. Kerstin Emma Schirp, *Jude, Gringo, Deutscher: Das abenteuerliche Leben des Werner Max Finkelstein* (Berlin: Books on Demand, 2002).
6. The photograph on page 18, showing the five Grunberg daughters, comes from Werner's book, as do the photos of Frieda on pages 215 and 241. Reproduced with permission of Kerstin Emma Schirp.

Picture credits

All images from the Robins family archives, except for:

17: Kerstin Emma Schirp, *Jude Gringo Deutscher*
33: Source unknown
45: Landesarchiv Berlin
47: Landesarchiv Berlin
51: Hans-Ulrich Fluss
61: Wolfe Harris
68–69: Isaac Robins
76–77: Eugen Fischer, *Die Rehobother Bastards*
94: Wikimedia Commons
103: Source unknown
125: Wikimedia Commons
130: Baur, Fischer and Lenz, *Human Heredity*
164: http://www.eugenicsarchive.org/html/eugenics/static/images/2217.html
165: Wikimedia Commons
200: Wikimedia Commons
202–203: Eugen Fischer, *Die Rehobother Bastards*
204–205: Santu Mofokeng, *The Black Photo Album*
215: Kerstin Emma Schirp, *Jude Gringo Deutscher*
225: Landesarchiv Berlin 227–228: Landesarchiv Berlin
230: Hans-Ulrich Fluss 231: Hans-Ulrich Fluss
232: Source unknown 235: Landesarchiv Berlin
237 and 238: Michael Robins
239: Wikimedia Commons
240: Kerstin Emma Schirp, *Jude Gringo Deutscher*
246: Wikimedia Commons
248: Wikimedia Commons
251: Source unknown
283: Kerstin Emma Schirp, *Jude Gringo Deutscher*

Bibliography

Agamben, Giorgio. *Homo Sacer: Sovereign Power and Bare Life.* Translated by Daniel Heller-Roazen. Stanford: Stanford University Press, 1998.

Angrick, Andrej, and Peter Klei. *The 'Final Solution' in Riga: Exploitation and Annihilation, 1941–1944.* Translated by Ray Brandon. New York and Oxford: Berghahn Books, 2009.

Arendt, Hannah. *The Origins of Totalitarianism.* Florida: Harcourt Publishers, (1951) 1968.

———. *Eichmann in Jerusalem: A Report on the Banality of Evil.* New York: Penguin Books, 1963 (1977).

———. 'We Refugees', in Marc Robinson (ed.), *Altogether Elsewhere: Writers on Exile.* New York: Harvest Books, (1943) 1996.

Bank, Andrew. 'Fathering *Volkekunde*: Race and Culture in the Ethnological Writings and Teachings of Werner Eiselen at Hamburg, Berlin and Stellenbosch Universities, 1921–1936'. Paper presented in the Department of Sociology and Social Anthropology, Stellenbosch University, 12 February 2015.

Barthes, Roland. *Camera Lucida: Reflections on Photography.* Translated by Richard Howard. Paris: Hill & Wang, 1980.

Bauman, Zygmunt. *Modernity and the Holocaust.* Ithaca, New York: Cornell University Press, 1989.

Baur, Erwin, Eugen Fischer and Fritz Lenz. *Human Heredity.* Translated by Eden and Cedar Paul. London and New York: George Allen & Unwin, MacMillan, 1931.

Berenbaum, Michael, and Abrahm J. Peck (eds). *The Holocaust and History: The Known and the Unknown, the Disputed and the Reexamined.* Washington DC and Bloomington & Indianapolis: United States Holocaust Memorial Museum and Indiana University Press, 1998.

Black, Edwin. *War Against the Weak: Eugenics and America's Campaign to Create a Master Race.* Washington DC: Dialog Press, 2003.

Braude, Claudia Bathsheba (ed.). *Contemporary Jewish Writing in South Africa: An Anthology.* Cape Town: David Philip, 2001.

Breckenridge, Keith. *Biometric State: The Global Politics of Identification and Surveillance in South Africa, 1850 to the Present.* Cambridge: Cambridge University Press, 2014.

Cohen, Roger. The *Girl from Human Street: Ghosts of Memory in a Jewish Family.* London: Bloomsbury, 2015.

Cole, Josette. *Crossroads: The Politics of Reform and Repression 1976–1986.* Johannesburg: Ravan Press, 1987.

Dubow, Saul. 'Afrikaner Nationalism: Apartheid and the Conceptualization of "Race"', *The Journal of African History*, Vol. 233, No. 2, 1992.

———. 'Racial Irredentism, Ethnogenesis, and White Supremacy in High-Apartheid South Africa', unpublished, September 2015.

Ehmann, A. 'From Colonial Racism to Nazi Population Policy: The Role of the So-called

Mischlinge', in Michael Berenbaum and Abrahm J. Peck (eds), *The Holocaust and History: The Known and the Unknown, the Disputed and the Reexamined*. Washington D.C. and Bloomington and Indianapolis: United States Holocaust Memorial Museum and Indiana University Press, 1998.

Endelman, Todd M. *The Jews of Britain, 1656 to 2000*. Berkeley: University of California Press, 2002.

Fischer, Eugen. *Die Rehobother Bastards und das Bastardisierungsproblem beim Menschen. Anthropologische und ethnologische Studien am Rehobother Bastardvolk in Deutsch-Sudwestafrika*. 1913 (1961).

Giliomee, Hermann. 'Liberal and Populist Democracy in South Africa: Challenges, New Threats to Liberalism', Johannesburg: South African Institute of Race Relations, 1996. Cited in Claudia Bathsheba Braude (ed.), *Contemporary Jewish Writing in South Africa: An Anthology*. Cape Town: David Philip, 2001.

Goldhagen, Daniel. *Hitler's Willing Executioners: Ordinary Germans and the Holocaust*. New York: Alfred A. Knopf, 1996.

Gould, Stephen Jay. *The Mismeasure of Man*. New York: W.W. Norton, 1981.

———. *Hen's Teeth and Horse's Toes*. New York: W.W. Norton, 1983.

Grobbelaar, C.S. 'The distribution of and correlation between eye, hair and skin colour in male students at the University of Stellenbosch', *Annals of the University of Stellenbosch*, Section A, Vol. XXVIII, No. 1, 1952.

Hartmann, Wolfram, Jeremy Silvester and Patricia Hayes. *The Colonising Camera: Photographs in the Making of Namibian History*. Cape Town and Ohio: University of Cape Town Press, Ohio University Press, 1999.

Hirsch, Marianne. *Family Frames: Photography, Narrative and Postmemory*. Cambridge, MS: Harvard University Press, 2012.

———. *The Generation of Postmemory: Writing and Visual Culture After the Holocaust*. New York: Columbia University Press, 2012.

Judt, Tony (with Timothy Snyder). *Thinking the Twentieth Century*. William Heinemann: London, 2012.

Krouse, Martin. 'Confounding expectations? Thing of Beauty, The Black Photo Album', *Mail & Guardian* Arts Section, 22–28 November 2013.

Ley, Astrid, and Gunter Morsch. *Medical Care and Crime: The Infirmary at Sachsenhausen Concentration Camp 1936–1945*. Berlin: Metropol Verlag, 2007.

Mamdani, Mahmood. *When Victims Become Killers: Colonialism, Nativism, and the Genocide in Rwanda*. Princeton: Princeton University Press, 2001.

Mann, Michael. *The Dark Side of Democracy: Explaining Ethnic Cleansing*. New York: Cambridge University Press, 2004.

Marrus, Michael R. 'Review of "Britain and the Jews of Europe, 1939–1945" by Bernard Wasserstein', *The International History Review*, Vol. 3, No. 2, April 1981.

Mendelsohn, Richard, and Milton Shain. *The Jews in South Africa: An Illustrated History*. Johannesburg and Cape Town: Jonathan Ball, 2008.

Mofokeng, Santu. *The Black Photo Album/Look at Me: 1890–1950*. New York and Göttingen: The Walther Collection and Steidl, 2012.

Morris-Reich, A. 'Anthropology, standardization and measurement: Rudolf Martin and anthropometric photography', *British Journal for the History of Science* 46 (3), 2013.

Nguyen, Vinh-Kim. *The Republic of Therapy: Triage and Sovereignty in West Africa's Time of AIDS*. Durham and London: Duke University Press, 2010.

Olusoga, David, and Casper W. Erichsen. *The Kaiser's Holocaust: Germany's Forgotten Genocide and the Colonial Roots of Nazism*. London: Faber & Faber, 2010.

Pearson, Karl, and Margaret Moul. *The problem of alien immigration into Great Britain, illustrated by an examination of Russian and Polish Jewish children, Part I.* Annals of Human Genetics, 1925.

Porter, Theodore M. *Karl Pearson: The Scientific Life in a Statistical Age.* Princeton: Princeton University Press, 2005.

Postone, Moishe. 'The Holocaust and the Trajectory of the Twentieth Century', in Moishe Postone and Eric Santner (eds), *Catastrophe and Meaning: The Holocaust and the Twentieth Century.* Chicago and London: The University of Chicago Press, 2003.

Robins, Steven. 'Silence in My Father's House: Memory, Nationalism and Narratives of the Body', in Carli Coetzee and Sarah Nuttall, *Negotiating the Past: The Making of Memory in South Africa.* Cape Town: Oxford University Press, 1998.

Roseman, Mark. *The Past in Hiding.* London: Penguin Books, 2000.

Scheck, Raffael. *Hitler's African Victims: The German Army Massacres of Black French Soldiers in* 1940. Cambridge: Cambridge University Press, 2006.

Schmuhl, Hans-Walter. *The Kaiser Wilhelm Institute for Anthropology, Human Heredity and Eugenics, 1927–1945: Crossing Boundaries.* Boston: Springer, 2008.

Shain, Milton. *The Roots of Anti-Semitism in South Africa.* Johannesburg: University of Witwatersrand Press, 1994.

———. *A Perfect Storm: Antisemitism in South Africa, 1930–1948.* Johannesburg and Cape Town: Jonathan Ball, 2015.

Smith, Helmut Walser. *The Continuities of German History: Nation, Religion, and Race across the Long Nineteenth Century.* Cambridge: Cambridge University Press, 2008.

Spiro, Jonathan Peter. *Defending the Master Race: Conservation, Eugenics, and the Legacy of Madison Grant.* Burlington, Vermont: University of Vermont Press, 2009.

Steinmetz, George. *The Devil's Handwriting: Precoloniality and the German Colonial State in Qingdao, Samoa, and Southwest Africa.* Chicago and London: University of Chicago Press, 2007.

Stumbling Stones in Berlin: 12 Neighbourhood Walks. Published by Aktives Museum Faschimus und Widerstand in Berlin e.V. Koordinierrungsstelle Stolpersteine Berlin Kultureprojekte Berlin BmbH, 2014.

Wasserstein, Bernard. *Britain and the Jews of Europe, 1939–1945.* London and Oxford: Institute of Jewish Affairs and Clarendon Press, 1979.

Index